Jeep CJ

1972–1986

How to Build & Modify

Michael Hanssen

CarTech®

CarTech®

CarTech®, Inc.
838 Lake Street South
Forest Lake, MN 55025
Phone: 651-277-1200 or 800-551-4754
Fax: 651-277-1203
www.cartechbooks.com

Edit by Bob Wilson
Layout by Monica Seiberlich

ISBN 978-1-61325-734-0
Item No. SA396P
Library of Congress Cataloging-in-Publication Data

Names: Hanssen, Michael, author.
Title: Jeep CJ 1972-1986 : how to build & modify / Michael Hanssen.
Description: Forest Lake, MN : CarTech, [2017]
Identifiers: LCCN 2017003180 | ISBN 9781613253427
Subjects: LCSH: Jeep automobile–Motors–Modification–Handbooks, manuals, etc. | Jeep automobile–Maintenance and repair–Handbooks, manuals, etc. | Jeep automobile–Customizing–Handbooks, manuals, etc. | Jeep automobile–History. | Antique and classic cars–Conservation and restoration–Handbooks, manuals, etc.
Classification: LCC TL215.J44 .H36 2017 | DDC 629.28/722–dc23
LC record available at https://lccn.loc.gov/2017003180

Written, edited, and designed in the U.S.A.
Printed in the U.S.A.

Front Cover: *A group of CJs line up for a day on the trail at Rausch Creek Off-Road Park. These CJs are equipped with an array of modifications to improve off-road performance but maintain street drivability. Lift kits, mud tires, lockers, and much more keep these classic Jeeps moving on the trail.*

Title Page: *Four classic Jeeps navigate a steep rocky ravine on a fall day trail run. With the help of ground clearance, mud tires, low gears, and lockers, the Jeeps gracefully move up the rocky hill with little effort.*

Back Cover Photos

Top: *This 1984 CJ-7 underwent a recent T176 swap from a worn-out T5. The factory fit and strength plus low cost/hassle make this conversion an excellent choice. The T176's 3.52 low gear is not low by any means, but when combined with a TeraLow-equipped Dana 300, the ratios are very useable off-road.*

Middle Left: *Adapting a popular non-factory transmission to a Jeep transfer case requires the use of an adapter. Adapters from Novak are complete with all of the required components, including the rear mounting provision. (Photo Courtesy Novak Conversions)*

Middle Right: *An old trail trick to keep the underhood temperatures down was to stick a block of wood or steel under the cowl side of the hood hinges. The half-inch or so opened up a gap that ran fully across and allowed underhood heat to escape. Slow trail driving drastically raises underhood temperatures. You can feel the heat moving just by placing a hand on the hood.*

Bottom: *An often-competitive activity is to test the Jeep's suspension flexibility by driving up a one-sided ramp to measure ramp travel index or RTI. This measurement divides the distance traveled by the wheelbase of the Jeep, which is then multiplied by 1,000. A score of 1,000 means that the Jeep traveled up the ramp the same distance as its wheelbase length.*

CONTENTS

DEDICATION

I blame my father for all of this. He is the man who introduced a Jeep into my life when I was three years old.

ACKNOWLEDGMENTS

After many years of running a Jeep lifestyle website, jeepfan.com, I now find myself the author of a Jeep book. This lifelong obsession with the Jeep has kept me active in the Jeep community for more than 40 years. There have been so many people along the way who have tolerated my love of this vehicle and so many who have helped me grow my knowledge and ability. First and foremost is my family: my wife, Jennifer, and son, Austin, who have listened to countless hours of talk about Jeeps, many Jeep trail rides, responded to my "come hold this" requests with builds, and so much more.

My father, who truly is responsible for all of this, spent countless hours on his Jeep, which later became my first Jeep and my first build. He scared the wits out of me on the trail, took "the fam" to Jeep races, and taught me to drive the Jeep at an early age. His "learn by doing" (and making me do) approach, experience, and knowledge built the foundation I still use today. My late grandfather, whose creativity and ability to build something out of nothing, provided me with a valuable skill that is useful for Jeeps and more.

Special thanks to my favorite parts suppliers and installers who opened their doors to me: OK 4WD, Quad-ratec, and Jeff Daniel's Jeep Customizations. Rausch Creek Off-Road Park, who gave some Jeepers and me the run of the place to get some beautiful pictures. ARB/Old Man Emu, Novak, TeraFlex, and Genesis Offroad for making awesome products and helping me out. Eric Jankowski for his knowledge of factory Jeep information and keeping my facts straight.

Finally, I can't forget my close circle of Jeep friends: Ralph, Mike, Glenn, Matt, Bryan, Brian, Rich, and Mark, who always provide an opinion, advice, and a helping hand when needed.

The Jeep line has been in production for more than 75 years and has given us many models, each with its own special qualities, but perhaps the 1972–1986 CJ series could be considered among the more special Jeeps.

The 1972–1986, or AMC era, of the CJ lineup could be viewed as the CJ at its finest. The refinements in road handling, options that improved interior comfort, and the continuation of what made the CJ the off-road vehicle it always was contributed to the creation of a legacy.

Jeep enthusiasts enjoyed an era of CJs when parts were plentiful and the aftermarket made a plethora of upgrades and accessories that could satisfy everyone. Federal and state emissions regulations were relatively light in many areas, which allowed engine performance modifications and a variety of engine swaps. In 1987, Chrysler acquired American Motors and the CJ line was discontinued; it was eventually replaced with the all-new Jeep Wrangler YJ. The off-road Jeep crowd wasn't ready for the new toned-down Wrangler, which led to an increased interest in CJ modification.

The CJ remained a dominant vehicle on the trail well into the late 1990s but gradually faded after the introduction of the coil-sprung Wrangler TJ in 1996. Many CJs are still active in the off-road community, but most have been retired, some to rust away, and some preserved to remind us of this special

The new AMC Jeep emblem was found on Jeep vehicles after 1972. The red, white, and blue logo was so fitting of the 1970s, as America was celebrating its bicentennial.

era. The interest in the CJ continues today, perhaps not with the fever that it once had, but all you need to do is attend a Jeep show and look for the crowd. On the trail, the CJ still holds its own against the newer coil-spring-suspension Wranglers that have taken over the scene.

The CJ has been used in many ways other than just getting from point A to point B. The Jeep has served well in a military capacity, as a utility vehicle, a racer, an off-roader, a movie star, and more. For the purpose of building a perfect CJ, I home in on a single category, which may stretch a bit into a few others but focuses on one goal: building and modifying a CJ for the trail. A perfect trail Jeep is one that isn't totally purpose-built for the trail but rather built to get to the trail, run all day, and drive home. This kind of Jeep defines the true essence of what the Jeep was meant to be.

The Jeep community continues to thrive, possibly more than ever. The introduction of the four-door Wrangler in 2007 brought a Jeep into the lives of many who would have never considered a two-door Jeep. The new interest revitalized Jeep events all over the country; events such as the Bantam Jeep Heritage Festival held annually in Butler, Pennsylvania, which has seen record attendance. The number of Jeep-related events that occur throughout the United States and the rest of the world should be enough to satisfy any Jeep fan.

The stock CJ came with so much capability right out of the box, which continues today with the Wrangler, that most Jeep owners look at their Jeep's factory form merely as a blank canvas. A Jeep owner needs to start with only a few modifications to get his or her Jeep from stock to a well-equipped trail Jeep.

This modified 1977 CJ-7 is in its element on the trail. With minimal modification a CJ can become a considerably more capable trail Jeep from its already capable stock form.

The Bantam Jeep Heritage Festival is held annually in Butler, Pennsylvania, the town considered the birthplace of the Jeep. The festival holds a Jeep Invasion, where hundreds of Jeeps parade to Butler and line Main Street to kick off a weekend of all-Jeep events.

In the following chapters, I discuss the accessories and modifications that go into building and modifying a CJ. You will learn the kind of modifications that enhance your Jeep's performance, both on- and off-road. In addition, you'll learn about both the ease and complexity of a build. This will help you figure out if you want to take on a build or leave it to a professional. Most of the modifications and builds I cover can be performed in a well-equipped home garage; I provide tool tips and recommendations along the way.

I've been building and modifying Jeeps since 1984 and have been working on a 1978 CJ-5 I refer to as "Number 5" consistently since 1997. This Jeep has seen many modifications through the years and was continually run on the trail for 10 years. It has seen many versions of lift kits, engine rebuilds, and modifications, a frame replacement, lockers, tires, wheels, etc. The list goes on and on and is still going. In 2006, I semi-retired the Jeep from regular trail use, and now it serves as a joy to drive and reminder of the capability and heritage of this era. Look for Number 5 throughout this book.

Finally, safety is the number-one concern when working on your Jeep. Don't take chances, plan ahead, get help when needed, and be aware of your surroundings. Another word on safety is less about working on your Jeep and more about the safety of the modifications you are making; modifications often alter the way the Jeep drives. Lift kits and larger tires affect road handling and stopping ability. Low-quality or incorrect components can cause failures, damage, and potential injury.

A 2-mph traffic jam in the middle of nowhere. Jeep trail rides are unique in that the majority of the day is spent moving at a snail's pace. Low range, low gears, and good tires are part of the recipe in an off-road Jeep.

A 1978 CJ-5 modified, used, and loved for nearly 20 years at its final trail run at Rausch Creek Off-Road Park in Pennsylvania, before being retired from regular trail use. This Jeep has seen many types of trails and many stages of modifications.

THE AMC ERA: A BRIEF HISTORY

The Jeep brand has seen a few ownership changes since 1941, perhaps most notably the sale from Kaiser-Jeep to American Motors in 1970, which began a new and final era of the Jeep CJ series. The 1972–1986 CJ, often referred to as AMC-era CJs, began 1972 with the introduction of many changes to the line that included new engines, transmissions, and body styles.

The 1970 and 1971 models stayed the same, and after two years of planning for design changes, the 1972 model introduced the new AMC Jeep to the world, featuring a several-inch extension of the front clip to accommodate the length of the AMC I-6 and V-8. The CJ-5 remained a regular model in the series until 1983 when AMC, continuing to face criticism of the short Jeep's rollover reputation, decided to discontinue this nearly 30-year-old model.

An addition to the CJ lineup came in 1976 with the introduction of the longer 93½-inch-wheelbase CJ-7. The CJ-7 was the first CJ to arrive factory equipped with an optional automatic transmission, hardtop, air conditioning, and full-time four-wheel drive.

A final addition to the CJ lineup came in 1981 as a midyear model when Jeep introduced the CJ-8, also known as the Scrambler. The Scrambler was a hybrid Jeep/truck, extending the CJ into a small pickup truck whose unique fit in the market set it apart but at the same time isolated it, which resulted in moderate sales.

The AMC-era CJs were the first CJ models to run an I-6 or V-8 engine. The standard I-6 engines were workhorses in the CJ from 1972 to 1986, and the 304 V-8 was an option from 1972 to 1981. Production was low for 1981 models that came with a V-8, none of which were Scramblers. The new engines brought new transmission offerings to the CJ, most notably the automatic transmissions for the CJ-7 and Scrambler and T-18 heavy-duty 4-speed. Sitting at the end of the transmissions were two new transfer cases. The Dana 300 transfer case, offered from 1980 to 1986, is still considered one of the best transfer cases found in a Jeep.

A 1984 CJ-7 and its driver expertly maneuver a bed of rocks at the now-closed Paragon Off-Road Park. This pristine CJ runs a fuel-injected 4.2L I-6, with 33-inch tires, an Old Man Emu 2½-inch lift, and Powertrax No Slip lockers.

This 1978 CJ-5 is the perfect balance of original look with modifications. The Jeep runs 33-inch tires with original aluminum slot wheels. Under the hood sits a Ford 5.0L V-8, a popular engine swap in a CJ. The Jeep features many other modifications and accessories such as a Rock Hard front roll bar, high-lift jack, and side rocker protection. (Photo Courtesy Craig Brown)

A 1982 Scrambler white knuckle tackles some off-camber rocks on a trail. The added length of the Scrambler, especially in the rear overhang, is obvious. This Scrambler is mostly stock, with the exception of a 4-inch lift, 35-inch tires, and one-piece rear axles.

The AMC 304 was the first V-8 that was factory fitted into the CJ. The new engine provided extra torque and horsepower that, when combined with the relative light weight of the Jeep, pushed the CJ into muscle car territory. The engine used the 2-barrel Motorcraft carburetor and later the Ford Duraspark ignition system.

The Dana 300 transfer case provided a fully gear-driven four-wheel-drive system and a 2.66:1 low range. It gained a reputation as a strong and durable transfer case with many modification options. Lower gearsets, twin-stick shifters, and clocking rings are a few of the possible modification options.

All 1972–1986 CJs used the Saginaw steering box, combined with a drag link and tie-rod. Early years offered power steering as an option, followed by standard power steering in later models.

Attention was given to making the CJ safer and more street friendly, which led to many enhancements being introduced through the years. The CJ frame was strengthened in 1972, including boxed sections and more crossmembers to increase rigidity. Steering systems were changed to use the drag link/tie-rod configuration, and the Saginaw steering box offered optional power steering for the first time. In 1976, to further enhance the CJ's road handling, the frame was widened in the rear and included a front sway bar.

The 1972–1986 CJ models came equipped with the Dana 30 front axle. Rear axles were the Dana 44 from 1972 to 1975 and the AMC

The Wide Trak axles offered some additional width to the CJ, which improved handling and reduced roll-over risks. The additional width added approximately 1½ inches of track width on each side. A small drawback of the added width is that aftermarket wheels and tires would almost always exceed the width of the Jeep's fender flares, a problem in some states. Shown is the passenger's side of a front Wide Trak axle modified with a tie-rod flip kit.

Model 20 from 1976 to 1986. Interestingly, some of the late 1986 CJ models came equipped with a Dana 44 after the AMC 20 supplies ran out. Starting in 1982, in a further effort to improve CJ road handling, the CJ-7 and CJ-8 included wider front and rear axles that were referred to as the "Wide Trak" axles. With pressure for increased fuel mileage and lower exhaust emissions, Jeep was forced to use higher gear ratios that reduced its effectiveness off-road.

The AMC era brought some interesting model options including the Renegade, Laredo, Limited, and Super Jeep. These trim options brought special paint schemes, striping, and more to add to the "stand out from the crowd" nature of the Jeep CJ.

Adding a level of class to the Jeep line, the Limited package, offered only in 1982 and 1983, gave a more sophisticated look to the Jeep, while retaining the features that make the CJ a Jeep. This restored 1983 CJ-7 Limited is pristine in nearly every detail. (Photo Courtesy Eric Jankowski)

Jeep introduced the Renegade model in 1970 and continued it until 1986. Renegade models featured special decals, wheels, and interior options. An all-original 1985 CJ-7 equipped with an automatic, Trac-Loc, and factory air conditioning is a rare survivor. (Photo Courtesy Eric Jankowski)

The Super Jeep model was only offered in 1973 and was added to the Jeep line as a result of wheel supply problems due to the unexpected popularity of the Renegade model. The Jeep featured elaborate decals, special seats, and exterior additions.

Model Specifics

In breaking it all down, the AMC era splits into two distinct time periods and three distinct models. The 1972–1975 years and then the 1976–1986 years represent time periods that had distinct differences. The three significant models of CJs during this 15-year run are the CJ-5, CJ-7, and CJ-8. Note: The CJ-6 model was produced during the AMC era from 1972 to 1975 but was never a mainstream vehicle. In essence, the CJ-6 from 1972 to 1975 shared all the same parts as a CJ-5 of the same era, with some obvious exceptions such as bodies, tops, and a rear driveshaft. The next few paragraphs cover the important details of the time periods and models.

1972–1975

The earliest AMC-produced CJ-5 had an 84-inch wheelbase,

An iconic Renegade ad from 1973 shows the Jeep used in a more sporty form than utility. This early trend continued in the CJ series throughout its run. "The toughest four letter word on wheels" and "Only in a Jeep" were some favorite catchphrases from the era. (Photo Courtesy Fiat Chrysler Automobiles)

3 inches longer than the 1971 and earlier CJ-5s. The increase was inserted at the rear of the front clip. During the first few years of the AMC era, the CJ retained many of the design features found in the prior year's CJ-5. The most notable differences were standard electric wipers with an exterior-mounted engine, individual taillights and reverse lights,

The introduction of the CJ-7 allowed Jeep to offer options not found in previous CJ models such as an automatic transmission, a hardtop, full-time four-wheel drive, and added space. Early CJ-7 ads capitalized on the new details of the longer CJ. (Photo Courtesy Fiat Chrysler Automobiles)

a rear-mounted fuel tank, and Saginaw steering with a power option. The braking system was upgraded to 11-inch drum brakes using a newly introduced proportioning valve (1974). These early CJs had a stamped "Jeep" logo on the body in front of each door until later in the 1974 model, when the stamping was moved lower and used the plain Jeep lettering.

The Renegade model was continued and saw some changes in the striping features. In 1973 only, a new trim package called the Super Jeep was introduced when supply for the aluminum Renegade wheels ran short. This model featured colorful 1970s-style striping from front to rear. Interestingly, Jeep toyed with the idea of reissuing the Super Jeep in 1976 to celebrate America's bicentennial. A few were produced but were never available to the public.

1976–1986

The CJ lineup received many changes in 1976, including the introduction of the longer CJ-7 and eventually, in 1981, the even-longer CJ-8. A new floor layout was introduced to accommodate the larger optional automatic transmission. The frame was widened in the rear starting behind the front leaf spring mounts and reaching full width just before the rear spring mounts. The rear leaf springs were widened to 2½ inches and a front sway bar was added. These improvements helped the CJ's road handling and stability. To further improve the CJ's road manners, Jeep introduced front disc brakes with a power brake option, and in 1982 wider "Wide Trak" front and rear axles were added to the CJ-7 and CJ-8.

The CJs of this time period included many other notable details. The heater system was improved and air conditioning was optional.

1972–1975 Specifications

Engines: 232 I-6, 258 I-6, 304 V-8
Transmissions: T14, T15, T18
Transfer Case: Dana Model 20
Rear Axle: Dana 44
Front Axle: Dana 30

1976–1986 Specifications

Engines: 151 I-4 (Iron Duke), 150 I-4 (AMC), 258 I-6, 304 V-8
Transmissions: T150, T18, T4, T5, SR4, T176
Transfer Case: Dana Model 20, Dana Model 300
Rear Axle: AMC Model 20, Dana 44
Front Axle: Dana Model 30

The taillights were integrated to merge the brake lights and reverse lights. The wiper motor was moved to the inside of the windshield and the dash was redesigned to include heater controls, optional tachometer, and clock. Other interior additions included a locking steering column with an optional tilt and a radio.

Models

The AMC CJ era continued the use of the original CJ name, at first with just the CJ-5 model and later with the addition of the CJ-7 and CJ-8. Each of the three mainstream models share many features but all have their own unique detail that sets them apart.

1976–1983 CJ-5

The final run of the CJ-5 still included the 83½-inch wheelbase but was now equipped with a widened rear frame section, which was fully boxed starting in 1977, and a front sway bar to improve road handling. The rear springs were increased in width to 2½ inches. Notable CJ-5 Models were Renegade, Golden Eagle, and Laredo.

1976–1986 CJ-7

The CJ-7 was the first new CJ since 1955, and it was a near-perfect CJ featuring a 93½-inch wheelbase. The extra 10 inches were added at the rear of the door opening, widen-

A 1978 CJ-7 on the trail sporting its bright yellow paint and a list of modifications and accessories a mile long. The swapped AMC 360 V-8 runs through a T-18 transmission and a TeraLow-equipped Dana 20 transfer case. Both front and rear axles are swapped Dana 44s from a Scout.

The 1980s brought the Scrambler, a small truck like the CJ, that would gain an almost cult following after the discontinuation in 1986. The added wheelbase gave extra interior room, but the increased rear overhang could be troublesome off-road. Fortunately, the Scrambler shared nearly all the same components as the other CJs so modification options were nearly endless. This 1981 Scrambler sits in its owner's garage after the completion of an AMC 4.2L I-6 to AMC 401 V-8 swap.

ing the entrance to actually allow a person to enter the Jeep without special maneuvers. This extra space created increased room behind the front seats and allowed the rear seat to be mounted more forward to create useable room in the rear. The optional factory hardtop including lockable full metal doors with roll-up windows offered a quieter, more secure interior. The U-shaped door easily identifies the CJ-7. The CJ-7 had the

A rare Wedgewood Blue 1979 CJ-5 looks at home on the boardwalk at the Jersey shore. This Jeep is an unrestored survivor Jeep found in Oregon, equipped with year-correct Goodyear Tracker tires and 304 V-8. (Photo Courtesy Eric Jankowski)

same frame and suspension features as the CJ-5, with the exception of some added space in the middle. This model always had a tailgate and most often had a spare tire mounted to a swing-away body-mounted carrier. Notable CJ-7 models were Renegade, Golden Eagle, and Laredo.

1981–1986 CJ-8

The CJ-8, more commonly called Scrambler, was essentially a CJ-7 with 10 inches of wheelbase (103½ inches) added to the area behind the door and 14 inches added to the rear of the body to create a small truck-like bed. This Jeep featured a small-cab hardtop and the interior was equipped with a removable separator between the bed and front seats. The final year of the Scrambler was 1985 with an extremely limited run of only 2,015 built, with some likely carried over as 1986 models.

Spotting a Renegade

The Renegade was a regular model through the entire AMC era of the CJ. Renegade models frequently had special features and options such as decals, extra gauges, roll bars, and special wheels. Questions often arise about how to identify a particular year of Renegade. It's all in the decals.

- 1972 and 1973 have a black stripe down the center of the hood, along with a straight black stripe with white "Renegade" lettering along the side of the hood extending to the cowl, where it ends.
- 1974 and (first half of) 1975 have a black stripe down the center of the hood, along with a straight black stripe with white "Renegade" lettering along the side of the

hood extending to the cowl, where it turns downward 90 degrees and passes through the Jeep logo, ending directly below it.

- 1975 (second half) and 1976 saw the removal of the center hood stripe and the introduction of the single-piece decal that stretched across the hood from side to side.
- 1977 and 1978 introduced a large hood decal with separated "Renegade" lettering on the sides of the hood.
- 1979 and 1980 featured a much more complex decal arrangement. The center hood stripe returned, which was connected to progressive stripes that slightly changed in color and thickness. The "Renegade" lettering stood alone and a gradient stripe went under the door and behind the rear wheel.
- 1981 and 1982 changed the multi-colored striping to a tri-color design that created a U-shaped stripe over the

Another iconic ad from the 1974 Jeep Renegade model. The slight variation of the black side stripe and black hood decal only survived partway through the year. This Renegade look still remains a favorite today, where Wrangler JK versions of the same stripe are still made in the aftermarket. (Photo Courtesy Fiat Chrysler Automobiles)

The 1977 and 1978 scheme was a bit tamer than the prior years but still offered a look that made the Jeep stand out. The massive decal covered a large percentage of the Jeep's hood. (Photo Courtesy Fiat Chrysler Automobiles)

The new striping on the 1975 and 1976 combined the entire decal into one piece that stretched from one side of the hood to the other. The 1976 model year was the first year of the CJ-7 and the last year to offer factory aluminum slot wheels. (Photo Courtesy Fiat Chrysler Automobiles)

The gradient color striping on the 1979 and 1980 CJ is another favorite scheme. The light blue 1979 Jeep with blue-themed gradient striping made a look that still seems to work today.

hood with "Renegade" lettering on the sides of the hood. The tri-color stripe also went in a straight line below the door to the rear of the Jeep.

- 1983 and 1984 have a further change, where the multicolor hood stripe was only on the raised center section of the hood in a U-shape. The "Renegade" lettering was in all caps on the side of the hood, and there was a side stripe that went from the rear, under the door, and finally ended behind the front fender in a stacked-looking stripe.
- 1985 and 1986 were the final years of the CJ Renegade, and the hood design remained similar to the 1983 and 1984 style. The side stripe was changed to start at the rear of the front fender and curve over the rear fender, ending in the rear. ■

The final years of the CJ-7 Renegade featured a thinner hood stripe and capital letters on the side of the hood. The optional chrome grille finished the look of this 1985 white CJ-7 Renegade.

Choosing the Right CJ

Any of the three CJ models in any of the years discussed here makes an awesome off-roader, but each offers its own advantages and disadvantages. Some of these traits can be the source of debate among Jeepers and that could probably fill a volume on its own. For this book, I home in on a few of the key advantages (pros) and disadvantages (cons) of each to establish the baseline of the ingredients to building a CJ for maximum performance on- and off-road.

CJ-5

Pro: The short wheelbase of the CJ-5 is an advantage off-road when it comes to maneuvering through tight trails. The low breakover angle makes clearing obstacles that might high-center the Jeep easier. In more recent years, the CJ-5 has had a distinct advantage over the 93½-inch wheelbase found in the CJ-7, Wrangler YJ, and Wrangler TJ that are so popular on the trail by allowing the 83½-inch wheelbase to not get stuck in the 93½-inch worn trail obstacles.

Con: The short wheelbase can be a small disadvantage on hills because it causes the front to become very light from weight shift, resulting in poor traction. Perhaps a larger consequence of this short length is the lack of interior space. The CJ-5 offers so little interior space that Jeepers usually need to get very creative to find a space to stow all their gear. This is made worse when the Jeep has no tailgate. It is common to see CJ-5s on the trail with no rear seat to make way for storage.

Driveline modifications can be a challenge in the CJ-5. The short length can cause high driveshaft angles when longer transmissions or higher lifts are installed. These high angles can lead to vibration and universal joint failures.

CJ-7

Pro: The size of the CJ-7 is nearly perfect. Its longer wheelbase makes it more stable and its increased interior space gives more room for people and gear. Perhaps a favorite characteristic of the CJ-7 is a doorway that one can actually enter. The added wheelbase is a bonus for the rear driveshaft for its added length that makes it less prone to vibration when the Jeep is lifted. The CJ-7 was also available with an automatic transmission that is preferred by some off-roaders. Swapping transmissions and transfer cases is much easier in the CJ-7 thanks to the added wheelbase.

Because the CJ is known for its ability to rust effortlessly, a rusted CJ-7 body can be replaced by a substantially newer Wrangler YJ body with minimal modifications. These bodies are relatively easy to obtain and are often in good shape because rustproofing has improved in the years following the AMC era.

Finally, much of the aftermarket caters to the CJ-7 because of its popularity. Most components are interchangeable across the CJ line, but items such as tops, seats, and body protection are often aimed at the CJ-7. The CJ-7 and Wrangler YJ share many interior and body components including tops, doors, and roll bars.

Con: Because so many Jeeps run this similar wheelbase, tough spots on trails are frequently even worse with a CJ-7 because the ruts are usually the exact same size as the wheelbase of the Jeep. The CJ-7 is the dominant Jeep of the AMC era, so if you are the type of person who likes to stand out with a unique Jeep, a CJ-5 or Scrambler may suit you better.

CJ-8

Pro: The pickup truck style of the Scrambler gives you much more room to carry gear. The added wheelbase helps on the hills and improves street ride quality. The longer wheelbase reduces driveline angles to reduce vibration from high lifts. The Scrambler production numbers were low, making this Jeep increasingly rare. Scramblers often gather more attention from Jeep fans than other AMC-era Jeeps.

Con: The increased wheelbase creates a larger breakover angle that increases the chances of high-centering the Jeep on an obstacle. Larger lifts and/or tires help with this. The Scrambler has a large rear overhang, which can be trouble off-road. The addition of a substantial aftermarket rear bumper helps prevent body damage. People occasionally "bob" a Scrambler to remove the excess body.

The Scrambler was designed to be a two-seater, which limits interior room. Adding a full roll bar can be a challenge when the small cab's hardtop is retained.

The Perfect Out-of-the-Box CJ?

An examination of all of the years of the CJ will conclude that the 1978 and 1979 CJ-5 and CJ-7 were the epitome of the CJ. These two years offered a V-8, strong reliable transmissions such as the T18 and GM TH400 automatic, large front disc brakes, and 11-inch rear drum brakes. One little exception to

this is the somewhat rare 1980 CJ-7 with a V-8 and an automatic. This combination included the Chrysler TorqueFlite automatic (TF999) and a Dana 300 transfer case, a formidable off-road package.

Putting It All Together

In truth, any year and any model CJ makes a perfect Jeep for on- and off-road use. Even a stock CJ is a blast to drive off-road and is very capable. In the following chapters, building and modifying a CJ from top to bottom for maximizing performance on- and off-road is discussed in depth. Jeep owners tend to tinker with their Jeeps continuously. From engine modifications, lift kits, lockers, and more, it's common for CJs to see many changes and phases. Not surprisingly, CJs still remain a favorite Jeep for many, even with modern Wranglers everywhere.

Considered the best years of the CJ, the 1978 and 1979 CJs offered strong I-6 and V-8 engines, tough transmissions, and usable gear ratios. After 1980, the CJ became less off-road friendly out of the box due to fuel mileage and exhaust emissions requirements.

A small number of 1980 CJs were available with a 304 V-8 until the 304 was discontinued. This, combined with the newer Chrysler automatic and Dana 300 transfer case, made this Jeep extra special and extra rare. This 1980 CJ-7 is perfectly modified to perform well both on- and off-road.

CHAPTER 2

ENGINE

Engine performance modifications in the Jeep community are rather different from most other forms of automotive enthusiast engine modifications. A Jeep engine is most often modified to provide increased low-end torque rather than increased high-end horsepower because the needs of the trail are different from those of the dragstrip. Jeep engines tend to run at slow speeds and slow vehicle movement on the trail, which puts extra stress on the cooling system.

High-compression, high-horsepower engines usually do not tolerate the kind of driving conditions Jeep owners might expose their Jeeps to.

Even though the CJ series was discontinued years ago, it is possible that local and federal emissions laws are still applicable. Research into emissions laws should be done before digging into modifying your Jeep's engine to avoid violating laws and rules, which could result in the inability to pass a smog test. Many aftermarket parts are smog legal and

many do not alter emissions systems at all. Typically, swapping an engine of a newer model year is permissible by emissions laws, as long as comparable emissions equipment is retained. With the advanced age of the AMC-era CJ, it's hard to imagine swapping an older model year engine into the Jeep.

Factory Engines

Factory Jeep engines were briefly discussed in Chapter 1, so here I dig more into "actually useable" Jeep engines, including the advantages and disadvantages of each. Two 4-cylinder engines were offered in the CJ during the AMC era. Although both were functional engines, their lack of power and torque make them poor choices in a modified CJ, so they should be avoided and/or swapped. In the following few paragraphs, I discuss the I-6 and V-8.

AMC I-6

The 232 and 258 I-6 engines are similar in design and use many of the same components. The 258 was a far more popular engine in the AMC-era CJ than the 232. The engine is well known as reliable and provided a

This 1977 CJ-7 was a factory V-8 equipped Jeep with a TH400 automatic and Quadra-Trac transfer case. Of all the modifications, upgrades, and enhancements, the V-8 has remained stable with just enough performance modifications to perform well on- and off-road.

The AMC In-line 6-cylinder powered the CJ and so many other Jeep vehicles reliably and effectively for more than 30 years. This Jeep's 258 is showing its age and use from all the years of mud, grime, and dirt present on it. These engines were true workhorses that were capable of 250,000 miles from brand new to totally abused.

The AMC Tall Deck V-8 engines were often accused of being copies of other manufacturers' engines when in reality the engine was its own creation. The thing that separates the Jeep from other types of automotive enthusiast crowds is that a dirty, muddy engine is considered more attractive than shiny parts. Evidence that the Jeep is used the way it is intended only makes onlookers more interested.

significant amount of torque for its size, thanks to its long compression stroke. The 258 has proven itself as a workhorse engine in a CJ and can provide years of reliable service to its owner. The low-end torque of this engine and the low gears of a CJ is a near-perfect combination. However, there are some gotchas with this engine, and perhaps the biggest one deals with the horrific carburetor system found on 1981 and later CJs.

AMC V-8

The AMC 304 V-8 is a fun engine for a CJ and even in totally stock form can provide plenty of power and torque to throw a CJ around on the street and trail. Although the 1970s smog-laden V-8s weren't known for their performance, with a little help they can come alive. AMC V-8 engines were popular in the AMC muscle cars they came in, such as the Javelin and AMX. Thanks to those cars, a space was created in the performance aftermarket for the AMC V-8, and many upgrades and modi-

fications are available. V-8–powered CJs running fenderwell headers and glasspack mufflers are an icon of the late 1970s.

Modify, Rebuild or Swap?

Before modifying your factory Jeep engine, consider its condition. Is it worth modifying, is it too far gone and not worth rebuilding, or even further swapping? Some inspection and a few tests should be performed on your Jeep's engine before making this decision. A good-condition engine that is ready to modify should stand up to the added performance from the modifications. A rebuild candidate may be a fair-running engine but due to maintenance neglect or excess wear, this engine would benefit from a rebuild, along with modifications. A freshly rebuilt engine can be as good as new and can revitalize a Jeep. In the case that the engine may cost too much to rebuild or is beyond rebuildable condition, a replacement or swap should be considered.

Inspection and Testing

An engine in running condition is a good start, but how well it runs and how well it was maintained are just a couple of items that need further examination. Starting on the outside, inspect the cleanliness of the engine. Excess grease and gunk on the outside of the engine can mean

Finding grime like this inside your engine may mean a rebuild is in order. Grime in the rocker arm area usually means it's everywhere. Changing oil and filter according the manufacturer's specifications prevents this, even on an old engine. Complete disassembly and professional cleaning is the only real way of removing the contamination.

there were unfixed leaks from old gaskets or worse, cracks. This grime hides problems and can cause the engine to run hot or possibly even catch fire. This book doesn't focus on the specifics of rebuilding engines; consult an appropriate guide specific to your engine for more detail.

Compression

Compression testing can indicate the condition of the valves, valveseats, and piston rings. This simple test is performed using a compression tester that threads into the spark plug hole, cranking the engine (without it starting), and noting the pressure measured. Pressure numbers vary across engine types and years. In reality, the actual pressure number isn't as important as the consistency (10-percent variance) of pressure among cylinders. If each cylinder measures a similar pressure, the engine's valves, valve-

Test an engine's compression with the ignition system disconnected and all spark plugs removed. Thread in the compression tester and crank the engine using a remote starter switch or with the aid of another person on the key. Be sure the transmission is in park or neutral. Take note of each cylinder's pressure and compare after the test is complete. Similar pressures in all cylinders indicate good balance and even wear, desirable if the compression is within specification, which is around 120 to 140 psi for both the I-6 and V-8.

seats, and piston rings could be considered in sound condition.

AMC I-6 and V-8 engines in good condition generate pressures greater than 100 psi with 120 to 140 psi being within spec. A consistent low reading across all cylinders could be normal but may indicate a flat, worn-out engine. If a cylinder measures low, adding a teaspoon of oil to the low cylinder and repeating the test will indicate if bad rings or valvetrain cause the low pressure. No change in pressure from the oil test can indicate a holed piston or blown head gasket. Low pressures might warrant a full inspection and rebuild.

Engine Oil

Draining and inspecting the oil can give an idea of the conditions inside. Most people know that the engine oil provides lubrication to the close tolerances of the engine's bearings but it can also suspend contaminants within. New oil is a nice, clear amber color and quickly turns to a blackish color from contaminants. Inspecting the oil for its texture and smell can indicate a problem; gritty oil can be a sign that the oil is very old, along with an old filter.

If other fluids come out with the oil, such as coolant, this indicates the

likelihood that there is a gasket leak or crack in the block. Frothy or milky oil can contain coolant or water. If the Jeep was driven in deep water, it's possible that water has entered the engine through the vents.

Coolant

Draining the coolant from the engine and inspecting it for rust or corrosion can indicate the condition of the cooling system within the engine and radiator. The presence of rust can indicate the water-to-coolant ratio was too weak and the water was causing the cast iron to rust. In addition to rust, a weak coolant ratio can result in corrosion to copper components. Periodic testing of the coolant ratio is simply done using an inexpensive coolant tester.

Interior

Interior inspection of the engine is definitely more involved and requires some disassembly of the engine. Starting with the valvecover(s), remove the cover and inspect the rocker/valve area and components. If this area of the engine is covered with grime and old, thick, sticky oil (known as sludge), this is a good indication of very old oil, overheating, and/or poor-quality oil.

Inspection of the interior of an engine is a good indication of the extent of a rebuild. The removal of the oil pan or intake manifold on a V-8 (requires draining antifreeze) gives a view of the condition of the interior of the engine. The smell or presence of non-oil fluids such as water, antifreeze, or gasoline can indicate trouble.

If the condition of this area is very poor, it's likely the rest of the inside of the engine looks the same.

A few products can be purchased to help remove sludge; many (if not most) aren't very effective and can result in engine damage by releasing stuck sludge into the engine, clogging bearings and passages. Proper sludge removal is generally best done by full disassembly and cleaning of the engine.

Summing It Up

An engine that passes the inspection and tests could be considered worthy of modification. A minor rebuild during modification, such as new gaskets and seals, should be considered, as well as replacement of certain components that are typically a hassle to replace when the engine is fully assembled, such as the thermostat, hoses, belts, and water pump.

Rebuilding

If, after inspection, a rebuild is in order, it is best to pull the engine and further inspect crankshaft and connecting rod clearances to determine if machine work is needed. Consult an engine rebuild guide for your particular engine to determine inspection specs.

If the engine checks out, a rebuild can be far less expensive than a new engine and can be performed by a do-it-yourselfer to save some expense. Certain things such as engine cleaning should be performed by a professional to ensure all contaminants are removed from even the hard-to-reach places in an environmentally sound and efficient manner.

In addition, consider a professional valve job while the engine is out and apart, again another overlooked job so easily done at this

Bent pushrods from a past broken timing chain combined with age, dirt, and grime made this engine run poorly, and after years of neglect a rebuild was needed. Bored .020 over, cleaned, and new bearings made this engine like new again. During assembly, a new performance cam, intake, and a fresh coat of factory color paint made this engine ready to go back into place.

time. If rebuilding an engine is not in your bag of tricks, a good engine shop should be able to perform the rebuild, including checking proper clearances and machining if needed.

Replacement or Swap

If the existing engine is beyond repair, a decision to replace the factory engine with a same type or swap to another type needs to be made. Typically, replacing the engine with the same type is the least expensive option because the expense of a swap and the costly items such as adapters, radiators, mounts, exhaust, etc., that go with it will not be incurred.

If the choice is replacing the engine with a similar type, consider factors such as engine size; perhaps an AMC 304 would be best replaced

with a 360 that bolts right in.

Finally, deciding to install a used replacement engine in good shape is considerably less expensive than a crate engine.

Performance Parts and Modification

Increasing the performance of your Jeep's engine can be achieved with a variety of additions and modifications. Because the goal is to build a Jeep that performs well on- and off-road, the modifications are not to build a 1,000-hp race engine but rather a good-torque and good-power engine. The beauty of off-roading a Jeep is that horsepower is not always as important as it may be in other automotive circles.

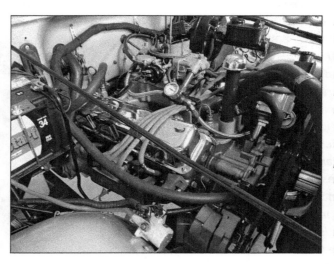

A rebuilt AMC 401 in this Scrambler provides enough horsepower to easily propel this Jeep in the passing lane. The nature of the 401 and thoughtful performance additions keep the engine producing plenty of high horsepower for some fun while maintaining the low-torque "tame" for those slow, controlled trail maneuvers.

Much of the day on the trail is spent moving at slow speeds and excess horsepower usually results in poor drivability, overheating, and broken parts. This fact allows a Jeep owner to invest a reasonable amount of the Jeep funds into performance parts that actually make a difference without going overboard. The saved funds can be put into things that matter more on the trail, such as traction systems, gearing, suspension systems, and everything else.

Here, I generalize on performance parts and focus on common modifications that enhance performance.

Factory Engine Modifications

Because most Jeep owners find themselves with a factory engine, much can be done to both the AMC V-8 and I-6 to enhance their performance. It is fortunate that both of these engines (for the most part) can serve the Jeep well with no modifications, but really, why would you want this? Because the engines are so usable out of the box, this suggests that anything that is done only serves to make the engine better.

AMC I-6

The most common I-6 in a CJ is the 258-ci (4.2L), which is a good engine with excellent low-end torque. The biggest drawback to this engine is the Computerized Engine Control (CEC) system found on the 1980s-era 258. The performance of these systems was barely adequate when the Jeep was brand new; the last CJ rolled off the assembly line more than 30 years ago so it's safe to assume performance will be considerably worse.

Clifford Performance has a long-standing excellent reputation

The 1980s CJ I-6 brought with it the dreaded CEC system. Seemingly miles of vacuum lines and incomprehensible carburetor system made this engine a poor performer even at its best. Swapping the CEC for a better system can free up much space.

for combining proven components to improve the Jeep's I-6; this shop is a good starting point for ideas and solutions.

Stroker Engines and Kits

Perhaps the ultimate in AMC I-6 performance comes from a stroked 4.2L. Stroked engines use larger bore pistons and a longer stroke crankshaft to increase the engine displacement up to 4.7L. Stroker I-6 engines can make up to 300 hp and 350 ft-lbs of torque. Hesco, Clegg, and Golen produce crate stroker engines and stroker kits that provide significant power and efficiency gains. The options available from these companies range from direct drop-in replacement crate stroker engines to turnkey multi-port electronic fuel injection (EFI) engines to full-on supercharged engines.

I-6 Induction System

Replacing the whole CEC is the best start for a 258, and best results come from either installing an aftermarket intake with a performance carburetor/throttle body fuel injection or installation of an electronic fuel-injection conversion from a 4.0L HO engine.

A few aftermarket performance parts companies, such as Offenhauser, make aluminum intake manifolds for the AMC I-6, and perhaps most notably, Clifford Performance with its extensive line of AMC I-6 performance products. These manifolds allow installation of performance carburetors or throttle body fuel-injection systems.

Typically, the manifolds are designed to use 4-barrel carburetors but can be adapted for other carburetor

This CJ-7 runs a perfect example of a performance I-6 that is well paired with the Jeep's transmission and drivetrain. A CEC-less, rebuilt 258 running a Clifford intake, Howell TBI, header, and TFI ignition lead the swapped T176 transmission and TeraLow-equipped Dana 300 transfer case.

The Howell TBI system is specially tuned for the I-6 in the CJ and provides computer-controlled efficiency to make the engine run at its best. TBI systems provide for quick starts and smooth trail running, especially in situations that flood most carburetors. The Howell kit includes all sensors, fuel pump, and components to easily swap out a troublesome carbureted system.

types. Unless the I-6 is capable of handling a large 4-barrel, that is, the engine was stroked and/or is running performance heads and a performance cam, a small 4-barrel carburetor should be the limit.

For a more stock engine, many Jeep owners have used the Weber 38/38 2-barrel carburetor with excellent performance results. The more adventurous Jeep owners convert the I-6 to a Howell EFI throttle body injection (TBI) system. This complete system brings the CJ a bit more modern. The TBI system performance is excellent off-road and improves starting in both hot and cold weather.

Mopar makes an EFI system for the 258 that is essentially a fully contained induction conversion for the Jeep I-6. This system replaces the entire induction system with a modern fuel-injection system nearly identical to the one found on the 4.0L HO engine that Wranglers, Cherokees, and Grand Cherokees ran until 2006. This system requires a fair amount of wiring and sensor installation but is installable by most DIY-type Jeep owners.

4.0L Head Conversion

The 4.0L engine used in Jeeps from 1987 until 2006 used an improved head design that is compatible with the 4.2L engine, with a minor modification to seal off the small, triangular cooling passages on the intake/exhaust side of the head with epoxy. A common practice is to lightly stuff the ports with packing peanuts (which dissolve), seal with epoxy, and smooth the epoxy when dry. With this swap, use of a 4.0L exhaust manifold or header is required; the stock intake may be retained if desired.

This swap, when combined with a performance carburetor, TBI, or MPI setup from a 4.0L, wakes up a tired 4.2L and increases engine efficiency and off-road performance. The longer stroke of the 4.2L combined with the head improvements can yield an I-6 with more than 200 hp.

I-6 Camshafts

A few high-performance camshafts can be found for the I-6 from companies such as Clifford, Comp Cams, and Crower. Cams that improve the low-end torque (in the 208 duration and .448 lift range) are the best choice for a Jeep that sees the trail and street. Clifford performance makes a complete cam kit for the Jeep 258 that includes all the components such as springs, pushrods, and lifters. This kit increases the I-6 torque curve to produce a flat torque curve off idle to 4,500 rpm, especially useful off-road at slow speeds.

I-6 Exhaust

Headers versus manifolds is a debate that will last as long as engines still have them. The I-6 was known to crack factory exhaust manifolds, but on the flip side headers are known to blow gaskets and leak exhaust. Proper headers increase flow, resulting in better horsepower and torque. Clifford, Hedman, PaceSetter, and Borla make quality headers for the I-6 in various constructions and configurations.

Stainless and ceramic coatings provide long life and good looks. Some I-6 headers use a 3-into-1 tube design to provide a dual exhaust; the traditional 6-into-1 remains most common. Performance differences between the two can be negligible and insignificant to the dual-exhaust routing headaches that occur.

A good muffler can also help with performance and make the Jeep sound a little better. A loud exhaust

A Clifford header provides smoother exhaust flow from the I-6 with some added tone to give the Jeep's sound some personality. Headers can increase torque and power 30 percent, depending on configuration and engine specs. Dual- and single-outlet headers are available for the I-6.

gets old very quickly on a trail Jeep; consider a muffler that sounds good but is quiet enough to not annoy. Flowmaster mufflers combine good flow with good sound and solid construction that can handle the punishment of off-road use.

I-6 Ignition

The Jeep I-6 used a points system until 1976 and the Motorcraft electronic ignition system until 1986. The Motorcraft system worked well but was prone to sudden failure without warning. Many Jeep owners made it a regular habit to carry a spare ignition module in case of a failure.

The high-energy ignition (HEI) system is considered the most reliable classic ignition system and only requires a single wire for power. A GM HEI-style distributor can be adapted to work in the I-6 with only a gear modification. These conversion distributors can be found ready to go and are easy to install. Davis Unified Ignition makes a top-of-the-line HEI-style distributor for the Jeep I-6 that provides the ultimate in ignition performance.

An alternative to a complete HEI swap is adapting a Ford TFI ignition to a Duraspark distributor.

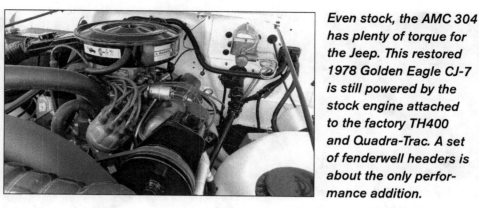

Even stock, the AMC 304 has plenty of torque for the Jeep. This restored 1978 Golden Eagle CJ-7 is still powered by the stock engine attached to the factory TH400 and Quadra-Trac. A set of fenderwell headers is about the only performance addition.

AMC V-8

Like the Jeep I-6, the factory 304 V-8 is a good starting point in a CJ, even in its stock form. The messy emissions controls and equipment of the 1970s stifled the small V-8, but with a little help this engine can provide plenty of low-end torque and some extra horsepower to make the Jeep feel like a muscle car. Swapping an AMC 360 or 401 is a bolt-in job and can provide a larger boost to the Jeep than might be possible with the 304. The AMC V-8 has a fair amount of aftermarket performance parts available, and finding a proven combination is not a difficult task.

The Generation 3 or Tall Deck AMC V-8 was used from 1970 until

A few varieties of the high-output electronic ignition systems are available for I-6, including a less common but effective Ford TFI conversion. This system uses a more modern ignition system with a similar function and performance to the GM HEI system. The TFI conversion uses some of the stock components while most importantly replacing the Ford Duraspark module.

1991 and was available in 304-, 360-, 390-, and 401-ci configurations. These engines share most components such as cylinder heads, intake manifolds, camshafts, etc. A 304 or 360 are probably the most common and easiest to find. Both provide a good start to a Jeep engine build.

V-8 Stroker

Unlike the I-6, the AMC V-8 engine has few stroker options available, built mostly of homegrown combinations using mixed parts and special crankshaft grinds. The cost and compromise may make it not worth it for a Jeep used on the street and trail. Power and torque gains found in the I-6 stroker make the work make more sense. In contrast, the AMC V-8 running in its factory sizes serves the Jeep easily, even with light modifications. I suggest you skip this option; it's just not worth the effort to stroke an AMC V-8 for a CJ.

V-8 Induction System

The stock AMC V-8 used a Motorcraft 2-barrel carburetor that was surprisingly well suited for both on- and off-road use. These carburetors were well known for reliability and maintenance-free use. A variety of intake manifolds were used on the CJ V-8; design differences were often

A shiny new Edelbrock Performer intake manifold provides the perfect performance enhancement for a V-8 in a Jeep. This AMC version is destined for Bryan Sterner's 1980 CJ-7 that is running the stock 304. A proper-size 4-barrel carburetor and matching Edelbrock Performer camshaft completes the package.

Holley carburetors have always been known for their exceptional performance, except when used off-road. The front and rear fuel bowl combined with the bowl venting location often caused fuel to dump into the throttle body when ascending or descending hills, resulting in flooding and stalling. Holley answered the call of off-roaders with a specially designed off-road carburetor called the Truck Avenger, featuring special metering blocks and off-road crossover vent tube.

The Edelbrock Performer Series carburetors are based on the Carter AFB and come in a variety of flow capacities. The integrated side-bowl design of the carburetor makes its off-road performance excellent compared to most other performance carburetors. The pre-tuned bolt-in design makes this a popular aftermarket carburetor.

to accommodate emissions systems such as exhaust gas recirculation (EGR).

Companies such as Edelbrock, Offenhauser, and Weiand make performance manifolds for the AMC V-8; most are made to work with 4-barrel carburetors and can be adapted to work with modern throttle body fuel-injection systems. The Edelbrock Performer series intake with its matching camshaft make an excellent combination to make some extra torque and horsepower from the engine that is nearly perfect for an on- and off-road Jeep. Most aftermarket manifolds can be purchased with or without emissions capabilities.

A small (470 to 670 cfm) 4-barrel carburetor or throttle-body fuel-injection system added to a V-8 running an aftermarket intake and cam provides better throttle response and starting. Two excellent carburetors for use in a Jeep are the Edelbrock Performer and the Holley Truck Avenger. When either is combined

with the combination above, optimum performance on- and off-road can be achieved.

The Edelbrock carburetor is based on the Carter 4-barrel but is specially tuned for the Performer Series products. The integrated main body side bowls and simple design make this very effective in a Jeep, especially off-road.

The Holley Truck Avenger is based upon the Holley 4160 with several modifications to make it perform in off-road conditions. Most notable is the crossover vent tube to prevent flooding on ascent and descent and spring-loaded needle and seat to control fuel flow. The Holley Truck Avenger is available in three CFM sizes. A 470-cfm suits the 304 and a

670-cfm suits the 360 and 401. Avoiding the tendency to over-carburete an engine; using the 770-cfm pays off in the form of performance and no tearing eyes from fumes.

Holley, Howell, and MSD produce electronic throttle body fuel-injection systems that replace the carburetor and can provide a high level of all-around performance, most notably in off-road conditions and starting in both cold and hot environments. These systems can operate with full, minimal, or no tuning; often through the use of the many sensors, the system tunes itself constantly while operating. A small drawback of these systems is the complexity of installation and the added potential points of failure.

Throttle body injection (TBI) systems offer a modern replacement to a traditional carburetor. The Holley Pro-Jection TBI was a popular system in the off-road community. Its simple design, easy starting, and steady engine performance at any angle were just a few of the positive features. This Holley Pro-Jection system has been running on this 350 Chevy-equipped 1985 CJ-7 for more than 20 years. Holley replaced the Pro-Jection system with the updated Holley Avenger electronic fuel injection (EFI) system.

The dogleg port seen on this dirty AMC cylinder head is a unique feature of the AMC tall deck engines introduced in 1970. The extra port provided increased flow compared to the prior design.

In general these systems operate confidently, with most failures occurring with the fuel pumps. You can solve this by always carrying a spare on the trail. These systems can be expensive and the benefits may not outweigh their complexity and price.

V-8 Camshafts

A variety of camshafts are available for the AMC V-8. Many are made for strip or other racing applications, but a few exist that are perfect for the Jeep. As I mentioned before, the Edelbrock Performer Series components are nicely matched to each other. The Performer camshaft for the V-8 provides a nice power curve that increases low-end torque and mid-range horsepower. This mild build camshaft does not alter the low-end idle of the Jeep as a high-duration camshaft does, which is important when driving off-road slowly.

Other camshafts in the 204/214 duration and 448/472 lift ranges provide added low-end torque. In addition to upgrading a camshaft, upgrading the engine's timing chain to a dual roller completes the package.

V-8 Exhaust

The 1970–1991 AMC V-8 used a dogleg exhaust port that provided 20 percent better flow than prior-generation AMC heads. The factory V-8 used cast-iron exhaust manifolds that used a combining Y-pipe to exit the rear driver's side of the Jeep. The factory exhaust manifolds flow well for the purpose of a street- and trail-used Jeep; they can be retained and when combined with an upgraded exhaust, increase flow and torque.

Typically, a single exhaust is most common on trail-used Jeeps. The low-end torque on both the I-6 and especially the V-8 is better with a single exhaust system.

Although exhaust manifolds perform best on a street- and trail-used Jeep, a Jeep with headers, especially fenderwell headers, adds a cool factor that is hard to deny. Fenderwell headers exit the Jeep's engine compartment just behind the front wheels. A small muffler or cherry bomb muffler is typically used to quiet the exhaust. Almost all fenderwell header Jeeps are loud, so you need to be able to tolerate the noise that comes with the classic look.

Headers improve exhaust flow slightly over the factory manifolds, and the use of matched tube-length headers provides balance to exhaust output. Fenderwell headers are troublesome when used off-road because they may become damaged on obstacles and interfere with the often-used side rocker protection rails. In-frame headers allow for the exhaust to be

The small lobes and short duration on the stock camshaft in most engines made for smooth, fuel-efficient engines but at a cost to performance. Replacing a camshaft is an involved project that produces noticeable results compared to many other performance modifications. Choose a cam matched to the intake system for the best performance results. High-lift and long-duration cams sound nice but are difficult to drive off-road, as they sacrifice low-end torque for high-RPM horsepower.

Fenderwell headers hold both a performance enhancement and a visual appeal. Many 1970s-era V-8 CJs can be seen running these type of headers with small mufflers or glass-packs. With these headers comes a fairly loud exhaust sound, which is sure to wake the neighbors.

run within the frame rails, but space is tight on the passenger's side due to the transfer case drop.

Speaking anecdotally, many Jeep owners who have outfitted their Jeeps with headers of either kind have removed them to revert back to the factory manifolds. The reasons given for this are often constant exhaust leaks, excess underhood heat, and noise.

High-Performance Single Exhaust

An effective single exhaust using the factory manifolds must be fabricated by a professional shop or using sections of pipe and mandrel bends. Using 2-inch leader pipes running through a performance Y-pipe with a 3-inch outlet starts the system. Some run the leader pipe on the passenger's side forward and under the oil pan. An alternative is squeezing the passenger-side leader pipe over the front driveshaft and through the gap between the oil pan sump and transmission. To fit properly in the latter method, a lift kit is often essential and the pipe may need to be flattened slightly over the driveshaft. From the performance Y-pipe, the system exits the rear after passing through a performance 3-inch muffler and catalytic converter (if needed).

Flowmaster makes many varieties of mufflers that can fit a Jeep. Their durable construction and performance makes an excellent choice off-road. This free-flowing system can provide more low-end torque than a dual system. A single 3-inch pipe flows more than dual 2-inch pipes. ∎

To allow clearance for the front driveshaft and prevent the cross-over pipe from being too low, the passenger-side pipe routes forward, looping around the oil pan sump. After completing the curve, it joins the driver-side pipe at a smooth transition Y.

The 3-inch outlet leads into a performance Flowmaster muffler with 3-inch inlet and outlet. The 3-inch pipe continues from the muffler to the rear of the Jeep. Low-end torque from the single exhaust was an improvement over the old dual 2-inch exhaust system. The Flowmaster Y-pipe and muffler maintains the deep, throaty tone of the V-8, even though exhaust is only through a single pipe.

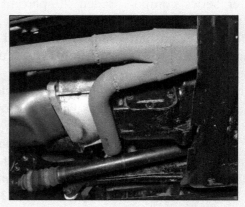

The performance Y-pipe setup keeps the crossover pipe up and out of the way of trail obstacles. This setup in a 1978 CJ-5 squeezes the pipe over the top of the front driveshaft for extra clearance and it passes in front of the T-18 leading to the Y-pipe collector. It was necessary to flatten the pipe at the driveshaft for proper clearance during suspension compression. The Flowmaster performance Y-pipe shown provides a maximized and smooth transition similar to a header collector from the 2-inch leader pipes to the 3-inch outlet.

V-8 Ignition

Early Jeep V-8s, including the I-6, used a points system until 1976 and the Motorcraft electronic ignition system until 1986. The Motorcraft system worked well but was prone to sudden failure without warning. Many Jeep owners made it a regular habit to carry a spare ignition module in case of a failure. The HEI system is considered the most reliable classic ignition system and only requires a single wire for power. As was discussed in the I-6 section, a GM HEI-style distributor can be adapted to work in the V-8 with only a gear modification. These conversion distributors can be found ready to go and are easy to install.

Davis Unified Ignition (DUI) makes a top-of-the-line HEI-style distributor for the Jeep V-8 that provides the ultimate in ignition performance.

Along with the performance distributor, a matched set of spark plugs and a performance set of spark plug wires from a company such as DUI, LiveWires, or Accel complete the ignition system upgrades. Spark plug gap should be set according to the distributor manufacturer. Popular performance spark plug manufacturers are E3, NGK, and Champion.

Converting to a GM-style HEI distributor increases spark performance and reliability. Davis Unified Ignition makes a ready-to-install premium version of the HEI conversion distributors.

LiveWires spark plug wires offer excellent HEI performance along with a mesh shield surrounding the wire to aid in protecting the wires from heat, wear, and objects. LiveWires are available in pre-made lengths for an HEI conversion on both the I-6 and V-8.

AMC V-8 HEI Installation

Installation of an HEI distributor is not a difficult job and can be done in an hour or two.

Begin by noting the No. 1 plug wire on the distributor then remove the stock plug wires and distributor cap, and pull the vacuum advance hose.

Locate the engine at top dead center (TDC) by removing the No. 1 spark plug and cover the hole with a finger. Rotate the engine in short starter bursts and feel for pressure on the finger from the compression stroke. Observe the distributor; the rotor should be at the location noted for the No. 1 plug wire. Look for the timing mark on the engine balancer, and rotate the engine to line up the mark with the timing-gauge "0" mark. This is TDC.

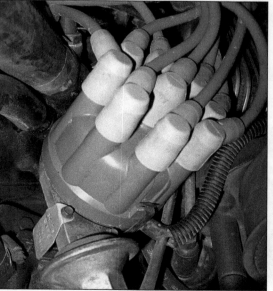

1 *From 1973 until 1980, the AMC V-8 was equipped with the Duraspark electronic ignition system. This system used a separate coil and electronic control module. The Duraspark modules were famous for sudden failures and could render a Jeep dead in the water. Most Jeep owners carried a spare module.*

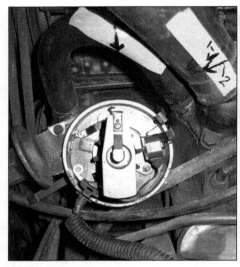

3 *The distributor hold-down is located below the distributor at the top of the timing chain/water pump housing. Loosen the bolt and remove the hold-down.*

4 *After the distributor wiring plugs are disconnected, remove the distributor by pulling it up from the engine. The rotor rotates slightly with the gear splines. Be careful not to allow dirt or items to fall into the distributor hole.*

2 *After getting the engine positioned at TDC, find a location to make a mark to note the position of the rotor. This aids in installation of the new distributor and hitting the proper location. A piece of tape with a mark on the coolant bypass hose is an excellent location.*

5 *A side-by-side comparison of HEI and Duraspark distributors. The HEI (left) uses a much larger cap that integrates the ignition coil for less loss.*

6 *The old Duraspark module and its wiring can be removed and no longer used. The original wiring harness has a positive lead (usually a larger red or yellow wire) that should be marked and set aside for reuse with the new distributor.*

7 *Like the module, the original coil and its wiring may be removed if no longer needed. The HEI coil is capable of higher output, allowing for increased spark plug gaps, resulting in a hotter ignition and larger spark area.*

8 *The oil pump shaft is driven by the end of the distributor and can be seen deep within the distributor's mount hole. It may be necessary to rotate the shaft slightly with a screwdriver to line it up with the new distributor.*

9 Install the distributor in the engine, aligning the rotor in the same position as the old one that was removed. In most engines, including the AMC V-8, this aligns the key at the bottom of the distributor gear with the oil pump drive rod, allowing the distributor to drop fully in. Rotating the engine with the distributor partially installed also allows it to drop in place. In this case, place the engine back at TDC before continuing. Replace the hold-down and lightly tighten.

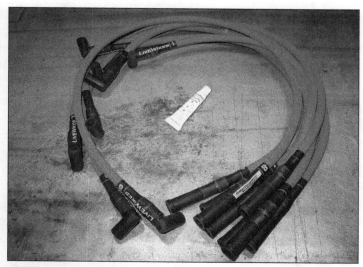

10 Install the HEI cap, tighten the clamps, and connect the distributor wiring harness to the cap. The HEI cap requires new spark plug wires. LiveWires spark plug wires are available for the HEI system in an AMC V-8. These wires are available in several colors and feature a protective outer mesh cover. Install the wires starting from the No. 1 position and following the 1-8-4-3-6-5-7-2 firing order.

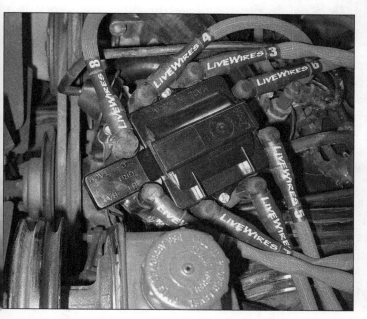

11 With the distributor installed and lightly clamped in place, move on to getting power to the HEI. The beauty of the HEI is its integrated design, requiring only switched battery power to operate. No harness, no ignition coil wire, no mess. One of the two harness connectors that were unplugged from the old factory ignition module has a large red or yellow wire, which is the switched power source. Connect this wire to the BAT terminal in the cap of the new HEI distributor.

12 Although (technically) the distributor just needs one switched power battery wire on many AMC-era CJs, the wire from the Duraspark harness makes for hard starting due to its power being momentarily cut off during engine cranking. The Jeep's wiring causes certain circuits to cut off during cranking to allow full power to the starter. The fix for this is using the existing starter solenoid's bypass circuit, which is engaged during cranking, providing full power to the distributor. Splice a lead from the terminal labeled "I" into the switched power wire to the distributor.

13 The HEI delivers a higher energy spark to the spark plugs, and increasing plug gap increases ignition speed and efficiency. Most HEI systems recommend setting the plug gap at .035 to .055 inch. Using a plug gap gauge sets the gap correctly. Installing new plugs is probably a good idea but not needed unless the original plugs are old and worn.

14 *Adjusting the timing is becoming a lost art form, and timing lights are becoming a thing of the past. After installing new plug wires and reconnecting the battery, attach the timing light and, with the vacuum advance hose to the distributor disconnected and plugged, start the engine. Use the timing light to observe the location of the timing mark on the harmonic balancer. Rotate the distributor to adjust to 5 degrees; when proper timing is achieved, tighten the distributor bracket.*

Fine Tuning the Timing

After initial timing is set and everything is in its place, drive the Jeep, running the engine normally then make several hard acceleration runs, from both a stop and a passing style. Note the engine performance and adjust the timing if the engine seems sluggish, pings, or is hard to start. Without a timing tape on the balancer to read the exact timing, a little experimentation will find the proper timing.

Sluggish, poor performance is often a case of the timing not being advanced enough. Rotating the distributor clockwise to advance will improve performance. Do this in small intervals, followed by a driving test. If the engine shows signs of pre-ignition (pinging) or is difficult to start, the timing is likely advanced too far. Rotating backward followed by a driving test will help you to find the optimum spot.

Additional Performance Parts and Modifications

Some general performance modifications and parts are nearly universal across many engine types.

Air Filters
Reusable air filters such as ones made by K&N, AFE, and Airaid pro-

K&N set the standard for non-paper air filters. These filters use a gauze type material coated with a special oil to remove contaminants from air entering the engine while improving airflow. These reusable filters come in many sizes and styles.

vide better filtering while increasing airflow. Driving a Jeep in off-road conditions exposes the air filter to dirtier conditions than street driving alone. Cleaning these filters more frequently ensures peak performance and longevity. For extra protection, installing a K&N pre-cleaner wrap around the air cleaner keeps larger debris off the filter element.

Snorkels
Some Jeep owners install a snorkel system to prevent water from entering the engine. No direct bolt-in snorkel systems are currently available for the CJ and most are fabricated using a matching air intake plenum combined with some creative plumbing to either move the air cleaner to the outside of the Jeep at a high location,

such as the windshield, or plumbing into the inside area of the Jeep's cowl.

The interior helps keep water out when fording streams, but driving through deep water may still submerge the filter. Hydrolock is a condition experienced when water enters the engine. Because water does not compress, the engine stops rotation until the water is drained, usually from the spark plug holes.

A snorkel alone is only half the equation for crossing deep water. The exhaust system should be routed to allow the engine to push out exhaust when underwater. Relying on the exhaust pressure when crossing deep water can cause excess pressure in the engine, resulting in stalling. A sudden change in pressure can cause the water to back up into the exhaust and end up within the engine's cylinders.

Cooling
A Jeep's cooling system is subjected to harsh conditions off-road. Slow speeds drive up underhood temperatures, and trail debris such as dirt, rocks, and mud can end up in the radiator fins, potentially causing overheating. A factory Jeep radiator can be upgraded to a more modern aluminum radiator for increased cooling efficiency.

Novak Conversions makes a direct fit aluminum radiator for the CJ. In addition, a large factory-style engine-driven fan or electric fans

The traditional style but increased capacity four-core radiator combined with a factory fan shroud and large engine-driven fan keeps my AMC 360 cool even on the hottest days on the trail. Good airflow and high-capacity systems are put to the test in Jeeps used off-road.

running with a proper shroud are needed to pull enough air through the radiator.

Flex-a-Lite makes a direct-fit, shrouded dual-fan system for the CJ. Note that these fans draw 19.5 amps, which can put a heavy load on a stock electrical system. A higher output alternator may be needed. Small flex-style performance engine-driven fans are typically insufficient for off-road use and should be avoided.

An old-school Jeep trick to help with underhood temperatures is the installation of 1/2- to 1-inch-thick blocks under the cowl side of the Jeep's hood hinges. This props the rear of the hood up, creating a nearly full-width vent that can drastically remove engine heat. The functional look created by this is rather unique and can be a conversation piece to the novice.

Some companies such as Royal Purple and Lucas make coolant additive to help increase cooling efficiency. There has been mixed reviews on the effectiveness of these products. If cooling problems are experienced, it may be worth a try.

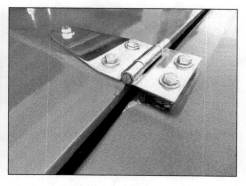

Finally, using a quality water pump with a proper pulley configuration is another important component to cooling in a Jeep. Spending some extra money in the area of cooling only lowers the likelihood of trail-related cooling issues.

PCV, Idle Mixture and Timing

The positive crankcase ventilation, or PCV, valve is designed to remove vapors from the inside of the engine. Most PCV valves draw engine vapors into the induction system to be burned with the fuel mixture. An old or defective PCV valve can hinder engine performance and cause excess vapor buildup within the engine.

Some carburetors and injection systems do not have provisions for adjusting idle mixtures but, if possible, adjust the idle mixture to proper specifications. A vacuum gauge is often the best device for adjusting the mix. Improper mixture, especially off-road, potentially causes the engine to run hot or have an excess fuel smell. An over-rich condition fouls spark plugs and leaves soot deposits in the exhaust system.

Proper engine timing affects many variables, including engine longevity, fuel economy, and engine power. Setting timing is a simple process using a timing light with the engine running. Rotating the distributor advances or retards the timing as needed.

An old trail trick to keep the underhood temperatures down was to stick a block of wood or steel under the cowl side of the hood hinges. The 1/2-inch or so opened a gap that ran fully across that allowed underhood heat to escape. Slow trail driving drastically raises underhood temperatures; even placing your hand there allows you to feel the heat moving.

Oil and Fuel Additives and Ethanol

Old Jeep engines have been left behind in the modern world. Most gasoline is unleaded and contains a mixture of ethanol. The early AMC era used engines designed to use the lead in gasoline to lubricate valve-guides and piston rings. The removal of lead and the addition of ethanol can sometimes cause issues. Lead substitutes can be added to the fuel to slow wear.

In recent years, zinc dialkyl dithiophosphate (ZDDP), a zinc-based additive found in engine oil, has disappeared from most brands. This oil component provided protection against wear for older engines, especially in a flat-tappet camshaft. Most newer engines use roller camshafts and other modern components that do not require ZDDP. It is claimed that adding a ZDDP additive such as Lucas Break In Additive replaces the missing ZDDP and prevents wear in old engines run without ZDDP.

Determining the effect of ethanol mixed into gasoline used in an old engine can make your head spin from the possibilities. Some older engines run normally; others experience performance and fuel-efficiency issues. Finding non-ethanol gasoline is becoming more difficult and there are other ways of making your Jeep's engine more tolerant of the mixed gas.

Most aftermarket carburetors perform well with mixed fuel and can be adjusted using mixture screws and jet changes. Both stock and aftermarket TBI and EFI injection systems typically perform well with mixed fuel, especially more advanced systems that run oxygen and MAP sensors.

Pretty, Shiny Stuff

Why not finish off your Jeep's underhood with some items to show off your hard work? A set of aluminum or chrome valvecovers and a matching air cleaner dress up the engine a bit. Degreasing the engine helps keep the engine cool and prevents the possibility of the gunk smoking or catching fire from the heat. Once the engine is clean, a fresh coat of engine paint can finish the package.

Putting It All Together

Starting with the engine, I put together a recipe for a Jeep suited for maximum performance on- and off-road. As stated earlier, the factory engines provide for the Jeep in this capacity quite well. Retaining the factory engine, if possible, saves money and allows for upgrades to increase performance.

Based on that premise, this factory I-6 Jeep engine is equipped with the following.

- Aftermarket intake with a Weber carburetor or TBI
- Set of 3-into-1 dual-exit headers
- Performance Y-pipe running through a 2½-inch exhaust and a performance muffler
- HEI-style distributor, preferably a brand name or a conversion
- Set of performance spark plug wires and spark plugs
- Reusable air filter
- Factory-style engine-driven fan with a proper shroud

Based on that premise, this factory V-8 Jeep engine would be equipped with the following.

- Matched aftermarket intake and camshaft combination
- Off-road-friendly carburetor
- Set of factory exhaust manifolds feeding into a performance Y-pipe
- 3-inch single exhaust with a performance muffler
- HEI-style distributor, preferably a brand name or conversion
- Set of performance spark plug wires and spark plugs
- Reusable air filter
- Factory-style engine-driven fan with a proper shroud or a proper-size electric fan setup

Many of these elements would work well with a swapped engine, with the exception of a modern fuel-injected engine. Modern engines would likely not need any modifications because their out-of-the-box performance specifications are well suited for the Jeep.

Adding some pretty stuff to an engine, such as a nice set of aluminum valvecovers and an attractive air cleaner, cleans up the underhood look. Of course, a trail-used Jeep's engine does not stay clean for long unless it's cleaned regularly. This restored Jeep has an engine bay that you could eat off. It's nice to look at but isn't practical for the trails.

This modified I-6 provides loads of low-end torque perfect for both on- and off-road driving. The simple setup is easy to maintain and repair, if needed. Specs for the engine include a 258-ci I-6, Clifford manifold and header, Howell TBI, TFI ignition conversion, and Omix-ADA valvecover.

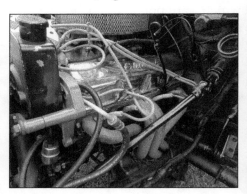

An AMC V-8 has no problem powering a CJ and performance modifications always add to the package. This factory-304-equipped CJ-7 runs that Edelbrock Performer Series combination that works so well. The Holley carb, intake, and cam combination result in extra-low-end torque and mid-range horsepower, which are well suited for an on- and off-road Jeep. The in-frame Hedman headers, dual exhaust, and HEI distributor finish the engine.

ENGINE SWAPS

Some people can't leave anything alone and Jeep owners have been swapping engines into their Jeeps since the earliest CJ. Engine swapping has reached a level of sophistication that allows even a relative novice to swap an engine into a CJ with great success. Engine swapping is one of the more popular topics resulting in questions and research by Jeep owners. There are no real limits to the swaps, but there are ones that make most sense, from the ease of installation to the cost of the project. Swapping an engine can snowball into a major project with major expenses, and problems can grow to the point that they can only be resolved with expensive solutions.

Luckily for 1972–1986 Jeep owners, AMC lengthened the CJ by 3 inches at the rear of the front fenders/hood area. These extra 3 inches allowed AMC to squeeze in the I-6 and 304 V-8, but more important, those extra 3 inches made a world of difference to the art of the engine swap.

A Jeep owner using the logic "I had this engine laying around" as a starting point for the swap usually ends up in a bad situation with a negatively impacted wallet. It is usually recommended to choose a swap candidate based upon what you want to do with your Jeep, research the details of the swap, plan the swap, and do it right. Swaps are not really for the mechanically challenged or

inexperienced DIY types. It is so much more than just bolting in an engine and hitting the key. The little details, such as exhaust, fuel lines, cooling, and clearance, are just the tip of the iceberg.

Because the goal here is to build a Jeep that works well on- and off-road, the engine you swap in should provide plenty of low-end torque, good highway driving power, efficient fuel mileage (realizing this thing is still a Jeep), and some extra power just for the heck of it. The swapped engine should match the driveline, including all components such as the transmission, transfer case, and axles. In

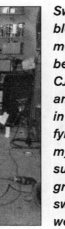

Swapping a Chevy small-block into a CJ is by far the most popular swap and has been a project since the earliest CJs. This circa-1980s father and son engine swap resulted in an overpowered and terrifying but fun-to-drive Jeep for my father and me. Aftermarket support for this swap is so great that a Jeep owner can swap in an engine during a weekend with proper parts.

AMC-era CJs had an extra 3 inches added to the rear of the front clip, increasing the frame, hood, and fender length. Those extra few inches at the bottom of the front flare allowed physically larger engines to fit in the Jeep's engine compartment.

A souvenir gained from the result of a swapped engine with a little too much horsepower and a young Jeep fan with a lead foot. These Dana 44 spider gears with sheared and broken teeth plus the not-shown repair bill and destroyed ring and pinion are a testament to the need for a well-thought-out engine swap.

addition, the engine swap shouldn't cost a fortune or add a level of complexity to cause potential problems and/or failures. A finicky engine on the trail in the middle of nowhere can ruin anyone's day.

In general, having access to the donor vehicle or all the components that made up the engine of the donor vehicle eases the swap and saves hours of parts searching. Missing components, including brackets, alternator, wiring, etc., slow the installation and end up adding to expenses. Swapping modern fuel-injected engines drastically improves the Jeep's drivability both on- and off-road, but these swaps are complex and carry even more importance to gather all the components before beginning. Take lots of pictures of the donor vehicle, take notes, and label stuff.

This book isn't big enough to be a comprehensive guide to swapping engines. It's a broad topic with many variables and options. Tried and true usually results in the best, most reliable swaps for both those new to swapping engines and the experienced. Exotic and strange conversions are best left for the seasoned and deranged Jeep enthusiasts.

You have two choices when swapping an engine into a Jeep: factory and non-factory. Both have advantages and disadvantages, such as larger aftermarket support, ease of replacement parts, and total cost of the swap. Consideration of both options should be thought out before beginning the project, and be careful of the outlying items that escalate the difficulty and expense.

Factory Swap Overview

Swapping a factory Jeep engine into another Jeep is the easiest swap to make. There is a special feeling of satisfaction with just removing the 4-cylinder engine and staring at the empty engine bay. Most swaps can use factory components and take little or no guesswork as to what fits. Swapping a factory engine usually comes in several forms: swapping a factory 4-cylinder with a factory I-6 or V-8, swapping a factory I-6 with a V-8, swapping a factory I-6 with a bigger factory I-6, and swapping a factory V-8 with a bigger factory V-8.

As stated earlier, having access to the donor Jeep makes the job much easier. Items such as engine mounts, radiators, throttle cables, and brackets can be potentially difficult and expensive to locate later.

If the original transmission is to be retained, most factory engines bolt to the transmission by using the

This 1980s CJ is still running the factory AMC 4-cylinder engine. The fan shroud extends several inches from the radiator to meet the little 150-ci engine. Anyone with experience driving a late-model CJ with a 4-cylinder understands why adapters exist.

Replacing a tired 304 with a rebuilt AMC 360 is just the trick in this CJ-5, which runs an Edelbrock Performer camshaft and manifold topped off with a Holley Truck Avenger 4-barrel carburetor. The smooth operation of the V-8 with its low-end torque has made this combination a favorite.

donor engine's factory bellhousing. Much of the factory wiring is usable with some minor modifications. Factory engine mounts specific to the particular engine being swapped should bolt directly to the Jeep's frame. As with the engine mounts, radiators bolt in and hoses can be readily obtained from parts dealers.

Engine mounts, among other items, degrade over time and should be inspected and replaced if needed during a swap. Polyurethane mounts are a popular replacement for the factory-style rubber mounts.

To Swap or Not

The highly popular Chevy small-block V-8 swaps can result in a Jeep with a reliable powerplant with proper power and that cool V-8 sound. Some swaps can have a high-horsepower engine with a lopey cam that sounds wonderful and scares the wits out of you; others have more reasonable daily-driver V-8s that are perfect for a CJ. Similar results from other make engines can be found. If this sounds good, you should also consider the added work and expense that follows a swap to a non-factory engine.

It's well known that the AMC V-8 can't match the aftermarket performance parts availability and the less expensive prices that separate the same part from the two manufacturers. For example, an Edelbrock Performer manifold for a small-block Chevy is about 40 percent cheaper than the same manifold for an AMC. This difference can accumulate when adding performance parts to an AMC V-8, but the price of adapters and the complexity of a swap often wash it away.

In addition, it's very convenient to be able to walk into an automotive parts store and get a part for an AMC V-8 or I-6 CJ. Fan belts, hoses, alternators, starters, etc., are simple to obtain without the guesswork encountered with other swaps. Try explaining to the teen at the counter of your local parts store that your Jeep has a Chevy 350.

Perhaps as AMC replacement parts and engines become harder and more expensive to find, swapping may be a necessary and more cost-effective solution. For now, though, sticking with AMC for the kind of Jeep you are building provides for the simplest, least expense project. ∎

Swapping a Chevy small-block into a CJ is by far the most popular non-factory swap, and a balanced-power engine results in good performance on- and off-road. This CJ has a later-model Chevy V-8 (indicated by the center bolt valvecovers) running a Holley 600 4-barrel carburetor and fenderwell headers.

A factory swap offers a fair amount of ease compared to swapping a non-factory engine. This crate AMC 360 is taking the place of an I-6 in this 1984 CJ-7. Using factory-style motor mounts, radiator, hoses, and more is possible with a Jeep-to-Jeep swap. After a short time mated to the factory transmission, a TF727 automatic was swapped in for strength and drivability.

Consider replacing some possibly old and worn items when swapping a factory engine. Throttle cables, engine mounts, radiators, and other general tune-up items may benefit the Jeep by being replaced. Old engine mounts tend to get brittle or separate completely. Aftermarket replacement and upgraded solid mounts are readily available. Replace any worn-out or brittle wiring with proper-size wire, perhaps even adding a secondary circuit block to distribute the power load better and make the wiring safer.

Non-Factory Swap Overview

There is technically no limit to what engine can be swapped into a Jeep, but most swaps just don't make sense from both practical and budget points of view. Novak Conversions in Cache Valley, Utah, is probably the best-known expert shop for Jeep engine, transmission, and transfer case swaps and conversions. Due to the vast amount of information about non-factory swaps, some high-level discussion is all there is space for within this chapter. Consider researching your conversion by starting with Novak and the many online Jeep websites and tech forums.

For the inexperienced, a swap may seem simple. However, a snowball effect often occurs when the list of incompatible components grows. The following items are just the obvious components that a swap can potentially impact.

Radiator

Most V-8 swaps require a higher-capacity radiator to properly cool the engine and to match up to the inlet/outlet ports on the engine. A Jeep that sees trail use puts extra stress on the

Electric fans can pull a large volume of air to keep the Jeep's engine cool; aftermarket support created the availability of bolt-in dual fans that include a proper-size shroud. Electric fans should be controlled by a thermostat and mounted to the rear of the radiator.

cooling system because of the continual slow speeds often experienced. Using a good fan, electric or engine driven, and fan shroud in addition to the proper radiator ensures that the Jeep stays cool. The small grille opening and narrow radiator space limits the radiator size; often three- and four-core radiators are used. A few companies make bolt-in swap radiators that are properly set up for the Jeep and provide proper cooling.

In recent years swap radiators are all-aluminum cross-flow styles, replacing the older copper/bronze construction, providing extra cooling power and good looks. Novak's KryoFlow HD radiators are properly sized cross-flow aluminum versions that are a direct bolt-in, designed to match the port needs of a swapped engine. Cooling problems are not something to take lightly and "going cheap" here usually has costly or big hassle results.

Mounts

Mounting the donor engine is likely the first big step in the installation. Locating the engine is often

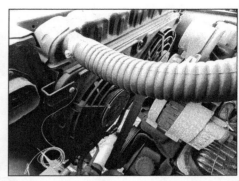

Conversion and higher-performance radiators ease a swap and provide the proper cooling to a higher-performance engine. Novak makes modern cross-flow bolt-in aluminum radiators for many types of Jeep engine swaps.

accomplished either by matching the engine to the original transmission location or by ensuring front (radiator) and rear (firewall) engine clearance. Altering the engine location that requires the transmission/transfer case to be moved requires modifications to the transmission mount or skid plate. Typically, a Jeep engine is mounted slightly offset to the driver's side to make room for the front driveshaft and differential.

Mounting a factory or non-factory engine in a CJ requires special mounts to properly secure the engine to the frame. These conversion mounts provide a solid mount that cannot separate as do the factory mounts. Mounts come in many varieties from bolt-on to weld-in for custom installations.

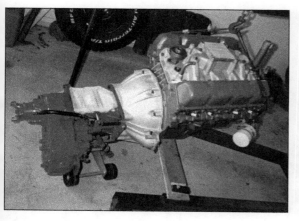

This is old picture of a freshly rebuilt AMC 360 attached to the factory T150 transmission and Dana 20 transfer case on the hoist ready to go into a 1978 CJ-5. The thought process of painting the transmission and transfer case red is questionable, but because the T150 was swapped with a T18, the red parts became black soon after.

The swapped Chevy bolts to the factory T176 transmission use an all-steel adapter bellhousing. Engine-to-transmission adapters come in a few forms, including this bellhousing adapter and adapter plates that can mount on the engine side or transmission side.

Several aftermarket companies, including Novak Conversions and Advance Adapters, make engine-specific conversion mounts that can either bolt on or weld in.

If the engine swap includes a transmission swap, all the components, including the transfer case, should be connected to properly locate the engine. The fact that the Jeep is so short is the biggest reason to have all the components together. Locate the engine as far forward as possible to allow for a longer rear driveshaft. This is especially important with swapped automatic transmissions.

Transmission/Transfer Case Adapter

As stated earlier, altering the engine location that requires the transmission/transfer case to be moved requires modifications to the transmission mount or skid plate. If you wish to retain the factory transmission, you should consider the durability of the factory transmission. For V-8 swaps, only a few factory transmissions are recommended. The T-18, T-176, T-150, and T-15 manual transmissions tolerate a moderately powered V-8, and any of the factory automatics perform well with a V-8 swap. The T-18 is the exception in regard to strength; this

transmission performs well with a higher-powered V-8.

Both the Dana 20 and Dana 300 transfer cases can handle the power of a V-8 swap and should be considered worth keeping. Adapting the engine to a factory Jeep transmission is usually accomplished using either an adapter plate or an adapter bellhousing. Many adapter styles are available from Novak Conversions and Advance Adapters and vary on type, based on application.

Using a non-factory transmission requires adapting the transmission to the transfer case. Similar to adapting an engine to a transmission, this swap usually uses special adapter plates and may even require changes to input gears in the transfer case or output gears on the transmission. Many transfer case adapters are available and vary on type, based on application. Once again, Novak Conversions

and Advance Adapters are truly the only games in town with this stuff.

It is common to retain the factory transmission from the swap engine while retaining the factory Jeep transfer case. For example, swapping a GM V-8 and using a GM factory used transmission such as the SM465 or TH350 only requires adapting to the factory transfer case.

Shifter Linkages

Relocating and/or swapping the transmission affect shifter linkages. Most manual transmissions have fixed shifters that may require altering the Jeep's interior transmission floor cover to match up to the new

Adapting a popular non-factory transmission to a Jeep transfer case requires the use of an adapter. Adapters from Novak come complete with all the components required, including the rear-mounting provision. (Photo Courtesy Novak Conversions)

shift tower. Blank covers can be purchased that have no holes, allowing for a clean, custom installation. Automatic transmission swaps often use an aftermarket shifter, which can make installation easy. Many styles are available and nearly all use cable linkages so interior location can be nearly anywhere.

Aftermarket automatic shifters from B&M, Hurst, and Lokar can add a great look to the interior of the Jeep; race-style gate shifters are most popular.

When using a factory transfer case, the Dana 300 can be outfitted with a twin-stick cable shift linkage that can make locating the shifter easier. Novak Conversions, Advance Adapters, and JB Conversions make Dana 300 twin-stick systems. The Dana 20 is more limited with aftermarket linkage; however, using the tube-style shifter mount allows custom lengths of the shift rods and tube to be fabricated, solving location issues.

Clutch Linkage

If your Jeep is going to have a clutch, making use of a factory-style bellcrank setup is possible, and a

The hydraulic clutch master cylinder mounts next to the brake master cylinder; depending on the year of the Jeep, a factory knock-out hole may exist to easily bolt up a master cylinder for a conversion. Filling the clutch reservoir is simply done by opening the cap.

This is an underneath view showing the clutch linkage and how it attaches to an engine using the factory mount. A non-factory engine requires a fabricated mount or aftermarket conversion mount to align the bellcrank to the clutch fork. Using a rod end provides smoother operation with less wear. Periodic lubrication of the moving parts is essential, especially if the Jeep sees frequent off-road use.

few companies make the proper engine-side attachment brackets to make this work without any fabrication. A later-model CJ may have been equipped with a hydraulic-style clutch, which can be more flexible and potentially require less maintenance and attention later. Many Jeeps can be retrofitted with a factory-style hydraulic clutch and some applications can use a hydraulic throw-out bearing from Centerforce or McLeod, requiring no clutch fork. Consider heat sources including the exhaust when routing hydraulic clutch lines and hoses.

Throttle Cable

If your swap uses a throttle cable, usually the stock cables or a different stock style works in most applications. Aftermarket throttle cable systems, such as ones offered by Lokar, can be used and work exceptionally

well. Electronic throttles require changing the factory pedal assembly to match the engine's requirements.

Automatic Transmission Kick-Down Linkage

The kick-down linkage used by some automatics can be a challenge in a swap. Factory-matched engine and transmission combinations usually make this easier from both a connection and operation perspective. In addition, aftermarket companies such as Lokar make excellent conversion cables and mounts to properly complete this job.

Exhaust

The exhaust can be a challenging part of an engine swap. There is limited space under a CJ, and fitting exhaust tubes and proper emissions

Some automatics, such as the TF727 swapped into this 1984 CJ-7, require linkage to provide input to the transmission for proper downshifting. Several aftermarket companies make custom transmission kick-down linkage cables, such as this one from Lokar, that fit most types of carburetors or TBI systems.

equipment (if needed) can be difficult. Some swaps, especially a swap of a small-block Chevy V-8, have adapted fenderwell headers available from companies such as Hooker and Hedman to ease installation. These fenderwell headers offer long tubes and a variety of finishes. In addition to a classic look, fenderwell headers save underhood clearance issues and in-frame room but are often loud and a low-hanging hazard on the trail.

Short-tube headers or factory manifolds are often used to run exhaust within the frame rails. Keeping in mind the parts that need to run near the exhaust for both clearance and heat reasons saves later aggravation. The steering shaft, brakes, and brake lines are often a problem. Dual in-frame exhaust systems are possible in a CJ, but often issues with clearance from fuel lines and the transfer case are experienced. A well-thought-out, efficiently assembled single exhaust can save space under the Jeep and still provide the performance a Jeep owner is after.

To save ground and driveshaft clearance in a single-exhaust sys-

Fitting the exhaust on a swapped engine can present challenges, especially if keeping the exhaust within the frame rails running out the back. Shorty headers are shown here on a 1985 CJ; they're tight to the engine, providing maximum clearance to other components.

On the bottom right, a performance Flowmaster Y-pipe can be seen in this view of a V-8 single exhaust. A single exhaust can save valuable underbody space but can still perform like a dual. Keeping the crossover to maintain ground clearance is especially important because exhaust tubing is thin walled and damages easily.

tem, the passenger-side exhaust primary tube is often run forward and under the engine oil pan to join the driver-side Y-pipe.

Whichever exhaust system is chosen, a good exhaust shop should be able to fabricate a quality exhaust to fit nicely in the Jeep. Alternatively, a good welder can fabricate a custom home-built exhaust from mandrel-bent tubing sections and straight pipe.

Electronics and Wiring

Wiring a swapped engine is often done in the final stages of the project. Some of the Jeep's factory wiring may be used with minor modifications, especially in an engine swap from a non-computer-controlled engine. This job is much easier if everything was properly labeled when disassembled. Having a factory wiring diagram on hand during the swap makes locating wiring for items such as indicator lights and gauges easier. Take the opportunity to

A swapped engine likely has components in different places than the stock engine did. When swapping in a Chevy engine, you find the distributor on the rear of the engine nearly up against the firewall, nowhere near stock. Altering wiring to deal with location changes is part of the small details that add to the challenge.

replace important cables if needed, especially starter and battery cables.

If the swap involves a modern fuel-injected engine, consider the charging system needs due to the increased electrical draw of the fuel pump, engine control system,

The Optima might be the ultimate battery for the Jeep. Featuring strong cranking power, long life, and the ability to mount nearly anywhere are just some of the justification. A Red Top with dual terminals makes attaching a winch and other accessories easier. Winch cables sit at the ready on top of the battery on this CJ.

and injectors. Using the factory-matched alternator from the swapped engine maintains proper charging requirements.

A different engine may have additional power needs for starting due to more cylinders or higher compression ratios. This may require replacing the Jeep's battery with a stronger one. A favorite brand of battery among the Jeep community is the Optima. The Optima Red Top is a sealed battery that can be mounted in any position, and most models feature dual battery posts.

Fuel Lines

All AMC-era CJs used mechanical fuel pumps. Swapping an engine can require the use of an electric pump even if the engine is not fuel injected. In addition, swapped engines may require fuel lines in a different location than factory. A CJ, depending on its original engine, can have fuel lines on either side of the frame rail, entering the engine compartment at the cowl area. Later CJs have a fuel return line that can potentially be needed by the swapped engine.

Some fuel-injection systems require larger fuel lines than are on the Jeep from the factory. If larger

replacement lines are needed, using hard fuel lines is recommended to avoid damage from trail debris. In the end, a swap likely requires creating your own custom lines or modification of the existing lines.

Retaining the factory fuel-venting system such as the check valves and charcoal canister should be considered because many places that require emissions testing also inspect the Jeep for the presence and operation of this equipment.

Fuel Pumps

Many swapped engines that have engine-driven fuel pumps have a pump that is not in the same location as factory. Along with the need to relocate the fuel lines, an engine-driven pump on a swapped engine may pose clearance issues. In these cases, replacing an engine-driven pump with an electric pump can solve the issues. An electric pump can help with clearance issues, hot starting, and vapor lock. Properly wiring an electric pump using an oil pressure switch to maintain safety in the event of an accident or fuel line break is important. Typically, an electric pump is wired to operate only if the engine is producing fuel pressure.

The mechanical engine-driven pump found on CJ engines provides years of trouble-free service. On occasion, engine-driven pumps that rely on a diaphragm to pull the fuel will vapor lock, a condition where the fuel evaporates in the line, causing stalling or hard starting, from high underhood temperatures experienced by slow off-road driving. Swapping an engine may put the fuel pump on the other side of the engine so you need to run new or altered fuel lines.

An electric fuel pump such as this Carter can be an easy solution to a swap engine requiring fuel lines in a different configuration than stock. The Carter pump features an internal regulator and does not require a return line. This pump is mounted above the skid plate to avoid damage from objects on the trail.

Popular Non-Factory Engine Swaps

Using a non-factory engine can set a Jeep apart from factory-engine-equipped Jeeps. The project can be as satisfying as it can be maddening. From clearance issues to finding the proper part are the realities you face when taking on this task. Luckily, many have come before us to perfect this art, and a small group of these people created products that can make this project much less expensive and stressful. Some engines have so much aftermarket support that a swap could be done in a weekend; others, not so much. Choosing wisely saves time, stress, and money.

Chevy Small-Block V-8

The small-block Chevy (SBC) V-8 has probably been the most swapped V-8 in Jeep CJ history. Its compact size, massive aftermarket and manufacturer support, and reliability are only some of the reasons. The SBC has been well supported by the Jeep community for years, and many conversion products are manufactured to make this swap almost painless. Companies such as Novak Conversions and Advance Adapters make nearly every non-standard component to complete this conversion.

Almost any size SBC is a good choice for a CJ, but the 350 is likely the most popular. This size has many options for compression, overbore, and even strokers.

A 383 is a common crate engine and performance upgrade that provides some extra torque beyond the 350 thanks to the longer stroke. Even a junkyard 350 that is in good running condition can be outfitted with a few performance parts to spice up the engine to perform exceptionally well in an on- and off-road CJ.

Common performance upgrades to yield the desired results on an SBC are a performance cam, intake manifold, and carburetor. This small investment into a few replacement components increases both torque and horsepower. The Performer series of performance components from Edelbrock make a perfect package for an SBC in a Jeep CJ.

GM Small-Block Generation III+ V-8

According to Novak, the GM small-block Generation III+ V-8 is surpassing the SBC in Jeep conversions. This engine, introduced in 1997, has won over many SBC loyalists. Available in many displacements and horsepower ratings, Novak Conversions considers this engine a nearly perfect swap engine. According to its website, "The fact that one of these engines can be installed into a Jeep with such success makes the decades-rich tradition of engine swapping more exciting than it has ever been."

This Chevy 350 spent part of its life swapped in a 1970 CJ-5 until it was pulled and re-modified to better suit a trail Jeep. The engine sports an Edelbrock Performer cam and intake, along with the Holley TBI. Unlike in most other auto hobbies, Jeep engines look better with age and clean is not a requirement.

The GM 4.3L V-6 engine is a similar swap to a Chevy V-8, and the modern powerplant shares many of the same adapters and mounts with the V-8. A TBI (shown) or MPI setup can provide good power for a CJ.

Installing these engines consists of a more complex swap due to the need to deal with engine electronics, a high-pressure fuel system, and much more. A big advantage of a modern engine swap is the likelihood that the engine in its stock form will produce more horsepower and torque than a performance-modified SBC. In addition to performance, the modern engine adds reliability and excellent off-camber performance from the fuel injection.

Both the SBC and Generation III+ V-8 are compatible with many of the factory and popular swapped transmissions with a properly programmed PCM.

GM V-6

In addition to the Chevy V-8s, a different and popular GM swap is the 4.3L V-6, part of the 90-degree V-6 family found in many GM cars and trucks from 1978 until 2014. The 4.3L V-6 was introduced in 1985 and was the final displacement used until 2014. The 4.3L came in several versions; the most notable differences were in the induction system, which included carburetors, throttle body fuel injection, and multiport injection.

The 4.3L V-6 is an excellent engine for a Jeep; it provides good power and torque for both trail and road use. The small size fits well within the Jeep's engine compartment, allowing the engine to be located forward to better fit a longer automatic, especially advantageous in a CJ-5. These engines use the same motor mounts as an SBC and share the same rear bolt pattern, allowing the use of the same adapters as the SBC. Challenges in swapping in this engine in its MPI form include proper computer programming and wiring. Many of these swaps use mostly homegrown solutions to computer and electronics issues.

Howell and Painless make replacement harnesses to simplify wiring the EFI engine. A common practice is to convert the 4.3L engine to a small 4-barrel carburetor and aluminum intake, such as an Edelbrock Performer, or to an aftermarket TBI fuel injection, such as the Howell TBI.

Jeep 4.0L

Because the Jeep 4.0L wasn't a factory engine in the CJ, it is included here in the non-factory section. The 4.0L was a descendant of the AMC I-6 with many improvements over the original. It's hard to believe they have the same roots. The 4.0L has a slightly smaller displacement than the 4.2L, thanks to an improved head design, better camshaft profile, and, best of all, multiport fuel injection. Jeep introduced the 4.0L in 1987, but it wasn't until 1991 that the engine reached its 190-hp "high-output" status. It was also in 1991 that this engine appeared in the Wrangler and the 4.2L was discontinued.

Swapping a 4.0L into a CJ is relatively easy and only a few non-stock components should be needed, such as a crank position sensor, wiring harness, and electric high-pressure fuel pump. In addition to the fuel pump, fuel lines need some mod-

The Ford 5.0L is an interesting swap in a CJ. The swap is more complex than a carbureted one, but the end result yields a fantastic engine well suited for the Jeep. Getting the complete set of components from the donor car or parts yard saves a lot of hassle with the swap. Novak Conversions can help with this swap with advice, motor mounts, and adapters.

ification to match up with the MPI system. The factory 4.0L used a bellhousing-mounted crank position sensor, which is not present in a factory CJ. Hesco makes an alternative sensor system that mounts to the front harmonic balancer, an adapted part that saves time and headaches. The 4.0L uses the factory engine mounts and bellhousing bolt pattern, allowing a bolt-on to nearly all CJ transmissions.

The 4.0L is considered by some to be the perfect off-road engine in the CJ and Wrangler series. The MPI, engine improvements from the 4.2L, good horsepower, and low torque create an excellent combination for a Jeep used both on- and off-road. When the 4.0L was discontinued at the end of the Wrangler TJ in 2006, Jeepers everywhere were worried about whether a new engine would live up to this engine's reputation.

It took until 2012, when Jeep introduced the 280-hp Pentastar V-6 in the Wrangler JK, for Jeepers to love an engine again. Considering the close match to the CJ 4.2L, this swap makes good financial and feasible sense. Hesco has put much research

into this swap and can provide guidance and products to make it a simple, perhaps weekend, project.

Ford

The Ford Windsor V-8 was produced from 1962 until 2001 and evolved to become the well-known 302, also known as the 5.0L that appeared in the Mustang as well as many other Ford vehicles. The readily available Ford V-8 can be swapped into the CJ, although not as easily as the GM because parts interchangeability is more difficult and the engine is slightly longer. A 5.0L Mustang EFI engine swap makes for an interesting and impressive conversion in a CJ. The engine wiring for the EFI system can be a challenge; use any resources available.

Specialized conversion motor mounts and exhaust headers are available to help facilitate the installation; both Novak Conversions and Advance Adapters make mounts for Ford engines. Ford V-8 engine swaps go well with the T-18, T176, and T150 transmissions that the factory offered in a CJ, along with other Ford transmissions such as the NP435.

Mopar

Swapping a Mopar V-8 can provide a reliable engine with plenty of torque and a vast amount of aftermarket support. Mopar engine swaps are essentially separated into three categories: Classic LA-style V-8s, 1992–1998 fuel-injected engines that were based on the original LA-style engine, and modern Powertech V-8 engines that replaced the LA engine in 1999.

The Mopar LA V-8 and pre-1999 engines are longer than the Chevy but measure almost the same as the AMC V-8. The rear-mounted distributor can present an issue in the CJ but usually makes it. Similar to the Ford, swapping a Mopar V-8 is not nearly as popular as a GM engine but components exist from both Novak Conversions and Advance Adapters to do these swaps successfully.

The modern Powertech V-8 and Hemi found their way into the Jeep lineup as factory options in the Jeep Grand Cherokee. Although these impressive engines are part of the Jeep family, swapping into a CJ is not a popular or easy choice and should be reserved for the expert. These swaps are very complex and involve a considerable amount of wiring, electronics, and computer systems. In addition, modern factory-matched transmissions need to be used for these engines to operate properly.

Diesel

There is a portion of the Jeep community that loves the idea of a diesel engine powering the Jeep. A diesel engine is well known for its fuel efficiency, reliability, and long life, in addition to massive torque that mixes well with off-road driving. A few companies specialize in diesel swaps, such as Jeff Dan-

There are die-hard diesel engine fans out there and they love them in their Jeeps for the increased longevity, torque, and fuel efficiency. Jeff Daniels' Jeep Customizing specializes in swapping the 3.9L Cummins 4BT diesel into a CJ. This one sits waiting for its transplant into a new host.

iel's Jeep Customizing and Bruiser Conversions, including diesels that run on bio fuels. Diesel swaps may require changes in gearing and transmissions resulting in the differences in the power curve over a gasoline engine. The Cummins 4BT seems to be the most popular CJ diesel swap due to its size and performance.

A caveat to a diesel swap is the excess weight of even a small engine. These engines require heavier springs to accommodate the extra weight without bottoming out the suspension. In addition to dealing with the weight, swappers need to deal with extra components, including the intercooler, turbo, exhaust, and cooling. Vibration, exhaust fumes, and hidden costs are a common complaint from those who have swapped a diesel into a CJ.

Crate versus Used

There comes a moment when a swap is about to be undertaken when you really have to decide whether to use a fresh new crate engine or one that lived a previous life. On the surface, a crate engine can seem to be

a large up-front expense, but many have learned a lesson the hard way when the used engine turns out to be a dud. Careful inspection of a used engine to determine its condition and consideration for planned modifications can help determine which option is better.

Crate Engines

A crate engine is brand new or completely refurbished. Crate engines are often professionally built, tested, and best of all, warrantied. Purchasing a crate engine can take the guesswork out of home building an engine, as the specifications such as horsepower, torque, and internal components are clearly indicated. Crate engines can be purchased in varying stages of assembly, from short blocks all the way to full assemblies. A side effect of all this new stuff is the cost: Crate engines can go from reasonable prices on up and up.

Used Engines

Used engines often come in the form of a parts yard engine or direct from a donor vehicle. The condition

This AMC 360 crate engine upon arrival was professionally built with matched components and ready for installation into a CJ-7. Crate engines often come with a limited warranty, an advantage compared to a home rebuild.

of the engine can be a variable and a risk, especially if the engine cannot be run before removal. Many parts yards offer a limited warranty on a used engine; this alone can make a higher price a safer bet. Even better is if the used engine is still in the donor vehicle and can be inspected and run before removal.

Learning the methods of identifying an engine to determine its size, year, and specifications allows you to get the engine you are looking for. The AMC V-8 size is seen easily, thanks to the numbers cast into the side of the block near the motor mounts. A 401 is a favorite number for many enthusiasts. Later AMC engines may show sizes in liters. (Photo Courtesy Craig Brown)

Researching identification markings and tags aid in figuring out exactly what you may be looking at. Different engines use stampings and cast markings for identification. For example, GM engines typically are marked at the rear of the block on the driver's side. AMC V-8 engines may be the easiest to identify because nearly all of the engines have the engine size cast into the side of the block near the motor mount.

So which is better? If your budget allows it, a crate engine is the best bet. The warranty and peace of mind that

comes with a fresh engine goes a long way. A used engine that turns out to be a dud can be nearly as expensive to rebuild as the crate engine. On the good side, the type of Jeep you are building doesn't require an engine that produces high horsepower and isn't being pushed to the limit in competition. This fact proves that a good used engine serves a Jeep well.

Putting It All Together

Swapping an engine is not a complex or expensive project when done correctly and using a popular engine. Doing research and planning out the entire project before beginning saves time and money. From radiator to driveshaft, all components should be considered. For the best result, matching compatible parts ensures durability.

At the end of the day, an exotic or unusual swap won't fit the model Jeep that has been defined here. For a Jeep to have maximum performance on- and off-road, a traditional-style swap using a factory engine or a popular non-factory often produces the best, most reliable results.

The AMC 360 swapped into this 1978 CJ-7 is basically stock; the exception is an HEI distributor. Original intentions were to do some internal engine performance modifications, but the stock engine works so well. This Jeep is well suited for tackling the trails with its T18, TeraLow, lockers, and 33-inch Swamper tires. (Photo Courtesy Ralph Hassel)

TRANSMISSION AND CLUTCH

In a Jeep that sees off-road action, using the correct gearing can make a big difference in how it performs. Jeeps, like many other off-road vehicles, are unique in their use of gears from other varieties of motorsports. Off-road driving situations usually require the Jeep to maintain a slow, controlled pace to prevent damage. This is best accomplished by proper gearing. A Jeep uses the gear reduction in the transfer case along with the transmission to allow the slow, controlled pace.

This chapter covers the factory Jeep transmissions and popular swaps of factory and non-factory transmissions. Detail on factory transmissions,

including each one's "swap-ability," is included with each type.

Jeep Transmissions

The purpose of the Jeep's transmission is to allow the vehicle to be driven at different speeds within the engine's speed capacity. A lower gear is used for moving at slow speeds, and higher gears are used as the vehicle's speed increases. Most transmission gears are identified by the gear ratio, which is a ratio of engine rotation to transmission rotation. AMC-era CJ transmissions operate at a 1:1 ratio in the highest gear with one exception, the T5, which is an overdrive

transmission. Often, more-modern swapped transmissions have an overdrive gear at approximately .75:1.

In many other types of vehicles, performance transmissions consist of close ratios and the ability to shift gears very quickly. In a Jeep, a transmission is usually judged by its low gear ratios and overall strength. Wide, low gear ratios often provide a lower ratio to the lowest gear that is very useful in slow off-road driving. Manual transmissions that include a "granny" low gear are among the

The shifter on a T-18 is deceptive in that first gear is really a granny-style gear and is not usually used in normal driving. Transmissions that feature a super-low first gear are often driven like a 3-speed. The T-18 with a straight shifter in a CJ is often a good indicator of a swapped transmission because the factory T-18 shifter is curved.

Off-road driving usually involves climbing over objects that would be impossible for most other vehicles; this requires a slow, controlled pace to prevent damage to components. This driver relies on his Jeep's gearing as he maneuvers his Scrambler over some boulders at Rausch Creek Off-Road Park.

Automatics allow smoother control over difficult obstacles by allowing the driver to use one foot on the gas and one foot on the brake. This allows the Jeep to continue movement without the need for clutching; coming off objects is gentler through the use of constant braking. In counterpoint, an experienced driver with a properly geared Jeep with a manual transmission can accomplish the same thing.

most preferred. These super low gears allow for increased vehicle control without the need for extremely low axle ratios.

Manual transmissions tend to be preferred by CJ owners, but automatics can (and do) perform just as well. The debate as to which is better is like debating chocolate versus vanilla; it truly is a preference of the Jeep's owner. A manual can offer greater control because the engine and drivetrain are constantly connected when the

Crawl Ratio

A measure of a Jeep's off-road capability frequently includes the crawl ratio. This ratio is a multiplication of the lowest transmission gear ratio by the transfer case low-range ratio by the axle ratio. For example: 6.32:1 (transmission low gear) x 2:1 (transfer case low range) x 4.11:1 (axle ratio) = 51.95:1 crawl ratio.

The higher the crawl ratio number, the lower the final drive ratio is. In most cases, a lower final drive ratio gives more control off-road because of the low ratio, which allows the engine to expend less energy to do the same amount of work. For example, a Jeep with a lower final drive ratio requires less engine effort to overcome an obstacle than the same Jeep with a higher ratio. This results in greater control for the driver.

Although there is no perfect ratio, an optimum ratio for this style of Jeep is typically between 50:1 and 70:1 in a manual-transmission Jeep and from 40:1 to 60:1 in an automatic-equipped Jeep.

In the late 1990s, crawl ratio was a novelty, and it seemed that there was no end to the lengths Jeepers would go to outdo each other with crawl ratios. As a result, competitive events called Slow Drags became a fad at shows and off-road events. Vehicles equipped with dual transfer cases and super-low gears appeared, some with crawl ratios significantly greater than 100:1, which are effectively useless in most situations.

In the end, a modification that has the biggest impact with the least expense and/or effort is often the best choice. Typically, a set of low-range transfer case gears that lower the final drive ratio satisfies this concept. ■

When comparing the biggest bang for the buck and/or effort, this graphic simplifies the three components that impact the crawl ratio. At the end of the day, a change of gearset in the transfer case has the largest impact on the overall ratio with no alteration of on-road driving. Of course, doing two changes or all changes continues to lower the ratio, along with the weight of your wallet.

clutch is engaged. Descents are better managed with a manual and the help of engine braking.

An automatic can provide constant power without the need to clutch to switch gears, and stalling on obstacles is essentially eliminated. Hill ascents requiring a gear change, whether it is up-shift or down-shift, are nearly instant and require no interruption in power with an automatic. In addition, an automatic is gentler on the driveline because the connection between the engine and transmission is only driven by fluid.

Because an automatic is not necessarily judged on its lowest gear, overall crawl ratios tend to be numerically lower than many manual transmissions. This is not nearly as important because the automatic transmission's torque converter effectively increases torque applied without increased vehicle speed, allowing more control. Navigating tough trail sections with an automatic is often performed with one foot on the gas and one foot on the brake, taking full advantage of the automatic's increased torque and lack of solid coupling to the driveline.

Choosing a New Transmission

Swapping a transmission can cause a snowball effect similar to an engine swap. Most of the time a swap requires an adapter to match the transmission to the engine, transfer case, or both. In addition, shifter (both transmission and transfer case) locations need to be considered, the skid plate/crossmember needs modification, and driveshafts likely need lengthening and/or shortening. Covering a transmission swap step by step is nearly impossible because there are so many variations possible and

This T-18 is being prepped for a swap into an in-process Scrambler restoration. The T-18 is a relatively small and readily available transmission that swaps easily into any AMC-era CJ. This one will eventually meet up with a Dana 300 transfer case through the use of an adapter. (Photo Courtesy Craig Brown)

so many variables. As was discussed in Chapter 3, Novak Conversions has perfected the art of Jeep engine and transmission conversions. Consulting them before starting a swap makes a swap easier and more apt for success.

The most commonly swapped factory Jeep CJ transmissions are the T18 and T176 manuals and the Jeep versions of the GM TH400 and Chrysler TF999 automatics. These can be swapped in with minimal expense and hassle because most don't require any adapters. Finding a complete donor vehicle adds to the ease of the swap. On many swaps from CJ to CJ, using the factory driveshafts from the donor CJ is usually possible.

Factory Manual Transmissions

From 1972 to 1986, seven manual transmissions were available, some in the same year ranges as options or with different engine configurations. From oldest to newest, they are: T14, T15, T150, T18, SR4, T176, T4, T5.

3-Speeds

The T14 is a lighter-duty 3-speed that was the standard transmission in 1972–1975 CJs with the I-6 engine; it ran a 3.1:1 low gear. Originally used in earlier Jeeps behind the Buick 225 V-6, this transmission uses a special bellhousing to match the AMC engine to the transmission. This transmission is usually a

This TH400 is outfitted with a short shaft needed to adapt a Dana 20 transfer case. It is waiting for installation in a CJ-7 restoration project. The strength of the TH400 and its availability make it an excellent swap candidate in a CJ-7 or Scrambler.

Swapping Considerations with a CJ-5

The CJ-5 has such a short wheelbase that often gets in the way of many things and transmission swaps are just another item to add to the list. Many transmission swaps are just not possible due the limited length behind the transmission and transfer case. The rear driveshaft may become too short to operate; this condition is worse if the Jeep is lifted because the rear driveshaft angle becomes steeper. Increased driveshaft angle puts extra strain on the universal joints and reduces suspension travel from universal joint binding.

The options for transmission swap candidates are rather limited. Sticking with shorter manual transmissions or smaller automatics will yield the best results.

The T18, T176, SM420, and SM465 are excellent swap manual transmissions for a CJ-5. Their compact size keeps the rear driveshaft longer and less prone to binding, vibration, and wear. Swapping an automatic into a CJ-5 is tough, even with the shortest of the automatics. A GM TH350 automatic is about the shortest swap candidate, which is truly the best choice of all other automatics.

If you want to use a transmission not listed here, make sure that you take plenty of measurements before begin-

The short CJ-5 can be a challenge for swapping, and even a relatively short T-18 as seen in a CJ-5 pushes the rear driveshaft length to a near minimum. A CJ-7 and CJ-8 are much more forgiving with rear driveshafts due to the longer wheelbase.

ning a swap of either transmission type. Take into account the length of the adapter and transfer case when planning a CJ-5 swap. Finally, other clearance considerations, especially with the exhaust system, must be made with a CJ-5 swap. The increased length of a swapped transmission reduces the available space to squeeze in a muffler. ∎

---

good swap-out type of gearbox. Its light duty and high ratio makes it a less-than-desirable choice in a CJ with anything other than a stock engine.

The T15 3-speed was offered with both the I-6 and V-8 from 1972 until 1975. The medium-duty transmission was equipped with a 3:1 low gear and used a special bellhousing to mate it to the AMC engines. This was known as a relatively strong transmission that worked well with V-8 engines. It could be outfitted with adapters to mate it with several swap engines.

The 3-speed transmission was a staple in the CJ until the T18 found its way into the Jeep in the early 77. This 1974 CJ-5 is still running its factory T15 behind the mildly modified 304. The 3-speed is fine for street driving and mild off-road use, but the high first gear and poor Dana 20 low-range ratio makes even moderate off-road driving more difficult. The smell of clutch is often in the air when Jeeps like this tackle a rock garden.

The high-ratio low gear combined with the factory-mated Dana 20, and its 2:1 low range makes this transmission a fine on-road combination, but off-road ratio suffers.

The T150 3-speed replaced the T15 and was offered with both the I-6 and V-8 from 1976 to 1979. The transmission is well suited to the I-6 and V-8 engines and makes an excellent swap transmission because many adapter methods exist. The T150 uses the standard Ford butterfly bellhousing mount and a 2.99:1 low gear. Similar to the T15, the high-ratio low gear combined with the factory-mated Dana 20 and its 2:1 low range makes this transmission a fine on-road combination, but off-road ratio suffers. A Jeep that was factory equipped with a T150 makes a good T18 candidate because of the compatible transmission bellhousing bolt pattern.

Although the 3-speed transmissions offered during the AMC era were very usable and durable, their off-road performance suffers due to their high-ratio low gears when combined with the factory Dana Model 20 2:1 low range. This combination usually makes for a numerically low crawl ratio, which is undesirable in a Jeep that sees regular off-road use. Off-road control of the Jeep is difficult when using these ratios, and frequently the clutch receives the most punishment due to excess use. To make matters worse, the poor crawl ratio is exaggerated even further when larger tires are added. In Chapter 5, I cover transfer case modifications that can provide a little help with crawl ratio results experienced in 3-speeds.

4-Speeds and a 5

Several varieties of 4-speed and a single 5-speed manual transmissions were used in the AMC era. Some strong and capable, some not so much.

T18: The T18 is technically a 4-speed but is often driven like a 3-speed. Featuring a "granny-style" low gear often using the 6.32:1 ratio, this transmission is a well-known favorite for off-road use. It's a truck-style, strong transmission used from 1972 until 1979 that came in two varieties. The 1972 to (some) 1976 T18 transmissions were equipped with the non-synchronized 4.02:1 low gear; the later 1976–1979 T18s were equipped with the non-synchronized 6.32:1 low gear. The T18 is easily adapted to GM engines through the use of adapters.

When swapping a T18 from another CJ, the process is nearly

This T18 in the process of being installed into a 1978 CJ sits in the hole where the transmission cover goes. The T18 will be soon mated to the TeraLow-equipped Dana 20 transfer case. The transmission's rear output gear can be seen on the lower left. (Photo Courtesy Ralph Hassel)

bolt-in, and adjustments to the transmission mount and driveshafts are the key needs, with other minor modifications. Using a T18 from a full-size Jeep usually requires changing the input gear due to the long factory adapter. Novak Conversions makes the proper input gear and its components. If the 6.32:1 low gear is desired, make sure the Jeep CJ donor transmission is later than a 1976. The Jeep T18 came equipped with a factory adapter to fit the Dana 20 transfer case; adapting the Jeep T18 to a Dana 300 is accomplished with an adapter and replacement shaft.

T176: The Tremec T176 4-speed, the strongest official 4-speed used in a CJ, was an optional transmission used with both the V-8 and I-6 from 1980 until 1986. Identified easily by its straight, hollow shifter handle, this transmission serves a Jeep with a mild V-8 or I-6 well, both on- and off-road. Its compact size, 3.52:1 low gear, and factory adapter to mate it

to a Dana 300 transfer case make it a great swap transmission. This combination results in a very useable off-road crawl ratio with no further modification.

For swap purposes, this transmission adapts well to non-factory Jeep engines, especially GM small-blocks and Gen I to III+ V-8 engines. The T176 can be a direct "bolt to" for many Ford engines. The T176 easily swaps in when using a Dana 300 transfer case. It is possible to adapt the T176 to a Dana 20 transfer case but the increased low range ratio of the Dana 300 makes swapping a Dana 20 transfer case to this transmission less desirable. In this case, swapping both the T176 and Dana 300 at the same time yields a better result.

T4 and T5: The T4 and T5 are light-duty transmissions, including a 4.03:1 low gear with the T5 featuring a .86:1 overdrive. These were used from 1982 until 1986 with both the AMC I-4 and I-6 engines and were

The T176 as seen in this CJ is always equipped with a straight, hollow-tube shifter handle that makes identifying it simple. The truck-like T176 has a solid shifting feel unlike the softer feel of the T4 and T5.

always mated to the Dana 300 transfer case. Using this transmission for engine swaps is not a popular choice due to the light-duty nature and the sparse availability of adapters.

Common factory replacements to this transmission are the T176 and Chrysler 999 automatic, which swap in using factory parts, including connection to the Dana 300. A T18 swap requires an adapter to mate it to the Dana 300. A common non-factory swap is either the SM420 or SM465 transmissions because they share similar bellhousings and overall size.

The SR4 is a very light-duty transmission that was typically found behind the I-4 "Iron Duke" engine made by GM. This transmission is best avoided and swapped out with a more robust transmission, like some of the other factory 4-speeds or either the SM420 or SM465 transmissions.

The T4 and T5 transmissions can be identified by their curved shifters located at the rear of the floor cover, as seen in this well-maintained 1985 CJ-7. The overdrive in the T5 was the only factory overdrive transmission found in the CJ.

This NV3550 was swapped from a Wrangler TJ into a CJ-7 and is sitting in the frame for a test fit. At this point, the project was waiting for the Advance Adapters conversion components to mount up the Dana 300 transfer case. (Photo Courtesy Craig Brown)

Non-Factory Manual Transmissions

Common non-factory transmission swaps are the SM420, SM465, NP435, NV3550, and AX15. Swapping in any of these requires adapters of some kind. The particular engine used in the Jeep also affects compatibility of these transmissions and adapter requirements. Because a low gear is often a desired option in a transmission, following is a list of the low gears found in these non-factory swaps.

- SM420, 7:1. Extra-low granny gear, high strength, and durability. Potential low parts availability due to age.
- SM465, 6.55:1. Extra-low granny gear, high strength, and durability. Used in many GM vehicles until 1991, it makes replacement parts and transmission availability better.
- NP435, 4.56 to 6.68:1. Varied low-gear ratios and large span of usage years makes finding replacement parts and transmission availability excellent.
- AX15, 3.83:1. A modern transmission equipped with an overdrive, available in factory post–AMC-era Jeep vehicles such as the Cherokee and Wrangler. This transmission can be adapted

to a Dana 300 transfer case easily.
- NV3550, 4.01:1. A modern transmission offered in a variety of Jeep vehicles featuring a .78:1 overdrive. This transmission can be adapted to a Dana 300 transfer case easily.

Factory Automatic Transmissions

The AMC era brought two automatic transmissions to the CJ. Both are reliable and useable and can serve a CJ well both on- and off-road.

TH400

The GM TH400 found in 1976–1979 CJs always mated to the BorgWarner 13–39 transfer case. This transfer case was commonly known as the Quadra-Trac transfer case. Common upgrades to the TH400 to increase performance are shifters, shift kits, performance converters, and coolers. Converting the TH400 from the Quadra-Trac to use a Dana 300 or Dana 20 is a common conversion. The Quadra-Trac's limited parts availability, reliability, and low-range options make this transfer case less desirable.

Because this transmission was used in many GM cars and trucks, shift kits come in many varieties and can improve the shift points and

Granny Gear or Overdrive

A transmission with an exceptionally low first gear may not be as desirable as a transmission with an overdrive gear. Either style results in increased performance but in different ways. A granny gear is useful off-road and an overdrive is useful for on-road driving. Because the desire is to build a Jeep that performs well in both situations, this decision is based upon other parameters.

Doing the math to calculate both the total crawl ratio and street highway RPM will aid in the decision. Highway RPM is a calculation of tire size to final drive ratio at an assumed 60 to 65 mph. The formula is as follows:

(Axle Ratio x Vehicle Speed x Transmission Ratio x 336.13) ÷ Tire Diameter

For example, here are a few highway RPM ratios for a vehicle with 35-inch tires and traveling at 65 mph:

- 5.38:1 differential, 1:1 transmission = 3,358 rpm
- 3.54:1 differential, 1:1 transmission = 2,210 rpm
- 4.88:1 differential, .78:1 transmission = 2,376 rpm

A Jeep with a 60:1 crawl ratio and a highway RPM of 3,358 makes for great off-road performance, but on-road driving experiences poor fuel efficiency and an uncomfortable ride. The poor highway RPM is often a direct result of low axle gears. Most factory Jeep engines and many other V-8 engines are most efficient in the 2,200- to 2,500-rpm range.

Using a transmission with more gears can increase street driving comfort and efficiency. An overdrive gear can allow the Jeep to run a lower ratio in the axle gears without sacrificing highway driving RPM engine speeds.

Another consideration to help with a decision is the transfer case ratio. Lower-ratio transfer cases lessen the need for an extreme low gear in the transmission or axles. This thinking refers to the idea of considering the total crawl ratio before starting a swap. Doing the math to calculate both crawl ratio and highway RPM helps in properly setting up the Jeep for both driving conditions. ∎

The TH400 found in this 1977 CJ-7 was there since it was new and it can be found nestled up in the frame. The Jeep originally was equipped with a Quadra-Trac but was converted to a Dana 20 years ago for increased efficiency and reliability.

shift characteristics by replacing certain components within the transmission. Be mindful of the kinds of shift kits you may consider installing in your Jeep's automatic. Many of these kits are designed for street performance and do not perform well when driving off-road.

In most cases swapping a TH400 requires a two-piece front driveshaft to clear the bottom of the automatic. A two-piece shaft requires adding an intermediate carrier bearing to the first section of the shaft. Most are attached to the frame, but some install a bearing mount that attaches to the engine/transmission. The latter prevents vibration because the fixed mount moves with the engine and not with the frame.

TF999

The Chrysler 999 automatic was used in the CJ from 1980 until 1986 and was found behind both the I-6 and V-8. This transmission in a CJ was always mated to the Dana 300 transfer case. Its relative short length, narrow pan width, and reasonable strength make it a good automatic for the Jeep. This transmission doesn't have the size of the aftermarket following as the TH400 or TF727 but a few choices of shift kits and shifters are available.

Automatic Transmission Swaps

Swapping an automatic into a Jeep that had a manual is a common swap, and it is usually combined with an engine swap. This can be easier than swapping a non-factory manual transmission because the automatic doesn't require clutch linkage and shifter location headaches. Using an aftermarket automatic cooling system and a shifter that uses a cable make installation of an automatic relatively easy (refer to the discussion of swaps in a CJ-5). Automatics tend to be long, and installation into a short CJ-5 can be a challenge.

Factory Automatics

Commonly swapped automatics include the factory TH400 and the TF999. As stated earlier, these can swap relatively easy because a donor vehicle with all the proper components can be transplanted to the receiving Jeep. A TH400 swap into a 1980 or later CJ requires an adapter for the transfer case or a transfer case swap.

Non-Factory Automatics

Popular non-factory automatic swaps into a CJ include the TF727, TH350, and TH700-R4. A TF727 from a later full-size Jeep yields a strong transmission with the proper attachment for a Dana 300 transfer case. This transmission requires a lift for proper front driveshaft clearance from the transmission's fluid pan.

The TH350 is a strong and compact GM automatic that is an excellent swap in a CJ. An adapter can allow the transmission to attach to either a Dana 20 or Dana 300; further adapters can be used to marry the TH350 to AMC engines.

The TF727 automatic, which is plenty strong to stand up to the power of a modified engine, can be found in many full-size Jeep models such as the Cherokee or Wagoneer. The TF727 factory mounts to the Dana 300 without an adapter, although the front driveshaft fitment on a CJ can be a challenge without enough lift.

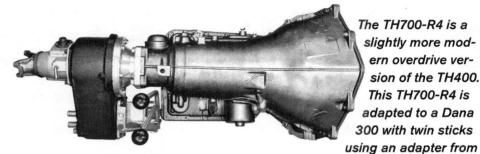

The TH700-R4 is a slightly more modern overdrive version of the TH400. This TH700-R4 is adapted to a Dana 300 with twin sticks using an adapter from Novak Conversions. The later versions of this transmission were known as the 4L60 and 4L60-E. (Photo Courtesy Novak Conversions)

The TH700-R4 is a 4-speed automatic that essentially replaced the TH350 in 1982, and features a .70:1 overdrive and a lockup converter. As a note, the TH700-R4 was renamed in 1990 to the 4L60 and later became the electronic-shifted 4L60-E in 1997. The TH700-R4 and early 4L60 swap into a CJ is relatively easily. The added overdrive and lockup converter helps with highway driving and fuel efficiency.

A more complex automatic swap is the 4L60-E. According to Novak Conversions, these are best installed with a more modern engine because the 4L60-E is electronically shifted and requires a throttle-position sensor that is not normally found on a carbureted engine. Otherwise, the 4L60-E is an excellent swap candidate and adaptable to Jeep transfer cases.

Similar to swapping a TH400, a TH700-R4 or 4L60 may require a two-piece front driveshaft for proper transmission clearance.

Automatic Transmission Upgrades

Upgrades to manual transmissions are rare but there are many options for automatics, from shifters to shift kits. Some require expertise for proper installation due to the complex inner structure of the transmission.

Shift Kits

A shift kit is a series of internal replacement components that alter shift timing and fluid flow. This can result in firmer, quicker shifts often desired in performance vehicles. Most automatics, including factory and non-factory, can be outfitted with a shift kit to improve performance. Mild shift kits are probably the extent that you should use in a Jeep that is driven on- and off-road.

Some Jeep owners prefer automatics that are modified to stay in a particular gear regardless of RPM. There are manual shift kits available for most automatics that can do this, including ones that can reverse the shifting pattern allowing quick shifts from first to reverse.

Torque Converters

Performance torque converters are often used in performance vehicles with automatics. Converters with higher stall speeds do not work well off-road, as they require increased engine RPM for movement, which often causes launching forward, potentially causing damage. The increased stall speed may also cause higher transmission temperatures, putting a further strain on the fluid and internals.

Shifters

Aftermarket shifters are readily available in many varieties to aid in installation of a swapped automatic and/or add some quicker, more precise shifting. A factory-automatic-equipped CJ can benefit from an aftermarket shifter as well. A factory column shift can be inaccurate, especially if the driver is in a hurry. Aftermarket shifters usually come with the proper brackets and linkage for most transmissions, and their cable operation allows installation almost anywhere. Aftermarket shifters not only add performance, they look good and are fun to operate.

Cooling

Because a Jeep used off-road spends significant time moving at slow speeds and navigating trail obstacles, automatic transmission temperatures run higher than with traditional street driving. Factory automatics often are cooled with an internal cooling jacket within the radiator. This method works well in street driving situations but can actually cause higher engine and transmission temperatures when driving slow off-road. Installation of

B&M, along with others, make easy-to-install automatic transmission shifters that work well and look great. The B&M MegaShifter in this Scrambler provides a positive reverse lockout and ratchet shift action for quick gear changes.

an external transmission cooler that sits in front of the radiator keeps the temperatures down and extends the life of the transmission components and the fluid. Regular fluid maintenance is essential to keeping a Jeep automatic healthy.

Clutch

A proper clutch for a Jeep that is used on- and off-road doesn't have too

much pedal pressure but stays engaged properly when heavy torque loads are experienced. When swapping an engine or transmission, consider the type of clutch that may be installed and match it to the intended use of the Jeep. Driving off-road often requires excess use of the clutch when compared to normal street driving.

The Centerforce I clutch is an excellent upgrade to a Jeep. This clutch offers performance of an aftermarket clutch without the heavy pedal feel of a race-style clutch. The centrifugal weights increase clutch pressure at higher RPM while maintaining a stock feel at slower engine speeds.

Flywheel

An often-overlooked component, the flywheel serves as a gear for engine starting, providing rotational momentum for the engine, and as a surface to make contact with the clutch disk. When replacing a clutch and/or clutch disc, resurfacing the flywheel is recommended but

The factory column shifter found in the CJ is very old-school and perhaps confuses younger drivers. The factory shifter is somewhat un-precise and can be difficult to find the right gear when certain maneuvers are being made, but the space-saving location puts the shifter out of the way, which is always a benefit in a small CJ.

Behind the grille sits an external transmission cooler for the TH400. The biggest enemy to an automatic is overheated fluid, and off-road driving can heat up fluid in no time. An external cooler can cool the fluid more efficiently than one that is integrated into the radiator.

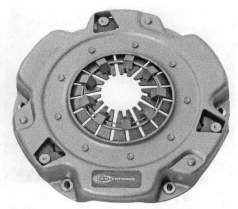

A complete setup from Centerforce includes a disc, throw-out bearing, and pressure plate. Either of the Centerforce clutches provides easy pedal feel with extra holding pressure at higher engine speeds through the use of centrifugal weights. (Photo Courtesy Quadratec)

frequently ignored. This can cause poor clutch performance and early wear. When swapping an engine or transmission, it is important that the flywheel match the installation. Engines are often externally balanced, meaning the flywheel is balanced along with the crankshaft and harmonic balancer. Although replacing a flywheel on an externally balanced engine disturbs the original balance, it is possible (and recommended) to have a replacement flywheel balanced to match the original.

Throw-Out Bearing

The throw-out bearing works by pressing on the fingers of the clutch to disengage the connection between the engine and transmission. This bearing sits just off the clutch fingers when there is no pressure on the clutch pedal. Adjustments to the clutch linkage properly locate the throw-out bearing to the clutch fingers. Riding the clutch or holding pressure on the pedal for

This new performance clutch pressure plate and disc is being installed into a CJ-7. A good clutch that provides proper grip without stiff pedal pressure is the most comfortable to drive off-road. The clutch is used very frequently off-road, and after a few hours your leg will feel it, if the Jeep is equipped with a stiff pressure plate.

extended times causes excess wear of the bearing. Replacing the bearing requires removal of the transmission. Heavy-duty bearings are desirable because the clutch in a Jeep sees excess use.

Mechanical Release Linkage

Most AMC-era CJs used a mechanical linkage to disengage the clutch. This linkage used rods connected to a bellcrank attached to the engine and body. Although this system was effective and simple, it carried its own set of problems, mainly wear and binding.

The rod that connected the pedal to the bellcrank was a plain metal-on-metal connection that became sloppy and eventually wore out. Replacements are readily available, but modified versions are superior. These performance versions use ball joints or spherical rod ends to control wear and provide smooth clutch operation. When swapping transmissions and/or engines, conversion mounts for the bellcrank are available from companies such as Novak Conversions and Advance Adapters.

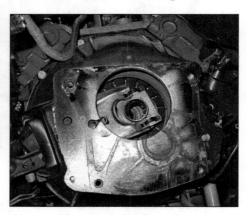

Along with a new clutch, a new throw-out bearing should be installed into the Jeep. Reaching this point requires removing the engine or transmission, not a simple job by any means.

The bellcrank mechanical linkage found in so many AMC-era CJs is fairly reliable but is prone to wear over time. Replacement rods that use rod link ends wear much better and provide better clutch feel. Frequent cleaning and lubrication keep these parts performing smoothly.

Installation of a body lift impacts the alignment of the mechanical clutch linkage, which needs to be adjusted after installation is complete.

Hydraulic Release

Some CJs used a hydraulic clutch setup that removes all the mechanical linkage but introduced a unit that could potentially leak and fail. Hydraulic clutches have become the norm in modern vehicles, and the components should be considered as reliable as the mechanical linkage. It's a popular upgrade on a CJ to convert to a hydraulic clutch setup using factory parts.

Installation of a hydraulic setup involves drilling and mounting the clutch master cylinder and mounting the slave cylinder to the engine. Several slave cylinder mounts are available for the Jeep for factory and swap engines from companies such as Novak Conversions and Advance Adapters.

Heat sources can be a concern with a hydraulic clutch installation. Care must be taken to ensure the clutch lines and slave cylinder are not

Engine or transmission conversions can go much easier when using a hydraulic clutch as on this CJ with a 350 Chevy swap. The slave cylinder can be mounted to the bellhousing using a custom or aftermarket bracket. Because the slave attaches to the master cylinder with a flexible hose, engine location is adjustable.

This 1984 CJ-7 underwent a recent T176 swap from a worn-out T5. The factory fit and strength plus low cost and hassle make this conversion an excellent choice. The T176's 3.52 low gear is not really low but when combined with a TeraLow-equipped Dana 300, ratios become usable off-road.

exposed to high heat. In engine and/ or transmission swaps, a hydraulic system can make getting the clutch up and running much easier because the only attachment is the hose.

Finally, Jeep owners often install some variety of high-body lift. This style of lift directly impacts the alignment of mechanical linkage, a problem not experienced by a hydraulic style.

Replacement

When replacing a clutch, it is always recommended to have the flywheel checked and resurfaced. In addition, replacing the throw-out bearing and pilot bearing while the assembly is apart is always wise. Getting back to these components is a considerable amount of work.

Putting It All Together

A lot of material was covered in this chapter, and it might seem like a lot to put together. In sticking with the established goal of building and modifying a Jeep for maximum per-

formance on- and off-road, you can establish a few things. Because the AMC V-8 or I-6 with moderate modifications was discussed in Chapter 2, here are a few transmission options.

Manual Transmission

If a manual transmission is desired, a factory T176 or, more preferable, a factory T18 would suit this Jeep well. The T18's strength and granny gear is a big advantage off-road. Use of either of these transmissions controls expenses with a big payoff.

A Dana 300 with a 4:1 gearset adds some extra numbers to the crawl ratio while allowing the Jeep to retain higher axle ratios for comfortable street performance. In front of the transmission, a Centerforce I clutch provides excellent feel and performance.

Ditching the factory mechanical linkage in favor of a hydraulic setup prevents wear and binding.

Finally, a set of heavy-duty driveshafts with long slip joints finishes the package.

Automatic Transmission

If an automatic is desired and the factory I-6 or V-8 engine is retained, a factory TF999 nicely attaches to a Dana 300 transfer case equipped with a 4:1 gearset. An external transmis-

sion cooler helps with heat buildup when driven off-road.

Installation of a transmission shift kit helps with the transmission's performance in all conditions. Retaining the factory steering column shifter conserves space within the Jeep. If the automatic is swapped or a performance shifter is desired, an aftermarket shifter can be installed in a convenient location. Most other types of automatics cause clearance issues or require high-price adapters.

Finally, a set of heavy-duty driveshafts with long slip joints finishes the package.

A T4 to TF727 swap in this AMC 360-equipped 1984 CJ-7 is in progress. This TF727, originally from a full-size Jeep factory, mounts a Dana 300 with no additional adapter. A transmission rebuild, new torque converter, and light shift kit makes this automatic perform well in a CJ.

TRANSFER CASE AND DRIVESHAFT

That extra lever on the floor in most Jeeps is for shifting the transfer case. A transfer case in its simplest form is a gearbox capable of directing transmission output to one or more output shafts. In the case of a Jeep CJ transfer case, its purpose is to allow for two- and four-wheel-drive operating modes with an addition of a low range to increase torque output and reduce speed. Several models of transfer cases were offered in the AMC era; all did essentially the same thing but each had its own set of unique features.

Jeep Transfer Cases

On the street, a Jeep is usually running its transfer case in two-wheel-drive Hi. In this position, most AMC-era transfer cases run in a straight-through fashion, meaning that no gear reduction is being done, and none of the lower transfer case gears are running. This mode provides efficient and quiet running for normal street driving, in contrast to the Dana 18 found in pre-1971 CJs, which ran most of the transfer case gears

all the time. In poor road conditions such as dirt roads, snow, or ice, four-wheel-drive Hi is used. This mode allows for nearly normal road speeds with the added traction and control of four-wheel drive. In more severe off-road conditions, four-wheel-drive Lo is used. This mode uses a gear reduction within the transfer case to increase output torque and reduce speeds.

Drive Mode Labels?

A few misunderstood drive mode labels exist in the realm of vehicles

The swapped Dana 20 transfer case shifter in this 1977 CJ-7 is a style that was found in the Jeep Commando with a TH400 transmission. The long throw U-shaped shift pattern makes for easy shifting but fitting a boot difficult.

The Dana 18 was the predecessor to the Dana 20. Its drop outlet for both the front and rear driveshaft required the internal gears to run constantly, causing excess noise and drag. The Dana 18 is a swap candidate for Quadra-Trac-equipped CJs because the double drop does not require swapping axles.

that are not strictly two-wheel drive. Terms such as all-wheel, four-wheel, full-time drive, etc., can be a bit vague to the novice. The term all-wheel drive has never been a term applied to AMC-era CJs; it refers to a drive mode in which some or all wheels are capable of driving the vehicle, perhaps entirely independent of each other. Newer, primarily street-driven sport utility vehicles and similar are often all-wheel drive.

Part-time four-wheel drive is most often referring to a vehicle that has a traditional transfer case such as the AMC-era CJs running a Dana 20 or Dana 300. These four-wheel-drive modes are only used "part time," meaning only when conditions demand the extra traction of four-wheel drive. In part-time systems, the front and rear axles are connected together physically within the transfer case. Full-time four-wheel drive is applied to a vehicle that can be driven in

---

Factory CJ Data

Transfer Case Drive Type
- Dana 20 and Dana 300 part-time transfer cases
- BW1339 Quadra-Trac full-time transfer case

---

any conditions and on any terrain in four-wheel-drive mode. These vehicles often have a transfer case that has the ability to automatically relieve the binding that occurs from front to rear through some mechanical means.

Vehicle Speed and Mode Selection

Usually, when in low range, the max speed of the Jeep is half or less than that of high range due to the gear reduction. Although there is no black-and-white answer to when different modes are to be used, experience and current conditions typically dictate the proper mode. It's important to remember that operating in four-wheel drive on dry pavement can cause binding of the drivetrain

due to the direct connection of the front and rear axles. Damage and/or wear to driveline components can occur if operated in this way for extended times.

Shifting

Shifting between modes can present itself as a challenge and a bit of a mystery for newbie Jeep owners. Most CJs equipped with a Dana 20 or Dana 300 have manual front lock-out hubs. These need to be manually engaged before four-wheel-drive operation works, regardless of the transfer case mode.

If the hubs are engaged, shifting from two-wheel-drive Hi to four-wheel-drive Hi and back can be done at most speeds. Shifting to and from four-wheel-drive Lo should only be done when stopped. Slow forward or reverse movement may be needed to allow the gears to mesh and properly engage. After extended or high-traction four-wheel-drive use, you might find it difficult to shift out of four-wheel drive; this is usually due to a level of driveline binding. The best cure for this is driving in reverse for several feet or finding some loose terrain to relieve the pressure.

Most Jeep owners keep spares of certain parts; some even hoard parts in case the need for a replacement arises. This ready-to-go Dana 20 sits tucked away in my parts archive just in case. This shot gives a good view of the shift mechanism and the tube assembly that holds it.

The Dana 20 shifter lever came in a few forms in the AMC era. Earlier models used a flat lever, while the later model used a round lever. The operation positions of the shifter in stock form are 4Hi, 2Hi, N, 4Lo, and, over time, wear would allow a 2Lo in between N and 4Lo. In 4Lo the lever extends rearward quite a bit, causing potential clearance issues with interior accessories.

Factory Transfer Cases

During the AMC era, three transfer case models were offered: two standard and one special option. The Dana Model 20 and Dana Model 300 are most common; the BW1339 Quadra-Trac is a less common option. Both the Dana Model 20 and Dana Model 300 transfer cases use full gearsets and operate as direct drive in two- and four-wheel-drive Hi modes. The Borg Warner 1339 Quadra-Trac transfer case is a chain-driven unit that provides full-time four-wheel drive.

Recalling from earlier, one way of judging a Jeep's off-road capability is by crawl ratio. The transfer case low-range ratio can have a large effect on the crawl ratio without the need for extra-low axle gears, which reduces on-road driving efficiency by causing higher engine RPM. A common modification to transfer cases is replacing the low-range gearset to improve crawl ratio without affecting on-road drivability.

Low gearset kits are available for both the Dana 20 and Dana 300. Both drastically reduce the low-range ratio that is so much more noticeable than an axle gear change. The result comes at a lower price than re-gearing the differentials and can be done at home with a good set of tools. In addition to the extra-low-range ratio, normal street driving is completely unaffected. (Photo Courtesy Ralph Hassel)

Sample Crawl Ratio

Let's establish a baseline CJ to calculate crawl ratios over the next few transfer case models and swaps. This CJ, with 33-inch tires, has a V-8 that runs at optimal efficiency in the low-2,000-rpm range on the highway and has a T18 with a 6.32:1 low gear. A 3.54:1 rear axle provides the proper ratio to the whole combination for on-road driving. You can plug the numbers into the RPM calculator formula: (Axle Ratio x Vehicle Speed x Transmission Ratio x 336.13) ÷ Tire Diameter ([3.54 x 65 x 1 x 336.13] ÷ 33) to arrive at 2,343 rpm at highway speeds. You should also recall that an automatic-equipped Jeep does not benefit as dramatically from increased crawl ratio.

Twin-Sticks

A Jeep owner can install a set of aftermarket shifters that allow for the two-/four-wheel drive mode and the Hi/Lo mode to operate independent of each other. Many of these sets even offer the extended ability to run rear-wheel drive or front-wheel drive only, with some internal modifications. These dual-shifter systems, referred to as twin-sticks, use some of the factory mount and parts of the new system. Several companies such as Novak Conversions, TeraFlex, and Advance Adapters make twin-stick shifter systems.

Dana Model 20

The Dana 20 replaced the Dana 18 and was found in 1972–1979 CJs. Its compact design and excellent

strength made it an optimal transfer case in a CJ. The biggest flaw to a factory Dana 20 is its mild low-range ratio at a mere 2:1. Sample Jeep crawl ratio: 6.32 x 2 x 3.54 = 44.75:1.

Several modifications are available for the Dana 20. Most common are different gearsets that reduce the low-range ratio. A popular home-grown gearset conversion has been developed using the 2.46:1 low-range gearset from the Ford Bronco version Model 20 transfer case.

The body of the Bronco version of the Dana 20 uses a driver-side front driveshaft output and is not compatible with the CJ passenger-side front output. This conversion requires the entire gearset from the Bronco transfer case and a bit of grinding of the transfer case housing to accommodate the larger gears. The increase in gear reduction from this swap is effectively similar to switching from 3.54:1 axle gears to 4.56:1 without the expense

Twin-stick shifters can give full control of the transfer case modes, including two-wheel-drive Lo and front-wheel drive. An experienced Jeeper can take advantage of front-wheel drive when navigating certain obstacles by holding the brake and steering when spinning the front tires to make the Jeep drag the front end left or right.

This rebuilt, TeraLow-equipped Dana 20 sits on a jack ready for mating to the T18 transmission already in the Jeep. The Texas-style mounting area makes identifying a Dana 20 easy, in addition to the external input gear that is usually mounted to the output shaft of the transmission. (Photo Courtesy Ralph Hassel)

A modification or rebuild of the Dana 20 should include a complete set of seals and gaskets to freshen everything up. Gear oil is well known for finding its way through gaskets and seals, causing the Jeep to leave its mark wherever it goes. Using a good RTV silicone and cleaning gasket surfaces ensures a good seal. (Photo Courtesy Ralph Hassel)

of re-gearing the axles and sacrifice of highway driving. Sample Jeep crawl ratio: 6.32 x 2.46 x 3.54 = 55.04:1.

Going even further with gear reduction sets is the TeraFlex Low 20. This kit replaces the Dana 20's gears with a custom aftermarket gearset. The Low 20 reduces the low range to 3.15:1, a much more usable low range for off-road conditions. Installation of this kit may require some grinding of the transfer case housing to clear the larger gears. Similar to the 2.46 conversion, this kit is less expensive than axle re-gearing and does not affect normal highway driving. Here's the calculation for a sample Jeep crawl ratio: 6.32 x 3.15 x 3.54 = 70.47:1.

Install a Transfer Case Gearset

Installation of a low gearset can be performed by an average DIY Jeep owner. Draining the gear oil and removing the transfer case is the first step in this process. Take your time,

1 *With the transfer case drained and removed, begin disassembly. Gear removal may require the use of dowels to push the shafts out of the case, allowing removal. Begin by removing the center gearset, followed by the front output gears then the rear output gears. (Photo Courtesy Ralph Hassel)*

2 *Most Dana 20 transfer cases require grinding to properly clear the larger diameter of the output gear. Using a Dremel grinder, gradually clear away enough material to give clearance to the gear. When complete, be sure to thoroughly clean the case to prevent any metal grindings from contaminating the gear oil. (Photo Courtesy Ralph Hassel)*

3 *Begin reassembly of the case by reversing the procedure. Using a light grease or petroleum jelly provides initial lubrication and helps hold bearings in place. Creating a wood dowel that is the same diameter as the bearing shaft allows the roller bearings to be placed in the gear. When the shaft is installed, it drives out the dowel. (Photo Courtesy Ralph Hassel)*

4 *With the rest of the gears installed, the installation is nearly complete. Make sure all the parts that go in are installed and the shift operation is functioning. Install a new gasket and bolt on the cover. (Photo Courtesy Ralph Hassel)*

follow the directions, take notes or pictures as you proceed, and it will go smoothly.

With the transfer case outfitted with its new gears, it can be mated back up with the transmission. Fill the case with gear oil and reattach the front and rear driveshaft. A quick test of the case's operation completes the project.

The drastic change in crawl ratio above is evident with only a gear change in the transfer case. On-road driving is not affected in any way by this change.

Dana 20 Shifters

Through the years, the Dana 20 used a few different shifting mechanisms in the CJ. Many are similar and interchangeable. Most of the shifter mechanisms were connected to the case through a tube; straight linkages connected to the shift rails. This design allows for custom extension of the tubes and linkage as needed when different transmissions are used. Twin-sticks are available for most Dana 20 applications.

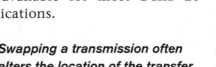

Swapping a transmission often alters the location of the transfer case, which results in the shifter location changing also. Many of the Dana 20 transfer cases use a tube to mount the lever mechanism, allowing custom tube and linkage arm lengths. This T18 required a few inches to allow the shifter to line back up with the factory floor hole. The threaded rod allows adjustment if needed.

The TeraLow-equipped Dana 300 in this 1985 CJ-7 sits idle between the dual exhaust. The Jeep's owner replaced the factory-style strap output yoke for a stronger U-bolt style. The Dana 300 had a larger drop than the Dana 20, which caused the need for a bump in the skid plate. It's common to see much rock rash on the bump section.

Dana Model 300

The Dana 300, which replaced the Dana 20 in the 1980–1986 CJ, is considered by most to be the most respected transfer case offered in a CJ. Much of its design is based on the Dana 20; however, the 300 differs in its use of an integrated input gear and simpler housing design. The standard 2.62:1 low-range-equipped transfer case operated similar to the Dana 20 with two-wheel-drive Hi, four-wheel-drive Hi, four-wheel-drive Lo, and neutral. Many modifications are available to make this excellent

Installation of a TeraLow 4:1 gearset into this Dana 300 from a 1985 CJ-7. Installation takes a few hours and can be done with usual garage tools.

transfer case even better. Sample Jeep crawl ratio: 6.32 x 2.62 x 3.54 = 58.66:1.

A few aftermarket companies make replacement gearsets for the Dana 300; most convert the Dana 300 from 2.62:1 to 4:1, which is a drastic improvement to crawl ratio without the need to re-gear the differentials. TeraFlex and Lomax are two popular companies that make quality 4:1 gearsets. Installation often replaces all the gears within the transfer case and requires minor grinding for clearance. Sample Jeep crawl ratio: 6.32 x 4 x 3.54 = 89.49:1.

As with the Dana 20, twin-stick shifters are available for the Dana 300 from a few manufacturers and in a few varieties. The twin-sticks allow for independent front and rear control and offer modes not available with the single shifter. The added modes provided by the twin-sticks add flexibility and are useful in certain off-road conditions. Front-wheel drive can be useful for dragging the front of the Jeep to the left or right when navigating obstacles.

For even more flexibility, a cable shifter is available for the Dana 300 from JB Custom Fabrication. The self-contained kit allows installation of the shifters in locations not possible with the case-mounted shifter.

In general, the Dana 300 is quite strong and can manage reliably with a variety of engines. A known weak part of the Dana 300 is the rear output shaft; replacement high-strength output shafts can be installed to correct this weak link. For tight installations involving a Dana 300, an ultra-short output-shaft conversion kit is available from TeraFlex to maintain the longest possible rear driveshaft.

Finally, a Dana 300 can be equipped with a clocking ring; rings

Clocking a Dana 300 increases ground clearance by moving the lower output shaft up and out of the way. This allows for a flatter center skid plate, lessening the potential from damage. This adapter/clocking ring from Novak adapts an SM420 to a Dana 300. (Photo Courtesy Novak Conversions)

are available from several manufacturers such as Novak Conversions, Advance Adapters, and NorthWest Fabworks. This ring mounts to the case input flange and allows the transfer case to be rotated several degrees. This is done most often to raise the lower output shaft, which allows for increased under center ground clearance. Rotating the transfer case affects several items, such as shifter orientation, which may warrant the use of a cable-shifter setup. Oil level and lubrication characteristics are also affected by rotation; follow the manufacturer's instructions to deal with this.

Quadra-Trac

A much-less-popular transfer case found in the AMC-era CJ was the NP 1339 Quadra-Trac, a first for Jeep to offer full-time four-wheel drive in a CJ. The NP1339 is operated by a chain and features an integrated limited-slip differential that allowed full-time four-wheel-drive operation. The driver could lock the center differential when needed to allow part-time four-wheel-drive operation with the use of a vacuum switch located in the glove box. A Quadra-Trac could be outfitted with an exterior-mounted planetary gear reduction unit that provided a 2.57:1 four-wheel-drive Lo mode engaged by a small lever found on the floor in front of the driver seat.

Because the Quadra-Trac was only available with the TH400, the Sample Jeep crawl ratio is 2.48 (TH400 automatic) x 2.57 x 3.54 = 22.56:1. Adapting a manual transmission to a Quadra-Trac is not realistic; it is said that this transfer case would never stand up to the output loads.

Mile Marker makes a conversion kit for the Quadra-Trac that replaces the internal center differential with a spool, allowing for installation of lockout hubs on the Jeep. This setup allowed for somewhat traditional two- and four-wheel-drive modes. To achieve two-wheel drive, the lockout hubs were disconnected rather than the transfer case, which ran the front driveshaft and differential constantly.

The Quadra-Trac was only available in the CJ-7 from 1976 until 1979 and only on those Jeeps with an automatic transmission. Because the output on the unit for both the front and rear is on the lower side of the transfer case, Jeeps equipped with the unit used offset differentials in both the front and rear.

Transfer Case Swaps

Swapping a transfer case is often part of a transmission swap because they usually require adapters and shaft swaps when being changed

Adapting a Dana 300 to a transmission is easy with the correct adapter. The integrated input gear of the Dana 300 made adapting it much easier than the Dana 20. Here is a T18 with its clockable Dana 300 adapter. (Photo Courtesy Craig Brown)

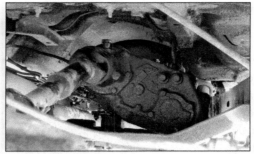

This 1977 Jeep is a good example of a swap of a Dana 20 instead of the factory Quadra-Trac. As a result, it was necessary to replace the rear axle with a center differential unit and install a two-piece front drive-shaft for clearance of the transmission pan. This Dana 20 is equipped with a TeraLow 3.15:1 low-range kit, and from its appearance it's obvious it has seen its share of trails.

alone. It may cost more than the benefit of the swap.

Dana 300

Swapping a Dana 300 into a Dana 20–equipped Jeep can be done with the use of an adapter. This swap isn't the most popular and often it is more cost effective to install a low-range reduction set in the Dana 20 already in the

Jeep. In the event that a transmission swap is underway, the decision should be made to either keep the Dana 20 or switch to a Dana 300. Adapting a transmission to either transfer case can be costly. Because a Dana 300 can be purchased relatively cheap, it may make sense to switch cases then. A similar thought could be applied to going the other direction (i.e., swapping a Dana 300 with a Dana 20).

Because the Dana 300 is so popular and well developed for the CJ, swapping a non-stock transfer case may not make sense. Exceptions to this thinking are when both the transmission and transfer case are being swapped at the same time. In some cases, retaining the transfer case originally installed with the swap transmission may make more sense. A big issue with transfer case swaps is the front output shaft location. Many vehicles use a driver-side drop; the CJ uses a passenger-side drop.

Quadra-Trac

Over years of use, the Quadra-Trac internal chain becomes fatigued and prone to failure. Parts availability has become tougher through the years, causing many Jeep owners to swap out the Quadra-Trac for a Dana 18 or Dana 20.

A Dana 18 was found in pre-1972 Jeeps and is a good swap for the Quadra-Trac because it uses

The CJ passenger-side transfer case drop can make it difficult to swap in non-factory transfer cases and axles because most vehicles used a driver-side drop. Jeep switched to the driver-side drop in the 1987 and later Wrangler series Jeeps, making the NP231 and NV241 transfer cases poor swap candidates.

Swapping out a Quadra-Trac for a Dana 20 requires a shaft and gear change in the rear of the transmission to use the Dana 20. This setup shows the replacement shaft, gear, and adapter required.

The two-piece front driveshaft allows the driveshaft to clear the transmission. The custom installation uses a center bearing mounted to the Jeep's frame. Although not always needed, this install uses a slip joint on both sections of the driveshaft to reduce vibration and allow movement of the engine.

the same front and rear output shaft drop and does not require a rear axle swap. The Dana 18 swap requires an output shaft change in the TH400.

A Dana 20 transfer case can be swapped in for a Quadra-Trac relatively easily with an output shaft change in the TH400 and some other modifications. The rear differential would need to be swapped with a readily available center unit, and provisions for the Dana 20 shifter need to be provided. Quadra-Trac CJs did not come with factory lockout hubs; after conversion, these could be installed to reduce drag from the front differential when driving in two-wheel drive.

In most cases, swapping a Dana 20 or Dana 18 instead of a Quadra-Trac requires a two-piece front driveshaft to clear the bottom of the automatic. A two-piece shaft requires adding an intermediate bearing to the first section of the shaft. Most are attached to the frame, but some install a bearing mount that attaches to the engine/transmission. The latter prevents vibration because the fixed mount moves with the engine and not with the frame.

The Atlas

Advance Adapters created the Atlas transfer case in 1996 and it's probably the ultimate in Jeep replacement transfer cases. These units are

based upon the Dana 300 and can bolt in as a direct replacement. The Atlas comes in a few versions featuring two and four speeds, with gear ratios from 2:1 to 5:1. Most are fully customizable to meet your Jeep's needs. The expense of the Atlas makes sense only for serious off-road use.

Jeep Driveshafts

A Jeep's driveshaft serves to transfer power from the transmission or (in the case of a CJ) from

the transfer case output to the axles while allowing movement of the axles within the suspension cycle. The universal joints allow the driveshaft to change angles; the slip joint allows expansion and contraction from suspension movement. These movements and seemingly simple purpose are actually rather complex and, if ignored, can cause breakage, vibration, and excess wear.

The factory Jeep driveshafts are capable of handling the stock engines found in the Jeep with reasonable off-roading and a light throttle foot. Upgrading any or all of your Jeep's engine, transmission, and transfer case can put an increased torque load on the driveshafts. They are often the first component to break when overpowered. It's not unusual to find a spare driveshaft or two in the back of a CJ on the trail, and it's not unusual to find a Jeep being driven home from the trail with only a front driveshaft.

This Jeep runs an Advance Adapters Atlas for superior strength and 4:1 low range. The Atlas, which is based on the Dana 300, is the ultimate aftermarket transfer case that is used by serious off-road-use vehicles. The aluminum case keeps the weight down while providing extra rigidity.

The CJ-7's extra 10 inches adds a comfortable space to allow the rear driveshaft to be longer, reducing operating angle and allowing more lift without vibration and wear. This Jeep runs a T176 transmission, which is quite compact for a 4-speed. A Scrambler adds another 10 inches compared to the CJ-7, which makes the driveshaft even longer for potentially long-swap transmissions.

In addition to upgrading and modifying the components listed above, larger tires, lockers, and lifts all put an increased strain on the driveshafts. The short rear driveshaft length found in so many CJs increases the operating angle, putting more strain on the universal joints, increasing the possibility of a failure. Upgrading the Jeep's driveshafts helps these components deal with the great amounts of torque generated. Several companies, including Tom Wood's and Reel Driveline, make replacement driveshafts with heavy-duty universal joints, thicker tubes, and heavy-duty/longer-travel slip joints.

Universal Joints

The CJ series used the Dana Spicer 1310 series universal joints, which are durable and strong. Upgrades to the joints require changing the yoke on the driveshafts, transfer case, and/or axle. Common upgrades from the 1310 are installation of the 1350 or 1410 universal joints. Usually, upgrades to universal joints are part of a driveshaft upgrade; companies such as Tom Wood's or Reel Driveline can provide available options.

Measuring your Jeep to fit a proper driveshaft is simple. Following the recommendations from the driveshaft maker is the best bet to ensure a perfect fit. Greasable joints are recommended, especially if the Jeep frequently sees mud and water conditions.

Angles

Operating angles are a complex subject that can be difficult to conceptualize. Many Jeep owners ignore angles and just put together a system that later causes vibration and/or failures. Depending on the style of universal joints, the proper operat-

A well-prepared Jeep owner has spare universal joints for both the driveshafts and front axle shafts in the Jeep when on the trail. Often a U-joint fails before other components. Assuming that when the joint fails it doesn't destroy the U-joint yoke, it can easily be changed on the trail.

ing angle varies. The angle should be considered from both the side profile and top profile. Use a magnetic angle gauge attached to the output yoke with no driveshaft attached to measure yoke angles.

Standard Universal Joint

A typical AMC-era CJ has driveshafts equipped with a single universal joint at each end of the shaft. This driveshaft operates most efficiently if both the output shaft yoke and axle input shaft yoke are on parallel planes from both the side and top. Some Jeep owners, in an effort to reduce the driveshaft angle, lower the transfer case mount. This causes the driveshaft planes to intersect, usually resulting in vibration.

Double Cardan Joint

Most AMC-era CJs were not equipped with double Cardan joints, which are often simply and slightly incorrectly referred to as constant-velocity universal joints. The exception is the Quadra-Trac equipped CJ-7s, in which only the front driveshaft ran a single CV-style joint at the transfer case output.

When ordering a custom driveshaft, measurements are needed to ensure a proper fit and performance. A magnetic angle gauge can be used to determine the operating angle of the driveshaft. Using the old one gives a good surface to measure from. If no driveshaft is available, a length of rigid angle can be used.

A common and effective upgrade to a lifted CJ is the addition of a double Cardan joint on the rear driveshaft. This style joint at the rear transfer case output reduces driveline vibration often experienced because of the short driveshaft running at a steep angle due to the suspension lift. Both the Dana Model 20 and Model 300 transfer cases can be refitted with a CV yoke. Installation of a driveshaft with a CV joint alone is not enough. Typical installation requires altering the angle of the rear axle to point directly at the output yoke, a difference in angle concept over a driveshaft with two universal joints.

Slip Joint

An extra-long slip joint allows a Jeep's suspension to travel farther when off-road without binding or potentially causing damage to the driveshaft. Maintaining the slip joint ensures proper operation and life. Jeep owners often remove the driveshaft to disassemble the slip joint to clean and lubricate the shaft and splines after a season of off-road driving. Water and mud can get into the splines, increasing friction and wear. Most aftermarket heavy-duty driveshaft slip joints pull apart without tools.

With a short shaft, using a CV joint can drastically reduce vibration and wear. Using a CV joint requires the rear axle angle to be raised and often requires a change of the rear output yoke on the transfer case to a CV style found on the Bronco version of the Dana 20.

To boot or not to boot is the question. This aftermarket driveshaft features an extended-travel slip joint with a boot to keep out the contaminants. Periodic cleaning, inspecting, and maintaining the joint keeps it operational.

A common question is "Should the slip joint have a boot?" There are often debates about this, but there really seems to be no correct answer. A boot can keep out contaminants but may stretch under extreme travel. A damaged or loose boot can keep contaminants in and cause rust and/or wear to the joint.

Putting It All Together

Either a Dana 20 or Dana 300 serves a Jeep well.

- Adding a low-range aftermarket gearset is such a big improvement to off-road capability without sacrifice of on-road driving that it seems like a "no brainer."
- Running a well-maintained Quadra-Trac, when equipped

with a low-range kit, performs well. It's not the evil transfer case it's made out to be. A part-time kit saves wear and increases efficiency.
- Replacing the factory shifter with a twin-stick setup allows more transfer case operating mode options while allowing easier shifting. The attractive look of the shifters is an extra bonus.
- Replacing strap-style yokes with U-bolts prevents strap failures.
- Maintaining the proper angles for the style of driveshaft you are running prevents vibrations and increases life.
- A replacement driveshaft with a thicker tube and longer slip-joint increases strength to handle more power and torque.

Finding the perfect setup in a transfer case and driveshaft is one of the easier modifications to contemplate in a CJ. A low gearset and strong aftermarket driveshaft make a Jeeper happy after a day on the trails.

Geometry Requirements

A standard driveshaft with two universal joints should operate with both the output yokes operating in a parallel plane with each other in both the side and top. Deviation from parallel causes increased driveline vibration and wear. For a Jeep running a CV shaft, the single joint side yoke is "pointed" at the CV. The CV joint can tolerate a higher angle and results in less vibration.

Straps versus U-Bolts

Somewhere around 1981, Jeep changed the driveshaft-mounting method from the U-bolt design to the strap design. Straps are cheaper and quicker to install but fail more quickly and more easily; the universal joint often forces itself from the strap when excess torque is applied. An easy upgrade is to replace the yokes on the transfer case and axles to use the older, stronger U-bolt style. Yokes for all the components are readily available either from the aftermarket or parts yard.

Maintenance

Driveshafts, especially the rear, experience constant use, which is hard enough on the small universal joint bearings, but regular off-road use adds the likelihood that water and contaminants may enter into the joint bearing caps. Regular maintenance includes greasing the joints and cleaning the joints by disassembly, if needed. In addition to the joints, the slip joint should be regularly lubricated and cleaned, if needed.

AXLE AND TRACTION SYSTEM

In the AMC era, the Jeep CJ ran only one version of the front axle and two different rear axles. The Dana 30 front axle served the CJ well through its years and, in fact, has remained in use in the Wrangler series. The axle was strong enough to tolerate off-road use and its small ring and pinion gave it excellent ground clearance.

The Dana 44 was found in the rear of the 1972–1975 CJ-5 and late 1986 CJ-7. Its 8½-inch ring gear and one-piece flanged axles offered good strength and reliability in a compact size.

Finally, the AMC Model 20 rear axle found in 1976–1986 CJs is a strong rear with an 8-7/8-inch ring gear, but several weak points with this model require some upgrades to fortify it for serious off-road use.

In 1982, Jeep introduced the Wide Trak axles, which added 3 inches to the axle width. The increased track width helped increase the Jeep's stability, improved road handling, and helped diminish the Jeep's roll-over reputation. From 1976 to 1979, Quadra-Trac–equipped CJs were fitted with an offset differential on the rear AMC Model 20 to accommodate the rear driveshaft exiting the NP1339 transfer case at the lower end.

Rocks are among the joys of off-road driving a Jeep. While they can cause damage in countless ways, Jeepers seek out the rock gardens on the trail and spend a significant amount of time traversing them in a slow and controlled pace, thanks to a proper crawl ratio.

Messing with axles might be a more frequent activity to a Jeep owner than messing with engines. Often you see a bone-stock Jeep with fancy, expensive axles equipped with all kinds of goodies stuffed underneath. Jeep swap meets such as the one at the Annual All-Breeds Jeep Show in York, Pennsylvania, are a popular place for locating that perfect one.

Cracking your differential open and seeing stuff coming out that looks like caramel indicates that water has gotten into the differential, either through the breather tube or worn axle seals. Off-road driving can expose the Jeep to deep water and mud that can work their way into the differential. If left alone, bearings and gears rust and/ or wear. Checking and changing the gear oil frequently in a Jeep that sees trail use keeps things properly lubricated. (Photo Courtesy Ralph Hassel)

Jeepers often upgrade the existing axles in their Jeeps or swap the factory axles out for higher-strength versions that tolerate the forces applied by larger tires and more powerful engines. Depending on your style of driving and the kind of off-road driving you do, it indicates the likely success or failure of the Jeep's axles and the potential need for an aftermarket axle upgrade.

Jeep Gearing

Gearing may be one of the most discussed and debated subjects among Jeep owners. The question "What gear are you running?" is as common as being asked, "Do you want fries with that?" at a fast food restaurant. Choosing the correct gear for your Jeep is a complex topic but can be boiled down to a few simple items: type of driving, type of engine, type of transmission, crawl ratio, and tire size.

Defining what axle "gearing" actually means is a good place to start. Simply, the axle houses the ring and pinion gears, which convert the rotation of the driveshaft to the forward and reverse rotation of the axle shafts. The ring and pinion convert the rotation using a ratio that allows the pinion to rotate at a faster speed than the axle shafts. A common ratio in a Jeep is 4.11:1. This means that the pinion rotates 4.11 times while the axle shaft rotates once. Increasing the ratio effectively lowers the amount of force required to rotate the axle shaft, thereby easing the workload on the engine.

Low versus High

A few frequently used terms can be confusing to an inexperienced Jeeper, mainly using "higher gears" and "lower gears" correctly. The term *numerically higher* refers to the ratio being greater, as in "4.56:1 is numerically higher than 3.73:1." Numerically higher gear ratios require more engine rotations to axle shaft rotations.

Most often, gearing is not referred to as numerically higher or lower. Gearing is referred to as simply higher or lower; *numerically higher* is the same as lower ratio. Much like a low gear in a transmission or transfer case, low gears are technically numerically higher.

Using the example above, "4.56:1 is numerically higher than 3.73:1" = "4.56:1 is lower than 3.73:1." In the end, lower gears allow for more vehicle control while increasing engine speed and torque. Navigating complicated trail obstacles with lower gears is much easier and, along with more control, results in less stalling and less damage potential.

The Big Picture

Because your goal is to build a Jeep for maximum performance on- and off-road, the compromise is even more important. Looking at the big picture will help with the decision of which gear to run. A high-crawl ratio results in maximum performance off-road but means little on the road (see Chapter 4). This leads to the big picture of the kind of Jeep being built.

Because axle ratios don't affect crawl ratio as much as the transmission and transfer case, and remembering highway ratio is typically 1:1, running slightly higher gears in the axle results in better street driving without greatly affecting crawl ratio. For example, running 4.11:1 gears instead of 4.56:1 drops engine RPM at highway speeds from 300 to 400, while only reducing crawl ratio five to eight points.

In the end, crawl ratio increased by increasing ratios within the transmission and transfer case, and running a reasonable axle gear, results in the best compromise. It is important to keep the tire size in mind with this calculation.

Both the factory I-6 and V-8 engines have good torque and run happily in the 2,200- to 2,700-rpm range on the highway; faster speeds just use up fuel at an increased rate. Determining the optimum highway engine RPM on a swapped or heavily modified engine is essential for this calculation. Many gear-ratio and RPM calculators can be found online. ∎

Driving Style

Finding the best ratio for a Jeep is the subject of many debates and, as with many things, there is no perfect answer. Gearing in the Jeep's axles is a matter of compromise, and unlike transmissions and transfer cases, there is not the ability to change axle gears with a shifter or without special tools. Labor costs to change an axle gear ratio can put a serious dent in your wallet; choose wisely. The compromise referred to is highway driving versus trail driving; go too low and you have to run high engine RPM to keep up with traffic; go too high and trail driving is miserable. Typical "usable" Jeep axle ratios run from 3.54:1 to 5.38:1. The difference of two points makes more difference at highway speeds and various tire sizes.

Tire Size

Larger tires effectively reduce gear ratios, which is important when choosing gears. For example, a Jeep with 33-inch tires and 4.11 gears is nearly equal to a Jeep with 35-inch tires running 3.73 gears.

Factory Axles

Jeep remained consistent with factory axles in the AMC era. The front was the Dana 30 and the rear was equipped with the Dana 44 and AMC 20. All of these axles were very capable of serving the Jeep well, even considering the weak hub design of the AMC 20.

Dana 30

The Dana 30 uses a 7.12-inch ring gear and is an open knuckle design that allows for a variety of outer knuckle designs to accommodate different brakes and hub configurations. From 1972 to 1976, it used 11

The Dana 30 is the longest-running axle in the CJ, continuing on through the Wrangler series. The open-knuckle axle came in the CJ in a variety of configurations of hubs, brakes, and widths. Its compact differential offers a fair amount of ground clearance. The Dana 30 is identified by its cover, which is kind of a baby Dana 44 design.

x 2–inch drum brakes with optional disc brakes in 1976, and starting in 1977 disc brakes were standard.

The 1976–1978 Dana 30 with disc brakes used the "big brake" design. The big brake disc used the 10½ x 1-1/8–inch rotor attached to the six-bolt bracket mounted between the knuckle and spindle.

The 1979–1986 disc brakes used a 10½ x 7/8–inch rotor with a two-bolt to integrated knuckle caliper mounting bracket.

The Dana 30 has 27-spline-count axle shafts, 5- or 6-bolt locking hub mounts, and a passenger-side offset. The Dana 30 uses two carriers that

are split between gear ratios: 3.73 and lower ratios use one style carrier and 3.54 and higher use another.

Dana 44

The Dana 44 uses an 8½-inch ring gear and one-piece flanged 30-spline axle shafts. The 1972–1975 used the 11-inch drum brakes; the 1986 used 10-inch drum brakes. The Dana 44, like the Dana 30, uses two carriers that are split between gear ratios; the 3.73 and lower ratios use one style of carrier and 3.54 and higher use another.

AMC 20

Most AMC-era Jeep owners find themselves with a Jeep equipped with the AMC Model 20, which isn't as bad as some make it out to be. A large, strong ring and pinion makes this axle capable at handling the torque of a V-8 engine and the demands off-roading. As mentioned earlier, the two-piece factory axles are prone to failure by shearing off the key where the axle shaft meets the hub. The force of the hub being installed creates the splines on the axle shaft. These self-made splines weaken through years of use, and shearing the key is possible even with casual street driving.

The AMC 20 was equipped with the larger 11-inch drum brakes until 1978 and the 10-inch drum brakes

The AMC 20 is easily identified by its round cover and is the most likely axle to be found under a CJ. Without proper modifications in a Jeep with larger tires, this axle's two-piece factory axle shafts barely stand up to normal street driving. Swapping them for stronger, flanged one-piece axles is a substantial improvement to longevity.

AXLE AND TRACTION SYSTEM

after. The differential carriers came in two separate versions: one for the 2.73 ratio and one for ratios from 3.31 to 5.13.

Traction Systems

Put simply, a differential splits engine power among the wheels and allows the wheels to move at different speeds when turning. This design alone typically allows engine power to move the wheel with the least traction. In its standard form, a differential has no traction control system and is referred to as an open differential. These perform well on dry, paved roads but easily cause loss of traction when conditions become severe.

AMC-era factory Jeep axles came with open differentials but were often equipped with special traction-aiding differentials as an option. Jeep often branded this option as a Trac-Lok axle, which is a form of limited-slip differential.

Limited-Slip

The "posi" (short for positive), or limited-slip, differential is the optional traction system that Jeep offered as the Trac-Lok differential. The limited-slip differential works by allowing a certain amount of torque to be applied to both wheels, even in low-traction situations. The limited-slip operates by using clutch packs on the differential side gears that limit excess slip from occurring when there is a loss of traction. This is an effective system for slippery road conditions and light off-roading, but in situations where a wheel may come off the ground, the limitations of the limited-slip are exceeded, causing loss of traction.

These Dana 44 Trak-Loc spider side gears "modified" by a younger version of me using a swapped 400HP Chevy 350 show the splines used by the clutch pack to provide extra torque to the slipping wheel. The factory Trak-Loc system worked well when new, but over time the clutches would wear and lose effectiveness. It's no comparison to a locker but surprisingly helpful in off-road situations such as hills and mud, where some speed and steady power is applied.

Locker

A locking differential causes equal torque to be applied to both wheels mechanically, regardless of traction, by locking the differential side gears together, effectively eliminating any differentiation. Lockers are extremely effective when off-road and provide maximum traction to a

wheel even if the other is in the air.

Lockers are available in a few varieties and operate in different ways but these can be divided into essentially two types: automatic and manual. Expense, convenience, and durability are all considerations when deciding on a locker for a Jeep.

Manual lockers offer the convenience of choosing when to engage the locker but often come at a higher price when including potential other components that are needed to operate the system. Automatic lockers can be much less expensive but often introduce less desirable characteristics to normal street driving.

Automatic lockers run in a normally locked mode but can unlock quickly to allow cornering without dragging a wheel. Most automatic lockers use the forward or reverse torque to hold the locker in the locked mode and only unlock during cornering when power is not being applied. If the driver is applying too much power during cornering, the locker locks, which causes the inner wheel to drag; the sudden locking can often be violent and cause erratic vehicle movement.

Most automatic lockers cause a clicking, ratcheting, or clunking

Installation of an Air Locker is often best left to an experienced shop due to the need for proper tools to set up the ring and pinion correctly. The air cylinder in the locker requires seals to be installed and a small portion of the carrier-bearing cap to be removed to allow the copper air line by. The air locker's signature air line gives away what is inside this Dana 44 front axle.

sound during cornering because the locker teeth are slipping over themselves. In addition to the clicking, lockers may suddenly engage, causing a banging noise that can cause the vehicle to pull left or right when accelerating. Rain and snow driving with an automatic locker can be a hair-raising experience. The locker stays locked in these situations, possibly causing the Jeep to fishtail.

You must be willing and able to deal with the characteristics of an automatic locker. Some manufacturers make automatic lockers that handle everyday driving well; these usually cost more and may be more prone to failure because of their complex design.

Some automatic lockers replace the entire differential carrier; other less-expensive versions replace the open differential spider gears. The latter is occasionally referred to as a "lunch box" locker. These lockers are

The Powertrax No-Slip automatic locker operates similarly to the Lock Right but offers smoother operation by using a synchronizing mechanism to eliminate the ratcheting sound often experienced by automatic lockers. (Photo Courtesy Powertrax)

typically not as strong as the full carrier design but can be and are used for years. Failure usually occurs with broken center pins, but, fortunately, most locker manufacturers offer high-strength center pins to help with durability.

In truth, driving style has the biggest influence on the reliability of these lunch box lockers. Even a V-8 powered CJ running 33-inch tires can run a lunch box locker successfully for years with proper throttle control. Lunch box lockers are a good introduction to an automatic locker without the expense; the Jeep owner can often install it with common tools.

The most popular differential carrier automatic locker is the Detroit Locker. This is probably the most heavy-duty automatic locker available. Installation requires special tools and skills. Popular lunch box lockers include the Powertrax No Slip and Powertrax Lock Right.

Manual lockers are the most popular style in a Jeep. These are engaged either by air, electronics, or cable. When not engaged, the manual locker operates as a standard open differential and allows normal driving. When engaged, the locker is fully locked and both wheels move at the same speed. Cornering with the locker engaged causes a wheel to drag, and a front axle equipped with a manual locker is difficult to steer at slow speeds when the locker is not engaged.

The Powertrax Lock Right is a simple automatic locker that can be installed by the Jeep owner using common garage tools. The locker is an inexpensive true locker that can provide extra traction with minimal expense. A Jeep owner running a locker of this type needs to know its behavior and realize that it's not as strong as a full carrier locker.

The Detroit Locker freshly installed in this 1978 CJ-7 has a swapped Dana 44 from a Scout. The Detroit is one of the strongest automatic lockers available due to its fully integrated carrier. Driving with an automatic locker requires some experience to be able to deal with the sometimes-odd behavior of the locker. (Photo Courtesy Ralph Hassel)

Like many others, this CJ runs an ARB Air Locker just in the front to allow steering in four-wheel drive to act normally. At the flip of a switch on the Jeep's dash, the locker engages and provides full torque to both front wheels, which, when combined with the rear Detroit locker, creates true four-wheel drive.

The most popular manual lockers are the ARB Air Locker (air), Eaton ELocker (electric), and OX Locker (cable and electronic). All are quality lockers that can serve a Jeep for many years. The decision that a Jeep owner needs to make is which locking actuation method to use.

An air locker requires an air compressor and air lines. Although the air lines and air coupling within the rear can leak, the system is generally very reliable. Electronic lockers require only a small wire to the axle to operate the locker. Cable styles require a cable to be run from the differential to the inside of the Jeep. This cable attaches to a shifter lever that engages and disengages the locker. Manual lockers require special tools and skills for proper installation.

Installing a Powertrax Lock Right

This locker is also known as a lunch box. Different axles require slight variations; follow the Powertrax directions. This install is on a factory AMC 20 differential equipped with Superior 1 piece axles.

With the Jeep properly supported, remove the wheels, drain the differential gear oil, and remove the differential cover.

Replace the cover and tighten the axle shaft retaining bolts. Fill the differential with gear oil and after replacing the wheels, the installation is complete.

Driving is different with an automatic locker. Clicking when cornering is normal and a pull to the left or right when shifting and/or heavy throttle use is normal and must be anticipated. Read the user manual for more driving directions.

1 *While the oil is draining, remove the brake drum on the driver's side and begin unbolting the axle retaining bolts. Carefully pull the axle shaft from the housing about 2 inches. It is not necessary to completely remove the shaft, just a few inches clears the splines in the spider side gear and allows the thrust block to move into the side gear.*

2 *With everything exposed, the spider gears, ring, pinion, and carrier are visible and ready for spider gear removal. On most AMC axles, removal of the carrier is not needed.*

3 *The cross shaft holds the spider gears in place and is removed by pushing the roll pin out from the ring gear side of the carrier. Complete removal isn't needed; leaving it partially in eases reassembly.*

4 *With the roll pin out of the way, remove the cross shaft. It's possible that the spiders will fall out, depending on position. Rotate the spider gears to allow them to be removed from the carrier.*

5 Press the center spacer into the side gear on the side the axle was pulled. Be careful not to push the spacer all the way into the axle housing. Remove the side gears, keeping the left and right shims in order. Remove the center spacer with the side gear.

6 Place the shims on the new Lock Right couplers and insert them into the carrier. Place the center spacer within the driver-side coupler.

7 Making sure the Lock Right spacers are set the correct way, push two shear pins in each driver and slide them into the housing, being careful the pins do not fall out.

8 With the drivers aligned and the shear pins pushed across to meet the opposite driver, insert the springs using a small screwdriver.

9 Making sure the springs are fully seated, rotate the assembly to install the remaining springs.

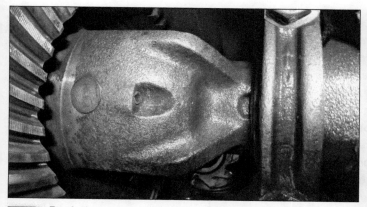

10 Push the removed axle back in to push the center spacer into place and install the new cross pin. It should go in with no force. If it feels blocked, it's possible the inner spacers are installed incorrectly. With the cross shaft installed, drive the roll pin back into place to retain the cross shaft. The pin should align flush with the hole in the carrier.

11 With the installation complete, clean up any old gasket material and apply RTV to the gasket groove and on the cleaned-up cover.

Spool

A spool is effectively a differential replacement. A spool either replaces a differential's spider gears or replaces the differential carrier. A solid connection is formed between the left and right axles and both remain locked in place, causing the engine's torque to be applied evenly to each wheel. A spool is impractical in a Jeep that is used on- and off-road because cornering causes one wheel to drag, resulting in excess tire wear and driveline stress.

Factory Axle Modifications and Upgrades

The factory axles can provide years of reliable off-road use on a Jeep. With some upgrades, they can handle 33- to 35-inch tires and moderately built engines. As mentioned before, driving style plays a big role in the survival of axles. A heavy throttle foot sends huge amounts of torque through the drivetrain. Large tires with aggressive lugs grab obstacles. This, when combined with the torque of a Jeep engine/transmis-sion/transfer case and a heavy foot, causes axles to break.

Because I focus on building and modifying a CJ that performs both on- and off-road, I want to point out that the factory axles will serve the Jeep and you well, with a few modifications and upgrades.

Dana 30

The Dana 30 front axle, in all its forms in the 1972–1986 CJ, features interchangeable outer knuckles. The outer knuckle comprises the components that extend from the ball joints and outward. This interchangeability allows installation of disc brakes on a drum brake–equipped CJ and

The five-bolt hub appeared in the early 1980s equipped with a weaker lockout hub. The five-bolt design isn't as much of a problem as the reduced material area for the lockout hub. Even aftermarket lockout hubs from companies such as Superwinch and Warn aren't as substantial as their six-bolt cousins. Swapping to a six-bolt design is a popular conversion.

The six-bolt hub is very strong and, when equipped with Warn Premium lockout hubs and hub studs, is nearly unbreakable because it's likely that a U-joint will fail before the hub. Checking the bolt tightness is essential. Often, failures are due to loose bolts.

Factory two-piece axles can be easily spotted by the presence of a stub sticking out of the center of the rear axle. Below the cover is a large nut that is used to force the outer hub to self-spline the inner axle shaft. The weak shallow splines created and small key are the only things preventing the axle from spinning within the hub. Over time, the entire assembly wears, causing failure. (Photo Courtesy Craig Brown)

One-piece replacement axles for the AMC 20 two-piece axles are available from several manufacturers such as Ten Factory, G2, and Revolution Gear and Axle. Installation of these kits is not difficult but having access to a press makes the job quicker and easier. (Photo Courtesy Quadratec)

swapping of the later, weaker five-bolt to a stronger six-bolt hub found on earlier CJs. Most popular locker types and gear ratios are available for the Dana 30, as well as stronger axle shafts with larger Dana 44 U-joints. Axle trusses are sometimes installed to increase the rigidity of the Dana 30, a significant improvement that can help prevent bent axles.

Lockout hubs can be a weak point on a Dana 30. Using Warn Premium locking hubs provides the best strength on a six-bolt hub spindle. In addition to premium locking hubs, changing the hub bolts to studs helps keep the hub firmly attached to the spindle. Warn makes a stud conversion kit with the properly sized studs and nuts. To go a step further, Warn makes a hub-conversion kit that replaces the bolt-on hub with an integrated design that is superior in

strength. Sadly, this conversion kit is no longer produced but can be found in the used market.

Dana 44

A Dana 44 is a strong, reliable rear out of the box with no modifications. The Dana 44 on all the AMC-era CJs uses the semi-floating flanged axle. Upgrades to this axle include a variety of limited-slip differentials, most popular lockers, trusses to increase axle rigidity, and rear disc brake conversions.

AMC 20

The most common upgrade to an AMC 20 is a one-piece rear axle conversion. This conversion replaces the factory two-piece design with a single, higher-strength flanged axle. A few varieties of this axle are made. Look for forged axles with rolled splines and

avoid those that require shimming. These tend to cause gear oil leaks.

Warn used to make a full floater kit for the AMC 20 that converted the axle to a full-floating style similar to the front axle. The wheel hub

The Warn Full Float rear axle kit replaced the factory axle and hub assembly with a high-strength front-like spindle and hub that supported the Jeep's weight. In this system, the axle shaft only provides rotation to move the Jeep. In the event of a broken axle, the shaft could be pulled from the Jeep without the hub moving out of place. In addition, lockout hubs could be installed, allowing the axle to be disconnected, especially handy if the Jeep is flat-towed.

This 1980 CJ-7 is outfitted with a rear disc brake conversion to increase stopping power and reduce brake fade experienced by drum brakes. This setup is a custom conversion, which uses parts gathered from other Jeep vehicles. The calipers are from a full-size Jeep and the rotors are stock CJ fronts. Mounts are custom fabricated. Custom setups require some fine-tuning and adjustment to get proper operation.

Disc Brake Conversion

A rear disc brake conversion is a popular modification that CJ owners make to their Jeeps. Replacing the rear drum brakes with discs increases stopping power, especially in wet conditions. Many Jeepers convert their Jeeps to disc brakes using parts from other vehicles such as Cadillac, Corvette, Geo, and Toyota. These home-made conversions require a significant amount of research and parts gathering and provide mixed results. It's definitely a project for the adventurous type.

A few companies make bolt-on conversions that do the job cleanly and safely. I usually recommend going this route to avoid trouble later, unless you know a proven combination. ∎

rode on a pair of bearings that supported the weight of the Jeep, leaving the axle used only for movement. In the event of a broken axle shaft, the axle could be removed and the wheel hub would support the Jeep and allow it to be driven. In addition, the full-float kit allowed running lockout hubs on the rear. This allows you to disconnect the rear axles for towing or other purposes. Full-float kits can still be found in the used market.

A number of Jeep owners use front Jeep spindles to fabricate home-built full-floater conversions for the AMC 20. This conversion requires a fair amount of fabrication, custom axle shafts, brake alterations, and more.

The AMC 20 axle tubes are known for their thin wall and tendency to spin in the center section. Welding the axle tube to the center section with small, intermittent welds can prevent this situation. A truss or gussets can be added to increase the axle's rigidity.

The AMC 20 can be outfitted with a variety of limited-slip differentials, most popular lockers, and gear ratios. In addition, a few companies make disc brake conversions. SSBC Performance Brake Systems makes a complete bolt-on kit.

Swaps, Replacements and Conversions

Swapping axles is a common practice with Jeeps, and the CJ is no exception. Often the swap is driven by the need to upgrade some aspect such as the strength of the axle as well as its width.

Wide Trak Axle

The Wide Trak axle found in the 1982–1986 CJ can be near bolt-in swapped to a 1976–1981 CJ. The only modifications that may be needed would be to the brake lines and parking brake cables. The 3 inches of additional track width adds some extra stability and wheel clearance to narrow track–equipped CJs. Swapping Wide Trak axles into 1972–1975 CJs would require more modification, mainly in the rear because the frame was wider in 1976 and later CJs. New spring mounts would need to be welded to the rear axle, and considerations would need to be made for the factory disc brakes on the Wide Trak Dana 30.

Aftermarket Specialty Axles

A few companies make bolt-in heavy-duty axles for the CJ. These are often even stronger than the factory axle they started out as. These axles are designed for the hard-core off-roader and can be very expensive. The most popular aftermarket axles are the Dana 44 and Dana 60 design. These feature many varieties of widths, brake configurations, and steering systems. Some of these axles can be purchased in a bolt-in form, which can save time and expense.

The Wide Trak axle is the perfect axle width for a CJ and puts larger tires and wheels in the "just legal" category in some areas. The added width increases stability and clearance for larger tires. Looking down the side of a CJ, you can see how a 33 x 12½ tire barely sticks out past the flare.

Aftermarket axles such as this Dynatrac Dana 60 are the ultimate in strength but come at a substantial price tag. These axles feature massive ring and pinion gears, thick welded axle tube, heavy-duty cover, and high-strength axle shafts. It truly is for the serious off-roader.

Modified Conversion Axles

Some Jeep owners choose to convert axles from other vehicles to work in their Jeeps. These conversions require special tools and fabrication skills to complete successfully. A Jeep owner should spend time doing research before jumping into a conversion. Many of these conversions require cutting the axle tubes and axles to narrow the track width to fit the CJ and/or adjust caster angles. Relocation or addition of mounts for the springs and brackets for sway bars/shocks is often needed.

The Dana 44 from other vehicles can be converted to work with the CJ. The most common donor vehicles are the full-size Jeep trucks, Wagoneer, Cherokee, and International Harvester Scout. Most of these axles are wider and require cutting to reduce track width.

Full-size Jeep axles from 1973 on used 30-spline shafts and had two widths. The narrow version measures 58½ inches; the wide track measures 65 inches.

Most full-size Jeep front axles are equipped with either six- or eight-bolt lug patterns, which requires swapping the outer knuckle to use the factory CJ Dana 30 knuckle to retain

Swapping axles from other vehicles such as a Scout requires relocation of the front and rear shackle mounts on the front of a CJ. Fabricating outriggers allows the springs to fit the original mounts on the axle. This 1980 CJ-7 uses a Scout Dana 44 front axle. In addition to the outriggers, a shackle reversal is built into the custom installation.

Spotting a Ford 9-inch is easy because it lacks a removable rear cover. Access to the ring and pinion is from the front of the axle by removing the third member. The compact housing adds extra clearance, and the integrated axle tubes are very resistant to bending. Installing a Ford 9-inch is typically a custom install potentially requiring cutting of widths, custom axle shafts, custom brakes, and mounts.

the five-bolt CJ lug pattern. The knuckle swap requires no modification but often requires special ball joint adjusters and/or spindle shims to correct camber.

Full-size Jeep rear axles are equipped with either six- or eight-bolt lug patterns. The wide track width

A front Dana 44 from a full-size Jeep fits in a CJ after the driver's side is cut down to match the proper width. The axle is not quite the width of a Wide Trak Dana 30 but is about 1/2 inch short on each side. Dana 30 outer knuckles can be swapped to the full-size Jeep axle, allowing retention of the five-lug hubs. The biggest challenge with this swap is obtaining the proper caster and camber angles due to variations in full-size Jeeps to CJ knuckles.

requires cutting and custom axle shafts to retain the five-bolt lug pattern.

Scout Dana 44s are probably the most popular axle swaps for a CJ. These are only slightly wider than the Wide Trak CJ axles and can be used with no cutting. The biggest caveat to running Scout axles is that the front CJ spring hangers need to be extended outside the Jeep's frame to match the spring mounts on the axle. Relocating the differential side spring mount on the Scout Dana 44 is not possible because the mount is part of the differential housing.

More Complex Swaps

The Dana 60 front and rear from some Dodge trucks can be modified to fit into the CJ. The Dana 60 is a massive axle designed for heavy trucks. The super strong 9¾-inch ring gear, thick axle tubes, and large

U-joints (front) make this axle nearly unbreakable for a CJ.

Another popular swap for the rear of a CJ is a Ford 9-inch rear with its strong 9-inch ring gear and easily removable differential section. Gear and differential changes are much easier on a Ford 9-inch because the differential section can be removed without the need to remove the entire axle housing from the vehicle. This axle can be found in many Ford vehicles, including the Bronco.

Breather Tubes

Jeep axles have breather tubes that allow ventilation of the axle due to heat and cooling experienced during use. These tubes usually extend up to the frame area to prevent water entering. Maintaining these tubes and extending them higher if needed helps keep contaminants out. In addition, when larger lifts are installed, it may be necessary to install longer breather tubes to account for the additional height.

Axle Maintenance

A Jeep that sees off-road use inevitably ends up in mud or water, exposing its underside to potential damage. Mud and water can enter the axles through old seals and become trapped within. Trapped mud and water cause components to corrode and wear, leading to premature failure. Changing axle lubrication frequently, depending on off-road use, prevents corrosion and ensures long life. If an off-road trip yields extensive water exposure, changing the lubrication immediately may be wise. Checking the seals on both the pinion and axle ends will help to keep the water and mud out.

Jeeps with front lockout hubs usually use wheel bearings that are installed in pairs and are serviceable. Disassembling the hub to allow removal of the wheel bearings for fresh lubrication should be part of regular maintenance on a trail-used Jeep. During this process, seals should be checked and replaced as needed.

Putting It All Together

I want to step back and recap the Jeep that has been built so far. It has a trail performance modified I-6 or V-8, a T18/T176 or TF999 transmission, and a Dana 300 transfer case equipped with a low gearset.

Because the goal is to build and modify a CJ to maximize its on- and off-road performance, building on the previous chapters, the recipe for a CJ's axles and differentials would be the stock CJ Dana 30 and AMC 20 as a first choice with just some enhancements. A factory Dana 44 has no further options, except a locker. These axles serve the Jeep build without the added expense or hassle from a swap, and it frees up some funds to equip these axles with some upgrades.

Lockers

For the best off- and on-road performance, a selectable locker is the only choice. This option is on the more expensive side but results in reliable off-road traction and smooth on-road driving. My selectable locker of choice is the ARB Air Locker because of its reliability and strength. The ARB Air Locker requires the addition of an onboard air source that can double as an air supply to inflate tires and potentially operate air tools.

I also believe that if a Jeep owner is going to the expense of installing the on-board air system and one locker, adding another makes the most sense. It is important to have the Air Locker installed by a qualified shop to ensure a good air seal and proper gear alignment.

Axle Upgrades

The Dana 30 front axle should be outfitted with six-bolt hubs and disc brakes, and the AMC 20 rear axle should be equipped with one-piece rear axles. Wide Trak axles are the preferred choice and can be an easy swap into the 1976–1981 CJ.

Gears

As discussed, 33- to 35-inch tires are optimum for the CJ, making 3.54:1 and 4.56:1 ratios the high and low extremes. That means that 3.73:1 and 4.11:1 are nearly perfect. These provide good crawl ratio when combined with the previously established components, and the slightly high ratio keeps engine RPM in its efficient range on the highway.

Those three switches on the homemade switch panel in this 1978 CJ-5 were often the difference between stuck or not. The front and rear ARB Air Lockers were at the driver's command and reliably performed through years of trail use. Often noted is the difference in the way a Jeep performs with the rear engaged, even in situations where the Jeep wasn't stuck. Running with the rear locked in rocky areas allows the Jeep to maintain firm traction, allowing slow, steady progress.

SUSPENSION AND STEERING SYSTEM

The AMC-era CJ retained a design similar to the suspension systems found in the CJ all the way back to 1941 and continuing in the Wrangler until 1995. A simple suspension consisting of leaf springs, shock absorbers, and a later-added front sway bar was found under all CJ Jeeps. This setup made modification easy and could be performed by nearly anyone with basic garage tools.

There are many brands of lift kits available for the CJ and kits of varying sizes from 2 to 6 inches. The most common lift size on a CJ is 2 to 3 inches. This size of lift performs optimally on all CJ models and does not require extensive additional modifications to the Jeep to accommodate an extreme lift. Manufacturers typically offer lift kits that contain all of the proper components to make installation straightforward and performance excellent.

Suspension Components

The AMC-era CJ used a simple suspension setup that was easy to modify and upgrade. Continuing a similar design from prior Jeep models, this era used leaf springs, shackles, and shocks to smooth out the bumps. Perhaps the biggest update was the addition of a front sway bar.

Springs

Leaf springs consist of a stack of several steel leaves curved in an arc. These springs serve as a means of locating the axle, supporting the vehicle's weight, and providing movement to allow the axles to conform to the terrain without transferring all the movement to the vehicle. Early CJ models used leaf spring packs that consisted of seven to eight springs which resulted in a very stiff ride. During the AMC era, Jeep started using wider springs with fewer leaves in the pack. This resulted in a softer ride, which made the Jeep more comfortable on the road but also allowed the springs to flex more off-road.

Replacing springs on a CJ is not a complex process but requires care for proper safety because the weight needs to be removed from the axle to remove the spring.

Lift springs are curved in a larger arc and effectively lift the Jeep's frame by increasing the distance between the axles and frame. Typically, lift springs allow easier suspension travel by using four on five spring leaves per pack and using more flexible spring rates. A quality lift spring pack usually uses Teflon pads to separate the springs in the

This 1985 CJ-7 sits in its stock form and is quite capable with no modifications, but the low ground clearance will cause more damage to the underside from smaller objects than to a lifted Jeep with larger tires. (Photo Courtesy Eric Jankowski)

The factory springs consisted of six to eight leaves and sat relatively flat. Over time, the springs can weaken and sag, causing a potentially backward arc, making driving feel and suspension travel worse. Aftermarket lift springs typically consist of four to six leaves and increase the spring arc to raise the Jeep.

The 4-inch leaf springs push useful spring arc to the edge due to the limited length of the CJ spring. Excess arc reduces the ability of the spring to extend, causing a loss of suspension travel. Keeping the spring closer to flat allows full potential of movement.

pack. This reduces friction during flex.

In addition, lift springs often use open-design spring pack clamps that allow the spring leaves to separate from each other during flex. All these tricks come together to increase suspension performance.

Spring lifts are the best choice when lifting your Jeep because everything above the axle moves upward, increasing ground clearance. This increase also allows for larger tires and longer wheel travel, which provides better traction on uneven terrain. Longer wheel travel, often referred to as axle articulation, allows the axle to move farther in the suspension cycle, which in turn allows the wheel and tire to stay in contact with the terrain. The result of this travel is better traction and a softer ride.

This suspension flexibility is often measured by using a single-sided ramp. The Jeep is driven up the ramp until a tire lifts off the ground. This ramp provides a measurement known as Ramp Travel Index (RTI); some Jeep events use RTI as a competition event.

A consideration must be made when installing lift springs because larger arcs inhibit downward wheel travel. A perfect spring setup is often one with minimal arc; this allows full travel up and down. Lifting a Jeep higher than 3 inches often results in an excessive spring arc, causing loss of off-road flexibility. Extreme off-roaders who use leaf-sprung Jeeps often resort to cutting into the fenders to allow for larger tires without increasing spring arc.

Choosing the best springs for your Jeep depends on the kind of

application you are planning, keeping in mind the things that affect your spring's performance, such as vehicle weight and spring rate. A Jeep on its own is a relatively light vehicle but adding trail gear, a winch, heavy bumpers, and other accessories could add hundreds of pounds, which affects lift height and ride quality. Many lift-spring manufacturers list the spring rates for their springs, and some offer lighter or heavier options. It's often best to contact the manufacturer or a well-known off-road reseller to determine the proper springs for your Jeep.

Leaf springs are strong, reliable, and require little maintenance. It is recommended that the springs receive a little maintenance after a season of off-road use. Checking the spring packs and leaf pads for damage, cleaning debris from between the leaves, and lubricating the leaf pads with some lithium-based grease, such as Energy Suspension Formula 5, keeps the pack in good operating condition.

Shocks

Although the springs provide the movement to the suspension, the shocks control and dampen the movement to stabilize the Jeep. Controlling fluid movement within the shock achieves this. Heat is generated during movement, and, in most cases, on a trail Jeep the heat is dissipated quickly to avoid aeration. Vehicles used in higher-speed environments may benefit from shocks using a remote reservoir that have superior heat handling.

Shocks are an often-overlooked component. Typically, when a lift is installed, new shocks are required to match the added height and spring rate. Most aftermarket shocks are nitrogen gas charged and provide

Rancho adjustable shocks allow the Jeep owner to fine-tune the characteristics of the shocks as needed. Street driving may require a stiffer setting to provide good handling, while a softer setting is desirable off-road to allow the suspension to react quicker to changing terrain.

The repositioned Rancho steering stabilizer on this CJ keeps it up and out of the way from trail obstacles. Careful repositioning keeps the stabilizer from hitting engine compartment components when the suspension compresses. There are many mounting options, but the U-bolt mount is most common. A single quality stabilizer is sufficient on a CJ with 33- to 35-inch tires.

This homemade shackle was on a project Jeep and was used to achieve several inches of lift with stock springs. Besides being ugly, these types of shackles drastically affect ride, handling, and are just plain dangerous. Needless to say, they ended up on the scrap pile and were replaced with more reasonable ones. (Photo Courtesy Craig Brown)

varying ride styles. Some provide variable valving, adjustable valving, mono-tube, twin-tube, and external reservoir designs to suit all kinds of applications. The twin-tube gas-charged shock is by far the most popular and appropriate shock on a trail Jeep.

The Old Man Emu (OME) Nitrocharger shocks are specially tuned for a Jeep using their springs. Rancho's RS9000 series shocks are adjustable for varying terrain, allowing for street driving settings and trail settings.

Steering Stabilizer

A steering stabilizer is similar in function to a shock absorber but serves more to dampen steering movement to provide driving comfort and prevent harsh steering movement. It was a fad years ago to equip a Jeep with multiple stabilizers to create a unique look with no real purpose. A properly designed, single stabilizer matched to a lift kit and tire size provides excellent performance.

Relocating the stabilizer to a higher position prevents it from sus-taining damage from contact with an obstacle. Stabilizers can mount to the tie-rod and axle in a few ways. Even from the factory, Jeep used a variety of mounting methods. Common aftermarket stabilizer mounting methods use U-bolt clamps that attach to the axle tube and tie-rod. U-bolt mounts can loosen over time and should be checked periodically. Mounts that bolt to the differential housing or the spring pack can provide a more positive connection that is less likely to loosen and move.

Shackles

Perhaps the simplest component on your Jeep, a shackle merely provides a movable joint to connect the spring to the frame. The movement of the shackle allows the spring to flatten out or increase its arc as the terrain changes under the Jeep. When a spring is completely flat, the shackle is at its fullest extension; when the axle is at its fullest droop or compression, the spring is at its maximum arc. Most lift springs should put the shackle at the proper pivot point to allow full movement. Shackles may be simple but can come in varying sizes and styles. Some take the DIY approach to shackles and use flat iron to create lift shackles. These are dangerous and extremely prone to failure.

Using shackles as a means of lift is not very effective because of the way the lift is measured at this point. A 1-inch-longer shackle only provides about 1/2-inch lift. In addition, longer shackles affect driveline angles, which can impact handling. It is recommended to go no longer than 1- to 1½-inch-longer shackles. Longer or shorter shackles can be effective at helping level the Jeep due to extra weight.

Crabtree Tool & Die makes superior-quality shackles for the CJ. A set was installed on this 1978 CJ-5 when installing the Old Man Emu lift. The 4-inch length results in about 1/2-inch lift to add some extra shackle travel. The center bolt keeps the shackle sturdy and makes installation less of a fight than with solid shackles.

Anti-kickback shackles use a boomerang shape or a set of triangular-shaped plates to prevent the shackle from moving in the wrong direction when returning from the fully extended position. This condition is somewhat uncommon in the CJ, unless it is equipped with exceptionally flexible springs.

One-piece (barbell) shackles are strong and function as well as the center-bolt style, even in longer lengths. The 6-inch shackles on this CJ offer 1½-inch lift compared to stock. One-piece shackles can be a fight to install when the springs are firmly bolted to the axle housing. When replacing springs, keeping everything loose helps installation of one-piece shackles.

The TeraFlex Revolver shackle was an innovation that allowed considerably more suspension travel through a clever design. The Revolver used a hinge that allowed the shackle to extend its length several inches. This allowed downward suspension travel to increase greatly, often challenging driveshaft slip joints, brake lines, and shocks. (Photo Courtesy TeraFlex)

Many aftermarket shackles come in a solid piece where the two sides are connected by a cross arm. These are much stronger but can restrict articulation movement because a twisting movement is restricted by the cross arm. It's a consideration, but often the strength outweighs the slight restriction.

Some shackles offer anti-kickback cross arms. These offset arms prevent the shackle from moving in the incorrect direction when the Jeep's axle is fully extended. When kickback happens, the spring wedges itself into place and prevents movement. The spring usually isn't damaged, but it requires some jacking and muscle to pop the shackle back into proper movement.

An ingenious approach to increasing a Jeep's articulation is the Tera-Flex Revolver shackle. This pivoting shackle sits within itself under normal driving conditions and acts like a regular shackle but can extend and pivot when the axle moves into full droop. These shackles allow several more inches of movement from the extension and the pivot. Moreover, they often require longer brake lines and shocks with extended travel.

Shackle and Spring Bushings

The springs attach to the Jeep by bushings installed in the spring eyes at the ends of the leaves; additional bushings are found at the shackle mount point. The purpose of the bushing is to allow smooth rotational movement at the end of the springs due to the springs' flexing. The bushings also serve the purpose of isolating the springs from the frame as well as reducing vibration and transfer of harsh movement. On a CJ, six half-bushings are used on each of the four spring and shackle sets. Factory springs used rubber bushings that hardened over time, deformed, and became brittle, which decreased their effectiveness.

When a lift is installed, the kit often comes with replacement bushings that are usually made of high-performance polyurethane.

These bushings, while slightly less soft than rubber, can increase suspension performance, feel, and durability. Some argue that rubber is softer and allows for better suspension flex and ride, but the larger presence of poly bushings says otherwise. It seems that, like many other things,

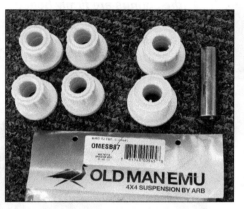

Fresh bushings are often included with a new lift kit or can be replaced if worn or brittle. The Old Man Emu lift kit installed on this 1978 CJ-5 included bright yellow polyurethane bushings for all four ends. Proper lithium-based lubricant such as Energy Suspension Formula 5 should be used with non-rubber bushings to avoid the material from breaking down.

Greasable shackle bolts allow the Jeep owner to keep the bushings lubricated, allowing free movement and reducing wear. When used off-road, a free-moving suspension allows the axle to follow the terrain more easily, increasing traction and improving handling. These Crabtree Tool & Die shackles include greasable bolts.

it comes down to personal choice. Checking and maintaining a Jeep's bushings keeps them at peak performance regardless of style.

A good addition to a poly bushing upgrade is greasable bolts. These bolts allow grease to be added to the interior of the bushing that allows smooth movement without squeaking. When installing new poly bushings, use proper grease according to the manufacturer. Most say petroleum-based lubricants should not be used with poly bushings. Lithium or synthetic grease yields the longest life from the bushing.

Maintaining the bushings extends their life, especially when the Jeep is used off-road. Water, mud, and other contaminants may get into the bushings, causing wear and noise. Periodic disassembly, cleaning, and lubrication keep them performing for years.

Bump Stops

Bump stops are designed to stop upward travel of the axle to prevent damage from the axle, tires, or driveline coming in contact with parts such as the engine, fenders, transmission, etc. Typically, the biggest concern is the tires (which are usually larger) coming in contact with the fenders. This can damage either component and it is best to prevent contact.

Many lift kits come with or recommend the proper-size bump stop, but a good rule for choosing bump stops is getting one near the lift size installed. A 2½-inch lift with 2-inch bump stops is a good combination, but it's recommended to measure the distance after a lift is installed. Larger tires or fender modifications can increase or decrease the stop needed.

The 2½-inch lift on the Jeep prompted installation of 2-inch bump stops to prevent the axle from moving farther up than it should. With the addition of larger tires, this is especially important because the larger tire comes in contact with the fenders, potentially damaging the tire, fender, or both.

Upgrades and Modifications

Upgrades and modifications to a CJ suspension drastically improve off-road capability and handling. Some suspension upgrades not only improve off-road manners but improve on-road manners as well.

Shackle Reversal

By design, the front springs of the CJ move opposite of forward movement because the shackle is located at the front of the Jeep. This means that when the suspension reacts to an obstacle while moving forward, the front axle also moves slightly forward. This design typically creates a rougher ride because of the contrary movement, which is accentuated even further when springs with a larger arc are installed.

Jeep owners sometimes relocate (or reverse) the shackle to the rear of the front spring to allow the axle to react in a more natural movement by allowing it to move to the rear with the obstacle. The reversal involves installing a fixed mount to the front

This Jeep is equipped with a M.O.R.E. bolt-on shackle reversal kit. This kit uses sturdy mount plates that attach using factory holes. Provisions to deal with winch mounts as seen here are available for the system. Shackle reversals can improve off-road handling by allowing the suspension to move with an obstacle instead of against it.

This shackle reversal uses custom rear shackle mounts on this 1980 CJ-7 that are partially outboard of the frame due to the increased mount width of the swapped Scout Dana 44. When using factory axles, bolt-on or through-frame rear mounts are available with the M.O.R.E. kit.

of the frame and installing a shackle mount instead of the rear fixed mount. Mountain Off-Road Enterprises (M.O.R.E.) makes an easy-to-install kit that properly installs the reversal for optimum results.

A downside to the reversal, and possibly the reason Jeep did not use the reversal from the beginning, is vehicle control during stopping. The natural movement causes the springs to move more freely, which causes the Jeep to nose dive during hard braking. To control movement, good shocks are essential with a shackle reversal. An additional concern is that the rearward movement of the axle often causes the tire to hit the inner fender with the potential for damage. A YJ spring conversion often helps or fixes this condition because it moves the axle slightly forward.

Wrangler YJ Spring Conversion

This popular conversion is easy on a 1976–1986 CJ; it yields improved road ride and increased off-road performance. Installing this conversion on a 1972–1975 CJ requires installation of new front and rear fixed-mount spring brackets, along with changing both the front and rear shackle mounts to accommodate the 2½-inch spring.

The Wrangler YJ uses a 2½-inch spring in the front, while a CJ uses a 2-inch. The YJ 2½-inch springs offer improved ride and flex that help both on- and off-road. The conversion isn't complex but requires some modification. Because the YJ spring is wider and longer, it requires different forward shackle mounts, which are available from a few manufacturers. Installation involves removing the factory shackle mount and installing the conversion mount. This mount is made to use the 2½-inch width spring and the additional length by moving the shackle forward approximately 1 inch. A recent redesign of the shackle mount no longer requires bumper modification.

Probably the most popular YJ spring conversion uses YJ springs from OME, which is a product of ARB, makers of the Air Locker. A few YJ spring options are available from OME, but the CS036R is perhaps the most popular choice for a CJ conversion. This model is the "heavy" version designed for use in the rear of a Jeep with a hard top; it uses loose spring clamps and nylon interleaf liners.

In fact, this model spring works perfectly in all four corners of the CJ. The spring rate and added height from the "heavy" model spring gives a nice 2 to 2½ inches of lift to the CJ along with a superior ride. Adding OME Nitrocharger Sport Shock Absorbers puts the entire package together.

A few companies offer an entire YJ conversion kit for the CJ that includes OME springs, shocks, and bushings, combined with conversion

A new set of OME 2½-inch springs for a 1978 CJ-5. These springs are YJ Wranglers, which use the 2½-inch width for all four springs. This conversion requires a front shackle mount to accommodate the longer Wrangler spring. These springs offer improved ride and flex compared to the factory 2-inch CJ front springs. In this install, all springs are the rear style (CS036R) with extra arc to maintain the full height of the lift.

front shackle mount and spring plates. This convenience can take the guesswork out of building a conversion system. OK Auto's Rock Equipment kit contains all the ingredients for this conversion.

Conversion shackle mounts come in several varieties. Rock Equipment conversion mounts are popular and were already on the Jeep from the prior lift. The mounts move the shackle 1 inch forward and use the bumper bolt to attach. A newer version is available that retains the use of the bumper bolt and doesn't require removing the factory crossmember rivet.

YJ Spring Conversion

Here's what you need:

- Lift kit using matched springs and shocks: 2½-inch lift for CJ-5; 2½- to 3½-inch lift for CJ-7 and CJ-8
- Extended brake lines
- 2- to 3-inch bump stops
- Heavy-duty steering box mount
- Tie-rod flip conversion
- 1/2- to 1-inch aftermarket shackles with crossbars; adjust to level the Jeep
- Caster wedge for front, if recommended by manufacturer
- Protective U-bolt plates
- Sway bar disconnects

Installing a YJ Conversion Lift in a CJ

Installing a lift in a CJ isn't particularly difficult. Maintaining a safe environment is most important. This procedure involves supporting the Jeep by its frame to allow the suspension to hang free. Using quality jack stands in proper locations is very important. I use jack stands to support the frame just behind the spring eye and add extra support at the front bumper with a high-lift jack. Don't take chances. (The procedure in the front and rear is nearly similar, so I cover just the front here.)

After both ends are completed and the Jeep is sitting back on its own weight, tighten the shackle bolts, fixed mount bolts, U-bolts, and anything else that was loose. After a brief driving period, recheck the bolts to ensure that they are tight.

1 *Remove the wheels. With the Jeep properly supported and the axle hanging free, begin removing or disconnecting the following components. Remove the shocks and remove/disconnect the sway bar links (front only).*

2 *Unbolt the U-bolts and remove them, along with the spring plates. At this point the axle is sitting free on the springs. It may be necessary to support the axle at the differential to prevent it from falling backward and binding the driveshaft universal joint.*

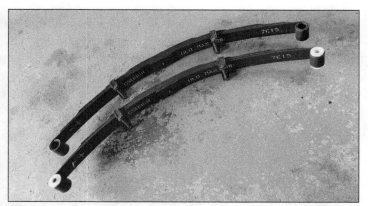

3 Support the axle with jack stands and unbolt the shackles to allow the springs to pivot away from the axle. Remove the fixed-mount bolt to allow the spring to be removed.

4 The OME springs come with three separate bushing pairs per spring and they are particular to where they go. The largest goes in the fixed mount, the upper shackle bushing uses the small edge bushing, and the lower uses the large edge bushing. Using the proper lubricant, install bushings into the springs and then install the sleeves.

5 The fixed-mount side does not move, so install the springs to the fixed mount first, leaving the bolt semi-loose.

6 The new Crabtree shackles weren't delivered yet so a set of stock used YJ Wrangler shackle plates was installed to get things up and running. Insert the top shackle bolt with the plates and bring the spring up to the shackle, allowing installation of the bottom bolt. Leave bolts loose for now.

7 Use steel shim plates that bolt to the springs' center bolt; these were installed during the spring prep process. Place the axle on the springs over the center pin to properly align the axle.

8 A new lift deserves new U-bolts because old bolts wear and different-thickness springs can cause a lack of threads when the bolts were trimmed to fit. Install the plates and loosely tighten the nuts.

9 At this point install the shocks and sway bar links. Gently tighten everything, but wait until the Jeep is sitting back on its own wheels to fully tighten everything.

Spring-Over Conversion

A quick way to gain 3 to 4 inches of lift is by locating the axles on the bottom side of the spring. This modification can provide increased wheel travel and articulation because increased height is achieved without increased arc in the spring; flatter springs allow further upward and downward movement.

When done correctly, a spring-over can provide 4 to 6 inches of lift while using stock springs; it will retain a close-to-factory ride. However, handling is compromised because of the increased center of gravity. Converting to spring-over requires modification to several components.

New lift and a new set of BFGoodrich Mud Terrains on US Mags aluminum slots keep the classic look of the CJ alive. The nearly 20-year-old lift was replaced and the Jeep is now ready for some action. Road manners of the OME springs and shocks are superior to the old lift that this Jeep ran for so many years.

The spring-over conversion is very cleanly done on this CJ. The original differential side mount was removed and a new one was welded on above. The lift results in about 4 inches of lift with no spring change. Steering rods are usually affected by this lift and here it's evident that the drag link may need a drop pitman to prevent contact with the spring.

Spring-Over Considerations

Many modifications need to be incorporated to spring-over a Jeep. Although this list may not be complete, it can give an idea as to what is involved with this conversion.

- Spring mounting pads must be relocated from the bottom of the axle to the top because the spring rides above the axle. New pads are usually welded to the axle; the original pads are removed to prevent clearance issues. A few companies offer bolt-on relocation brackets.
- U-bolt plates need to be modified to accommodate the change in the U-bolt orientation. Many conversions are made to use square-shaped U-bolts that cross the spring pack instead of the top of the axle tube.
- Shock mounts at the axle might need relocation or fabrication. In addition, longer shocks are usually necessary to deal with the extra flex.

- Driveshafts likely need lengthening to accommodate the added lift.
- Rear axle pinion angle needs adjustment to prevent vibration at highway speeds.
- Steering drag link and tie-rod may need adjustment or relocation because of the change in spring location.
- Longer brake lines are necessary, especially in the front.
- New or modified bump stops must be measured after the conversion is complete.
- Using lift blocks to further increase height is never recommended.
- Many aftermarket companies, such as Rocky Road Outfitters, make kits to help with this conversion, but it isn't for the novice. Many traditional spring-under lifts produce excellent results without the need for fabrication or safety compromises. ∎

AGR makes performance steering boxes for the CJ as seen on this CJ-7. This upgrade can increase steering performance with larger tires and front lockers. These boxes feature quicker turning by reducing the number of turns to reach lock and special valving for increased steering feel.

The M.O.R.E. heavy-duty steering box is a massive single-piece unit that replaces the factory plate steel mount well known for cracking. This mount requires drilling an additional hole in the frame crossmember for the mount and trimming of the crossmember for clearance of the power steering lines. The mount locates the steering box 1 inch forward to increase drag link to tie-rod clearance.

The AGR performance power steering pump in this CJ-7 is a perfect match for the AGR steering box underneath. The increased pressure and flow allows steering larger tires much easier, especially useful when using a front locker and navigating trail obstacles.

and can be dangerous if not done properly. Welding and some fabrication are usually required.

A few companies, including Rocky Road Outfitters, make quality spring-over kits that require little or no welding.

Performance Steering Box

The AMC-era CJ steering box is a Saginaw style that is used in many other vehicle types including GM cars and trucks. The presence of these steering boxes in so many vehicles created a market for modifications and upgrades. The steering box is an often-overlooked component, and many Jeep owners are unaware of potential upgrades. A few companies, such as AGR, make performance versions of the Jeep steering box that can improve steering power and handling, especially on Jeeps running large tires.

Steering Box Reinforcement

The factory steering box mount is a little insufficient for a lifted Jeep

with larger tires. The excess stress often causes the mount to flex, wearing the mount points and possibly causing frame cracking. A few methods of securing the steering box are available. Some secure the box to the frame while retaining the original mount, and some replace the mount with a substantial new mount.

M.O.R.E. makes a heavy-duty mount that replaces the factory mount entirely. This mount requires the addition of a front crossmember mount hole and often a bit of grinding because the mount locates the steering box forward about 1¼ inches to prevent drag link interference with the tie-rod, which is often experienced with a lifted Jeep.

Performance Power Steering Pump

To get the most out of a performance steering box, replacing the stock power steering pump with a steering box matched pump will

achieve the best performance. AGR pumps are matched to their steering boxes and provide maximum pressure and flow. These pumps use the stock reservoir and pulley; mounting is simple and the position is unchanged.

Tie-Rod and Drag Link Conversion

The factory Jeep setup attaches the tie-rod and drag link to the

A simple installation is flipped rods; it results in an extra 3 inches of clearance for both the drag link and tie-rod. The flip looks so natural that it makes you wonder why Jeep didn't do it this way from the factory.

bottom of the axle knuckles. In this location, both run essentially parallel to the axle and are extremely prone to damage from trail hazards. The tie-rod connects the axle knuckles together and the drag link attaches the passenger-side knuckle to the steering box. You can install a simple kit to relocate both the tie-rod and drag link to the top of the axle knuckles; you'll gain about 3 inches of clearance.

Installing a Tie-Rod Flip Kit

Because the three connection points use a tapered rod end, they only fit into the knuckle one way. The tie-rod flip kit comes with a proper-size reamer that tapers the hole from the other side for a proper fit. Small cones are inserted into the original tapered side to prevent the rod end from moving after installation.

Remove the wheels. Detach the steering stabilizer from the tie-rod. Loosen the clamps to allow the rods to rotate on the rod ends. Remove tie-rod and drag link ball joint end cotter pin and nut. Pop out the rod ends using a tie-rod puller, if needed. Don't beat on the rod end threads or you will be buying new rods. It is not necessary to remove the end from the drag link. Move the rods out of the way.

1 The flip kit comes with three cones and a proper taper reamer. This one has done a few flips, and markings are useful to prevent over-drilling. It is useful to insert the reamer into the bottom hole and make a mark as to how deep the tool goes to avoid over-enlarging the holes.

2 Using the tool by hand, gradually ream the hole from the top, testing fit as you go and moving toward the marking made earlier, leaving clearance to allow the tapered end to seat properly when tightened.

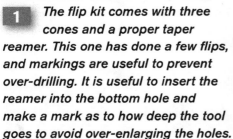

3 With the hole properly sized, install the tapered cones into the bottom of the ball joint mounts. These cones alter the bottom-up taper to the new top-down taper.

4 The cone sits firmly in the bottom hole and should sit nearly flush with the bottom of the steering arm. Test fit the rod end and ream further if needed. Install tie-rod and drag link into the newly created top holes. Tighten the nuts and install a new cotter pin.

5 Install tie-rod and drag link into the newly created top holes. Tighten the nuts and install a new cotter pin. Repeat the procedure on the other two ends, finishing up with a fresh shot of grease.

After installation, it may be necessary to adjust the mounting location of the steering stabilizer because of the tie-rod's location change. Jeeps were fitted with a variety of stabilizer mount styles; your results may vary. In addition, it's likely the steering wheel center, as well as toe-in, will need adjusting. The clearance gained is obvious. This modification is certainly worth the minimal effort and expense. After a brief driving period, check the tightness of the rod end nuts.

This Jeep is running a set of adjustable JKS sway bar disconnects. There are many varieties of disconnects and this type removes completely, leaving behind only the mounting studs. Wrestling with the mounts to reattach them after a trail run is a ritual among Jeep owners; a pry bar and hammer usually gets the job done.

Steering Shaft Upgrade

The factory steering shaft uses a coupler at the steering box end that is prone to wear, causing loose, sloppy steering. In addition to the coupling, the top of the shaft uses a non-greasable U-joint that wears and becomes loose. A few companies make replacement shafts that use greasable U-joints at both ends. These shafts, such as the one made by Flaming River, allow a custom fit and provide firm steering response and control wandering.

Sway Bar Disconnects

The sway bar connects the left and right side of the axle with a flexible rod; this is attached to the axle with links. The sway bar (or anti-roll bar) causes the opposite side of the axle to lower or rise with the originating side. This causes increased vehicle control by keeping the suspended part of the vehicle level during cornering.

This addition improved the Jeep's on-road performance dramatically but was a problem when off-road because it limited articulation. A simple fix was to create sway bar links that could be disconnected when off-road and reconnected when on-road.

Many aftermarket companies, including JKS Manufacturing, make a variety of connects that come in many styles and lengths. Sway bar disconnects that have a center tube that can be removed entirely are the most efficient. This type leaves behind only a small piece of the mount that prevents interference when disconnected. Installation of sway bar disconnects is relatively straightforward and can be done fairly quickly.

Spring Plates and U-Bolt Protection

Spring plates and U-bolts work together to hold the axle to the spring's mounting surface. Installing

The Rock Equipment U-bolt skid plates protect the U-bolts by attaching a steel skid to the spring mount, allowing it to slip over obstacles, preventing damage. When installing a new lift, it only makes sense to add some protection to an extra-low area.

Replacing the factory steering shaft with a Flaming River shaft eliminates the sloppy feel of the factory steering box coupler joint and the small bearing column universal joint. Checking the Flaming River shaft universal joint bolts is recommended after installation because they may not set properly, causing the joint to come apart.

A 1980 CJ-7 equipped with a set of U-bolt flip spring mounts, which reverse the direction of the axle to spring U-bolts to increase clearance and reduce damage. The bolt-on kit is pretty simple to install but may require replacement of the bump stops from the increased top-side mount plates.

Here's a perfect example of why using steel shims is preferred to aluminum. The old shim on the left that was removed from the Jeep is flattened and worn. The pressure and movement of the suspension slowly deforms the soft aluminum, causing the U-bolts to loosen and resulting in squeaking shims and suspension sloppiness. Steel ones bolt to the spring pack using the center pin.

Most lift springs slightly alter the tilt of the front axle enough to decrease or eliminate the proper caster angle. This angle forces the wheels to tend to stay centered, which when removed or reduced causes the Jeep to wander on the road, requiring constant steering correction. Installation of an angled shim between the axle and spring corrects the angle, thereby correcting the wander problem. Using steel shims that bolt to the spring using the center pin keeps the shim from wearing and squeaking.

a set of aftermarket spring plates that protect the U-bolts is essential on an off-road Jeep. There are many varieties, but the best ones provide a skid surface that protects the U-bolts while allowing the Jeep to slide over a surface. Rock Equipment makes an excellent set of skids that provide full protection.

An alternative to protective spring plates is a U-bolt flip conversion. This system moves the U-bolt plates to the top of the axle, both protecting the U-bolt nuts and increasing ground clearance. Dynatrac

makes a complete kit. Some welding and fabrication may be required for sway bar mounts and shock mounts.

Caster Correction

Finally, when lifting a Jeep, the axle angle is often altered; it may cause driveline vibration and/or poor road handling if left uncorrected. Poor handling is often due to incorrect front axle caster. A factory Jeep Dana 30 axle is set at about 4 degrees of caster; lowering that angle causes the Jeep to wander while driving on the road. This can be corrected

in a few ways. The most common is installation of aluminum or steel wedges between the axle and spring. This wedge tips the axle backward, setting the proper caster angle. (Steel wedges are preferable because aluminum squeaks and wears.) Some lift kits have a proper wedge already installed for the application.

Another method is a caster-correcting ball-joint sleeve. This oblong sleeve in installed in the upper ball joint mount and allows caster (and camber) adjustment. Although this method is effective, angle adjustment is limited to only a few degrees.

Body Lift

Installing a body lift is only really effective for allowing the Jeep to run larger tires with no suspension modification. The lift is achieved by installing taller body mount bushings instead of the factory bushings. This sounds simple enough, but many things can and will be affected by doing this modification.

These items may be affected:

- Brake lines may need to be adjusted
- Clutch linkage on most CJs attaches to the body and the engine; the body lift may cause binding
- Engine fan may come in contact with the fan shroud
- Steering linkage extension
- Fuel filler extension
- Shifter levers

A body lift offers no additional ground clearance to the chassis, with the exception of what the larger tire may give, and, aesthetically, they just look unnatural. In most cases, a body lift isn't the preferred option for off-road performance.

A lift can cause brake lines to pull tight during suspension movement. Many aftermarket companies, including Goodridge, make quality extra-length brake lines. Driveshafts and driveshaft angles may be affected depending on the size of the lift. A higher lift causes the driveshafts to extend and increase the angle in which they operate. Overextending a driveshaft can cause damage and potentially failure. A 2- to 3-inch lift does not usually cause an issue but checking is essential. CJ-5 and CJ-7 Jeeps have a relatively short rear driveshaft; the increased lift increases the operating angle and can cause vibration and potential U-joint wear and failure (see Chapter 4).

Coil Spring Conversion

A few companies used to offer coil spring conversion kits (from leaf springs) for the CJ. These kits required extensive modification and often fabrication to the Jeep's suspension system. Since the introduction of the Wrangler TJ in 1996, which was equipped with coil springs, the feasibility of these kits has diminished. The cost of the kit and the marginal gains achieved makes it something that has been virtually abandoned by the Jeep community.

Putting It All Together

Because the goal is to build and modify a CJ to maximize its on- and off-road performance, the photo below shows my recipe for a proper suspension in 1972–1986 CJs. This tried-and-true combination yields a trail-ready suspension system for a CJ that also drives well on the road.

This CJ has a 1-inch body lift to add a little extra height for look and clearance for the tires. The polyurethane bushings replace the factory pads and come in varying sizes. Installing a body lift is not as simple as installing the bushings. Many items that are not attached to the body often require adjustment, such as the fan shroud, clutch linkage, and fuel filler, to name a few.

An exquisite 1984 CJ-7. Years' worth of modifying and tweaking has brought this Jeep to a condition that maximizes its performance both on- and off-road. The 2½-inch OME Wrangler springs and 1-inch body lift pair exceptionally well with the 33-inch tires to give excellent ground clearance.

CHASSIS AND BODY PROTECTION

Using a Jeep as it was intended introduces the likelihood of trail damage. Rocks and tree limbs are just two things on the list of the many objects that can damage all parts of your Jeep and can come at you from all directions. Although a scratch from a pointy branch shouldn't ruin your day, a rock that crushes the Jeep's front differential cover is a different story. The aftermarket is full of chassis and body protection products that do their job to protect your investments, so when you hear "that sound" you know it's a rock scraping on a skid and not a vital part.

A proper suspension that allows freedom of movement makes a day on the trail a pleasure. Thanks to the suspension, tires, and traction systems, the Jeep's capability is drastically increased, causing a bit of a desire to try harder things. The rocks being navigated by this Jeep at Rausch Creek Off-Road Park are much larger than a stock Jeep can easily handle. Pushing the Jeep in this way introduces the likelihood of underside damage from trail objects.

Differential

A Jeep's axles, especially the differential housing, are likely to be the lowest component and most likely to come in contact with something on the trail. The differential covers are made of relatively light-gauge steel and crush easy, causing the cover to rupture and/or come into contact with the ring gear. Dumping gear oil is bad enough, but repair out in the woods is tough without a welder and a big hammer. You can protect the differential cover in a few ways; most common are guards, skids, and heavy-duty covers. It is equally important to protect both the front and rear differentials.

Differential guards often play a dual role by providing a ramp for the axle to skid up on and also by acting like a bumper to stop movement and prevent damage. Guards are typically constructed of heavy-gauge tube steel or steel plate and install using the existing bolt holes in the differential cover. A Jeep that sees trail use will definitely use the guards, both front and rear. You should inspect the guards periodically, and replace excessively abused guards to prevent failure.

It's obvious the differential guard on this Jeep has protected the fragile cover on the Dana 30 more than once. Rock rash on a guard reminds us of the damage potential that a seemingly innocent rock can bring. These types of guards serve as a bumper and skid at the same time.

The heavy-duty differential cover on this Dana 44 is an excellent alternative to the guard type. The thick metal cover provides a sturdy barrier to protect the gears within.

The AMC 20's rear helmet-shaped cover is well protected by this guard. Looking at the damage on the guard makes the small investment worthwhile.

Differential skid systems go a step further than bolt-on guards by extending the guard to protect the differential housing from the cover to the yoke. These systems typically mount to the axle tubes on the differential side and to the housing of the axle on the yoke side. These systems protect the entire differential housing, but the compromise is a slight loss of ground clearance.

Heavy-duty differential covers offer protection by replacing the original cover with a higher-strength reinforced cover. These covers are usually constructed of steel or aluminum. Heavy-duty covers are better than nothing but tend to be more prone to damage than bolt-on guards.

The AMC 20 axle uses an especially large round cover. This cover uses thin-gauge steel and has no form but is sort of dome shaped. This lack of form makes it weaker than Dana axles, which use a slightly thicker-gauge cover with curved shapes that add a bit of rigidity. Protecting the AMC 20 axle cover is extremely important because the rear cover can be easier to damage from backing up or falling off an obstacle.

Spring U-Bolts

The Jeep's axle/spring U-bolts are exposed to potential damage on their threads and fasteners because they are located on the bottom of the spring mounting plates. Dragging the fasteners over obstacles can break or bend the bolts, possibly causing the axle to come loose from the spring. For a first level of protection, the bolts should be trimmed flush with the nut to prevent excess threads hanging down that may get caught. It's easiest to mark the bolt when installed and remove one U-bolt at a time to trim. Most U-bolts are hardened and are difficult to cut with a saw blade; metal cutoff wheels work best. After installation, spray on some paint to slow rust.

Installing spring plate skids will provide considerable protection to the U-bolts by protecting them and providing a smooth surface for the obstacle to slide over. Several designs to the skids are available; some skids are integrated with holes to pass the fasteners through; others are a two-piece design where the skid bolts to the plate from the side. The side-bolt type holds up better due to the flat bottom with no holes and side-mounted bolts.

In Chapter 7, I discussed a U-bolt flip conversion, which changes the orientation of the U-bolts to put the threads on the top and the "U" on the bottom. This conversion can provide a considerable improvement in protecting the U-bolts. Depending on

Rock Equipment spring plates and their side bolt-on sliders protect the U-bolt fasteners and prevent damaged threads and bent U-bolts, as well as providing a smooth, flat surface to allow the Jeep to slide over an obstacle.

the application, this kit may require some fabrication to provide mounts for shocks and/or sway bar links. In addition, bump stops might need to be adjusted and a lift higher than 2 inches should be used to prevent the upper fasteners from making contact with the frame.

Center Skid Plate

Usually when Jeepers refer to a skid plate, they often mean the transmission/transfer case mounting crossmember. This crossmember dou-

bles as a third mounting point for the engine, transmission, and transfer case and as a skid plate protecting the transmission and transfer case. The center section of the frame between the front and rear wheels is a vulnerable area that can come in contact with an obstacle, causing damage. The center skid plate, which requires heavy protection, could be one of the most frequently custom-fabricated or augmented pieces on the Jeep.

The 1972–1975 CJs used a simple crossmember that provided minimal protection and was sometimes

equipped with a steel skid bolted to the bottom of the crossmember. The 1976–1979 CJ used a rather formidable crossmember that served as the skid plate; this wide heavy-gauge plate does an excellent job protecting the center section of the Jeep. The shape of the crossmember, six mounting bolts, and heavy-gauge steel makes it capable of supporting the Jeep. It does have limitations, especially with CJs equipped with an automatic, in which case the transmission pan was left exposed. The 1980–1986 CJs used a smaller crossmember that had a large drop to clear the Dana 300 transfer case.

A few companies, such as Barnes 4WD, make substantial replacement plates for the AMC-era CJs. These plates often attempt to flatten out the plate to provide a smooth, flat surface that is less prone to high-centering, which is when the center section comes in contact with the ground and the Jeep is stuck with the weight off the tires. Installing flat skid plates may

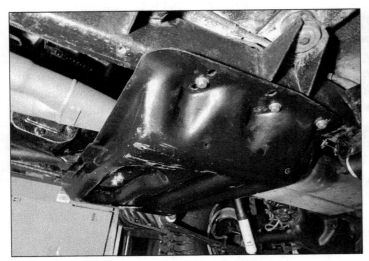

The center crossmember serves double duty as a mount and protection for the transmission and transfer case. High-centering the Jeep requires this crossmember to hold the weight of the Jeep while providing protection. The 1976–1979 CJ used this heavy-gauge, relatively flat crossmember skid that does its job.

The 1980–1986 CJ used a less substantial crossmember/skid plate than the late 1970s CJ did. The added bump to contour to the Dana 300 drop make this area low and vulnerable. This skid is quite capable of handling the trail; however, keeping that bump in mind when off-roading will avoid damage.

Unsatisfied with the factory center crossmember/skid plate, extra armor was added to it. This crossmember was originally a Dana 300 bump style that was to be installed into the Jeep that was running a Dana 20 not requiring the bump, so it was removed and pieces of plate steel were fabricated and welded into place. In addition, a forward piece was added to provide protection to the exposed underside of the T18 transmission. (Photo Courtesy Ralph Hassel)

A custom oil pan skid was fabricated for the AMC 360 in a 1978 CJ-7 to prevent damage from trail objects. The skid is created from a plate of steel bent to follow the contour of the oil pan from front to rear. The plate is attached to the pan using a healthy amount of heat resistant RTV silicone. (Photo Courtesy Ralph Hassel)

require some fabrication for proper fitment. Other even tougher center protection options are fabricated from tubular steel mounts that provide mounting places for a thick steel skid.

Fuel Tank Skid Plate

Starting in 1972, Jeep relocated the fuel tank from under the driver's seat to the rear between the frame rails. Although this move allowed for a larger fuel tank and a safer location, it exposed the tank to potential damage while on the trail. Most AMC-era CJs came with factory fuel tank skid plates that do a pretty good job for mild off-road use. Fortunately, many aftermarket companies such as Four X Doctor make a variety of replacement skid plates that offer a substantial amount of additional protection. A driver keeping this vulnerable area in mind when navigating a trail can go far to protect the thin-walled steel or plastic fuel tank.

An option to strengthen the fuel tank skid plate for the do-it-yourself crowd is to add thicker steel to the factory skid plate. The heavier steel is welded to the bottom of the skid; the extra armor helps reduce the chance of tank damage. When fortifying the factory skid, adding protection to the side of the tank helps avoid tank puncture damage.

Engine Oil Pan

No aftermarket protection plates are available specifically for the CJ from manufacturers, so Jeep owners often fabricate their own. The engine is usually under minimal danger from hitting an obstacle, but damage can occur from objects that may be thrown or wedged underneath. The thin wall of a typical oil pan can be punctured or bent easily.

Jeep owners can often get creative when fabricating parts for their Jeep. An oil pan armor plate made from heavy steel that is adhered to the oil pan using heat-safe silicone sealant protects the pan from objects that may puncture or bend the pan. Other homemade pan protection shields are fabricated using supports that use

The factory skid plate does a surprisingly good job of protecting the fuel tank, especially when the Jeep is lifted and running larger tires. The short rear overhang gives the Jeep an excellent breakover angle, helping to protect the tank. Knowing the underside of your vehicle is half the battle to protecting the underside. With years of off-road use on my CJ, the factory skid is still in good shape.

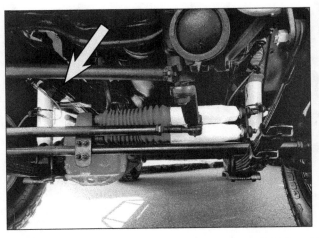

Thinking of a bump stop as protection is an often-overlooked item by Jeep owners. This Jeep is running a 4-inch lift with 35-inch tires and still using the stock bump stops (near the shock boots). It's likely this Jeep isn't used off-road or the tires and fenders would show the result of the two making contact.

The round shape next to the driver-side shackle is the front of the steering box. Its position often puts it in harm's way off-road when approaching an obstacle or steep angle change.

the pan's bolt holes attached to the protective shield that covers the pan.

Bump Stops

To recap what was covered in Chapter 7, proper-size bump stops prevent the axle from moving too far upward, causing the tires to come in contact with the body, possibly damaging the body or tires. See Chapter 5 for information on selecting the proper bump stops.

Steering Box

The AMC-era CJ steering box is mounted just behind the front bumper, low hanging, and prone to impact with trail obstacles, especially when changing grades and climbing obstacles. A few companies make steering box skid plates for the CJ, and Jeep owners often fabricate them. Some aftermarket front bumpers integrate a steering box skid into them. Replacing the factory steering box mount with a stronger one-piece bracket (as discussed in Chapter 5) helps support the steering box, if it doesn't have added protection, in the event it comes in contact with an obstacle.

Tie-Rod and Drag Link

The tie-rod and the drag link are two of the most vulnerable pieces on a CJ. These hollow rods connect the left and right steering knuckles, and connect the steering box to the passenger-side steering knuckle. Bending these rods can cause loss of steering, severe toe-in, or binding. The stock mounting location puts them just above the front springs in front of the differential, about level with the axle centerline. Obstacles on the trail can come in contact easily with these rods and cause damage.

Many Jeep owners carry spare rods along with them, and some clever on-the-trail repair methods have been used from angle iron to old wrenches. Converting these rods to mount them on top of the steering arms adds 3 inches of clearance to help keep them out of harm's way; this conversion is called a tie-rod flip kit (see Chapter 7 for more information).

In addition to flipping the tie-rods, stronger aftermarket rods are available. These rods are frequently constructed of stronger types of metal and can be equipped with easier-to-adjust threaded ends that use jam nuts instead of clamps.

Front Bumpers

The aftermarket is teeming with bumpers for the CJ, and many are great additions in both form and function. In the old days, the thin-wall tubular bumper seemed to be the normal upgrade; in recent years more formidable, heavier steel bumpers that were designed to stand up to off-roading have replaced the old tube steel. Bumpers frequently come in full-width versions to a more narrow, stubby width.

Full-width bumpers are approximately 54 inches; stubby bumpers measure around 42 inches. Stubby, narrow bumpers increase front tire clearance to allow a better forward approach to obstacles.

This Jeep fresh off the trail still runs its factory bumper with a few modifications, including the addition of a winch mount and custom fairlead mount. Factory bumpers lack the strength and rigidity found on aftermarket bumpers and they bend easily.

Shorter-width bumpers, also known as stubby, allow the Jeep to clear an obstacle that would normally hit the bumper. In addition to the added clearance, the short width allows the driver to place a tire on the obstacle for climbing. This Jeep has a 50-inch Olympic Rock Bumper that is sturdy but not too bulky or heavy.

Although tow hooks are essential, tow tabs are the safest style of pull point. A strap or line is securely attached to the tab using a D-ring shackle. This Jeep uses bolt-on tow tabs on the rear; they bolt directly to the rear frame crossmember.

This CJ has a front bumper that uses a stinger bar to protect the winch and grille area, adding a nice visual appeal. Some bumpers use a larger stinger bar to prevent forward end-over rollovers in extreme situations.

Some notable bumper manufacturers are Warn, Olympic, and M.O.R.E.

When choosing a bumper for your Jeep, you should consider the application and use of the Jeep. Overly large, gaudy bumpers add excess weight and bulk to the front of the Jeep with no real purpose. Heavy bumpers cause the front of the Jeep to sag, losing valuable ground and suspension clearance.

Many bumpers have provisions for tow points and winch mounts;

these are quite handy for a Jeep that is used off-road. Tab-style tow points are preferable for safety and efficient attachment methods. These attachment points allow using D-ring shackles, which stay attached to the bumper and keep the pull line secure. Tabs that pass through the bumper and are welded on both sides are the strongest.

Brush guards, also known more recently as stinger bars, are sometimes included on a bumper. These guards can serve multiple purposes.

Forward-facing, high stingers can provide a reference point for the driver as well as protecting the winch and grille area. High, forward-leaning stingers are designed to help prevent the Jeep from rolling end over end, and, in the event of a rollover, prevent damage to the hood/radiator area. This equipment is for the extreme off-roader or someone just looking for a mean look. A simple brush guard to protect the grille and winch is most practical.

Other options to look for in Jeep front bumpers include mount points that can accommodate aftermarket lights of a variety of styles. In addition, some bumpers integrate a 2-inch receiver mount to allow pull points, removable winch mounts, and whatever else fits into the receiver.

Some Jeep owners prefer to fabricate their own bumpers to fit their needs; this requires some skill with welding, cutting, and general metal fabrication. Aftermarket bumpers can be expensive, and sometimes a home-built one can be made for a fraction of the cost.

Rear Bumpers

Similar to the front bumper, many aftermarket rear bumpers are available for the CJ in many different configurations. Rear bumpers often integrate a spare tire mount, pull points, hitch receiver, and more. Some notable rear bumper manufacturers are Warn and Olympic.

AMC-era CJs had two spare tire mounts: fixed and swing-out. The CJ-5 equipped with a tailgate often came with no spare or a side body–mounted spare. The CJ-7 and Scrambler came with the body-mounted rear swing-out tire carrier. These carriers did not stand up to the weight of a larger tire and often stressed the mount area on the body, especially if the Jeep was badly rusted. All of these factory-mounting methods are best replaced with something heavy-duty.

Swing-away carriers come in many forms and use many methods of implementing a pivot and latching mechanism. There seems to be no end to the latch methods, but those that rate the highest are latches that apply pressure and securely lock with a handle. Pins and bolts can allow

The CJ-7 was the first CJ to come with a factory swing-out spare tire carrier. They are capable of carrying a 33-inch tire, assuming it or the Jeep's mount point isn't rusted away. The carrier on this Jeep is like new, and the added rear corner guards provide extra support to the carrier.

the carrier to wobble and rattle. Pivots that use bearings provide smooth operation and long life with no rattle. A lock to hold the carrier in the open position is a handy option when the Jeep is parked on an incline.

Rear bumpers not only carry tires but can also be equipped with provisions to mount off-road gear such as fuel and water tanks as well as high-lift jacks. They can also provide mounts for lighting and even integrate air tanks. Adding accessories to the Jeep's rear bumper, like the front, adds extra weight that may cause the rear of the Jeep to sag, losing ground clearance and possibly bottoming out the suspension. Jeep owners may install a

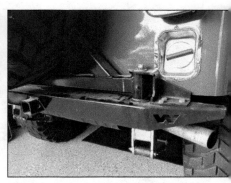

The Warn rear bumper on this CJ is a simple design with excellent function. The bumper bolts to the factory mounting holes on a 1976–1986 CJ and features a greasable bearing-equipped pivot to provide smooth swing-out operation and a positive pressure latch to keep it secure and rattle-free. The integrated 2-inch receiver allows use of compatible hitches and recovery inserts

heavier rear spring or an add-a-leaf to their existing rear springs to compensate for the added weight.

Side Rocker Guards

The body space between the front and rear wheel is referred to as the side rocker. This section is very vulnerable to damage from high obstacles over which the Jeep may be navigating, so protecting this section is essential for an off-road Jeep. Rocker protection is essentially available in two styles: body mounted and frame mounted.

The bumper-mounted custom swing-out rear tire carrier on this 1978 CJ-7 carries a tire and has attachment points for accessories such as a Hi-Lift jack, lights, and gear rack. His clever design uses a replacement front hub assembly to hold the spare, which can be used in case one gets broken. (Photo Courtesy Ralph Hassel)

The Sun side rocker guards on this 1977 CJ bolt directly to the body. The rounded bottom adds a substantial amount of rigidity capable of supporting the weight of the Jeep. These guards maximize ground clearance while protecting the side of the Jeep.

Body-mounted rocker protection attaches directly to the side of the body and usually wraps underneath to attach to the bottom of the body. These guards should be made of heavy-gauge steel to potentially support the weight of the Jeep if an obstacle comes in contact with the guard.

The advantage of body-mounted guards is the extra ground clearance they offer compared to frame-mounted guards. The guard spreads weight evenly over the entire body area. A disadvantage of the body-mounted protection is the need to drill holes into the Jeep's body for mounting. Body-mounted guards can serve as a jack lift point and a clever way of covering rust.

Frame-mounted protection, sometimes referred to as rocker skids, typically mount to the frame using arms that connect to the guard. They can either be bolted or welded to the frame. Frame-mounted guards can double as an entry step as well as protection. An advantage of the frame-mounted guards is that they don't require drilling into the Jeep body and keep an obstacle farther away. Because these guards sit below the body, there is a

The custom rock sliders on this 1978 CJ-5 are welded directly to the frame in three points. This style doesn't offer the ground clearance of body-mounted ones but does not require drilling into the body. Choosing this style makes sense on this Jeep because it has a fiberglass body that isn't exactly straight and rigid body-mounted guards would likely crack the fiberglass. The front mount arm doubles as a roll bar frame mount.

loss of ground clearance; this is not often a real issue with a lifted Jeep. Finally, frame-mounted guards are usually preferred on Jeeps with fiberglass bodies.

Many Jeep owners choose to fabricate a set of guards to suit their needs. Substantial guards can be fabricated using round or square tubular steel. When homemade frame-mounted guards are fabricated, they are often designed to provide a front roll bar frame-mount point.

Rear Rocker Guards

The rear corner of a Jeep is susceptible to damage from high trail obstacles and accidental damage

The rear corners are vulnerable from both backing into things and dropping off obstacles. The visually appealing heavy steel corners on this Jeep bolt to the body and add extra protection. Corners are typically available with pre-cut factory holes or blank for custom installs.

from backing up. Many Jeep owners learn the hard way what happens when they come off a high trail obstacle too quickly and the Jeep's suspension bounces, causing the obstacle to punch the rear corner.

Rear corner guards are form-fitting steel panels that are attached to the Jeep's body. Some are made of aluminum diamond plate; others are made of heavy-gauge steel. These guards can usually be purchased with or without factory holes for taillights, fuel filler, etc. Along with full-size corner guards, they can be found from partial height to full protection that extends from the rear to the door opening.

Entry Guards

Entry into a Jeep requires stepping over the door opening. Often, over time this opening sees a significant amount of wear. Installing a set of steel entry guards from Warrior Products or Kentrol protects the door opening.

Aftermarket wider flares can cover up larger, wider tires to keep water and debris from flying up. The ones on this 1984 CJ-7 from Xenon maintain a factory look, attach to the factory holes, and extend the flare width 2 inches wider than stock. In some areas, vehicle regulations mandate that tires are covered completely. This Jeep has 35 x 12½ tires on Wide Trak axles that don't protrude from the flare at all.

The Wrangler TJ used flares that were wider than a CJ and created a larger wheel opening. Many Jeep owners cut the CJ fenders to fit the flare, but the installation rarely is done cleanly. The TJ flare and fender is squarer, while the CJ is rounder. This owner took the time to painstakingly merge the CJ fender to the TJ flare shape, making a super clean factory-like look. They are certainly a conversation piece.

This Scrambler in-process project is outfitted with custom "flattie" fenders. These fenders add extra clearance to the tires and the tubular steel under-structure of the fenders makes them extra strong. (Photo Courtesy Craig Brown)

Fender Flares

When larger tires are installed on a Jeep, especially a Jeep with Wide Trak axles or aftermarket axles, the tires often stick out farther than the stock fender flares. In many areas, this can be a problem with vehicle safety codes. In addition, the larger tires can throw items that are not deflected by the flare. Companies such as Rugged Ridge and Xenon make wider replacement flares that add a few inches to the flare, providing proper coverage.

In more recent years, Jeep owners have used flares from the TJ Wrangler. In stock form, the TJ included larger wheel openings and wider flares. The rear TJ flares are almost a bolt-on addition to a CJ and retain a near-factory look. The front flare is a different story; the TJ fender opening is quite different and installation requires trimming and, depending on the quality of the fit, desired fabrication and bodywork are needed.

Flat Fenders

A more recent modification to a CJ includes modifying the front fender to a flat fender style to prevent large tires from making contact with the rounded part of the front fender and causing damage. In the beginning, Jeep owners trimmed the fender to get the flat fender look, but manufacturers have recently been producing bolt-on flat-fender fenders. Many of these fenders have a tubular steel understructure that makes the fenders strong enough to take the punishment of large tires and serious off-road use. Although some believe that the flat fender look goes against the CJ's style, the functional nature of these fenders may outweigh the unconventional look.

Roll Bars

Most Jeeps since 1976 were equipped with a roll bar from the factory, but interestingly it was an option. The roll bar wasn't standard equipment in a CJ until 1980, and then it was referred to as a lawyer-friendly "sport bar." The sport bar only covered the area behind the front seat and was usually bolted to the top of the fender area (1972–1978) or to the fender area and floor (1979–1986). The sport bar was capable of supporting the weight of the Jeep but was usually thought of as a "better than nothing" piece of safety equipment. As the Jeep aged and rust settled in, the bar's mount points became extremely weak and it's been known for a sport bar to punch through the body during a rollover.

Unless the Jeep is outfitted with a professionally designed, built, and installed roll cage, it should be considered a sport bar or sport cage. From here on, I refer to it as a "roll bar." Two varieties of roll bar systems can be used: add-on or replacement. The first uses the factory-installed bar and adds to it; the second replaces the entire factory equipment with a new system. Any addition to the factory roll bar adds rigidity and safety to the occupants; some fundamental considerations should be made when selecting a setup.

A bar that has a connection to the Jeep's frame provides the most protec-tion, but several non-frame methods provide a substantial improvement compared to stock. Weld-in roll bar kits are available from Smittybilt.

These provide plates and pre-bent tubular steel components that are welded in place to tie the factory roll bar to the frame. Most of these kits

Bolt-in Sport Cage

Rock Hard 4x4 probably makes the most popular and unique bolt-in cage kits for the CJ and other Jeeps. Their CJ front sport cage uses the factory back bar and the kit makes use of the exceptionally strong cowl area of the CJ by tying the front bar into the dash/windshield mount. This distributes the load across the entire dash and cowl area in the event of a rollover. Adding the floor tie-in mount kit further enhances this method.

Another unique feature of Rock Hard cages are the bolt-on bar clamps. These clamps surround the existing bar with a heavy steel clamp, making a rigid connection between the two. Rock Hard offers several clamp-style bars that can connect to a variety of locations.

In addition to the front cage kits, a family-style kit is available to offer increased protection to rear passengers. This kit mimics the family-style bar found in later YJ Wran-glers, while retaining the original factory CJ bar. This kit goes further by adding triangulation bars to increase the rigidity of the family bar. ■

An initial test fit of the bar gives an example of how the clamps work and what the system looks like. (Photo Courtesy Craig Brown)

This inge-nious roll bar system instal-lation is from Rock Hard 4x4. This system uses high-strength clamps that bolt extra bars to the existing factory bar.
Pictured is the factory bar out of the Jeep for some prep. (Photo Courtesy Craig Brown)

With paint and installation completed, the rear triangula-tion bars behind the front seats add rigidity without inter-fering with the occupants. (Photo Courtesy Craig Brown)

The clever method of attaching the front bar to the dash is an extra-strong mounting point that may be better than going directly to the floor. The extra cross bar above the dash pad connects each side. (Photo Cour-tesy Craig Brown)

are made for the 1979–1986 roll bar but may still require modification to properly install.

Most roll-bar frame tie-in methods are home fabricated and are sufficient for the kind of rollover a Jeep may experience on the trail. It is important to provide a bushing connection from the tie to the bar or vibrations are transferred from the frame to the body. Although this decreases the rigidity of the connection, it improves driving comfort. A few varieties of front bars are available and most require cutting and welding for proper fit. A few are bolt-in, most notably the system from Rock Hard 4x4; it uses locking clamps that securely attach the bar to an existing bar.

Kits that offer protection to rear seat passengers are available in both weld-in and bolt-in configurations. A Wrangler YJ family-style roll bar (1992–1995) fits with no or minimal modifications in a 1979–1986 CJ. The YJ roll bar uses a different rear bar to allow the use of shoulder seat belts. Although this style allows using the better seat belts, it removes the triangulation of the original bar, reducing its support strength. Many Jeep owners add triangulation bars, either weld-in or bolt-in, to increase rigidity.

Putting It All Together

Protecting the Jeep is an important part of modifying a Jeep for performance on- and off-road. Off-road use exposes the Jeep to many dangers. Proper equipment makes an off-road trip less stressful and more enjoyable. Chassis protection adds peace of mind to the driver. A Jeep owner can spend the whole budget on protection alone, but the following pieces are important and will not break the bank.

- Unless the Jeep is factory equipped with a 1976–1979 crossmember, you should add a center skid that is capable of supporting the Jeep.
- Differential guards on both the front and rear axles are a must. The tubular skid style seems to work the best.
- A tie-rod flip kit is an easy way to gain 3 inches of clearance to these relatively weak rods. An option is to add stronger aftermarket rods to further enhance this area.
- Use U-bolt skids with trimmed U-bolts to fortify this low area

and prevent damage.
- Add a heavy-duty steering mount to secure the steering box to the frame.
- Install a robust front bumper that provides good protection and tab-style pull points without being excessively heavy or bulky. Choose full-width or stubby to fit your style.
- Select a rear bumper that accommodates a swing-away tire carrier, has tab-style pull points, and a 2-inch receiver. The tire carrier should use a bearing pivot, be rattle-free, and have a positive lock open latch.
- Source a front sport bar to further protect the driver and passenger. Dash-mount systems save legroom and provide a strong mounting area.
- For side-rocker protection, the frame-mounted style is preferable

The Smittybilt sport bar in this 1978 Jeep looks cool and adds some extra protection to occupants but is not nearly as strong as a proper roll bar. The kit is weld-in and requires cutting for a clean installation. The lower mounts were tied to the frame for extra strength; in truth, it's a better-than-nothing approach.

Tying the roll bar to the frame, especially on a CJ outfitted with a fiberglass body, is important. Creating custom rear frame mounts for the factory bar that can be unbolted if needed is convenient. Rigid bar-to-frame mounts transfer chassis vibrations to the body, which may be lessened by using a bushing at the mount. Roll bar strengthening is always a compromise: rigidity versus interior interference.

TIRES, WHEELS AND BRAKES

The point is finally reached where all this stuff comes together to get the power to the terrain to get the Jeep moving. In addition to getting moving, stopping is another related topic that is an often-overlooked and neglected system in a Jeep. For many Jeep owners, tires and wheels are some of the first items changed. These, combined with a lift, give the most drastic appearance change to the Jeep with the least amount of work. It is not uncommon to find a CJ that has had no more modifications than just these few items.

Tire Types

A Jeep's tires are the final point before the terrain. They provide the connection between the drivetrain and the surface; if there is sufficient traction, the Jeep will move. If traction is insufficient the tires spin on the terrain, causing the Jeep to slip or, worse, get stuck. Tires may be one of the most important items on the Jeep that alone can make a significant difference in the Jeep's off-road ability. Reliance on grip from a small contact patch of a few square inches per tire means the difference of being stuck or not.

On the road, nearly any street tire provides sufficient traction in many street-driving conditions including rain and snow. In contrast, off-road conditions are where the differences in tire types become clearly evident. Throw a little slick mud at a street tire and you find yourself stuck in a hurry. A Jeep that is used off-road encounters terrain that would stop most vehicles in their tracks; tires often make this difference, perhaps even more than ground clearance.

Thanks to purpose-built tires, off-road driving through mud, rocks, and hills is easier and tackling more challenging trails is possible. In addition, modern designs and radial construction in purpose-built off-road tires still offer good street manners by not being too noisy or exhibiting poor handling.

Spend a springtime weekend at a Jeep-related trail event in the

Goopy mud sticks to anything it comes in contact with and fills the tread in a tire in an instant, causing the tire to become slick. Large voids between the tread blocks allow mud to be thrown away from the tire quickly, along with giving space for the tread to dig in and find traction. The key to mud driving is steady progress with enough wheel speed to keep the tires clean.

In addition to slippery surfaces such as mud, water, and roots, rocks are likely part of any trail. From large boulders to small rocks, they can all bring their own set of challenges and dangers. The Jeep's tires not only help get you over the rocks, they also provide the clearance needed to prevent damage. Tire size and type are important decisions that can make all the difference on and over the rocks.

All-terrain tires offer more aggressive tread than street tires but are designed for street driving in slippery conditions and less severe off-road conditions. The BFGoodrich All Terrain radial is a good example of semi-aggressive tread that provides good traction on-road in many conditions and performs well off-road in moderate conditions.

Northeast and you will understand the difference between mud tires and all-terrain tires. Soft ground combined with springtime rain creates a goop that is like grease. Throw in tree roots and hills and you will be wide-eyed with joy while running the trail with mud tires.

In contrast, spend some time on a rock bed at your favorite off-road area out West and it will be evident how mud tires work so well on rocks as well as the Eastern goop. When driving in a true off-road environment, the mud tire is truly an "all-terrain" tire.

Street

For the kind of Jeep being built here, street tires really don't fit into the parameters and are not fully discussed. At a minimum, an all-terrain tire belongs on this style of Jeep. You may ask why the Jeep would come with tires that are so limited to what the Jeep was originally designed for. In reality, Jeep needs to find a balance to allow the Jeep to appeal to the majority of consumers that prefer driving comfort to off-road prowess. Some studies have shown that only 15 percent of sport utility vehicles are used off-road.

For the first time in 2003, well past the CJ years, Jeep offered a special Jeep model called the Rubicon, built especially for off-road use. Even with its upgraded axles, transfer case, and tires, the Rubicon maintained a balance to keep its street manners. In the end, many like to consider the factory offerings as a template, giving true Jeepers a starting point rather than a finished product.

All-Terrain

All-terrain tires were created as a bridge between street tires and mud tires. This style tread is more aggressive than a street tire but lacks the large tread blocks and large separations between blocks found on mud tires. These tires typically run quieter on the street because of the tighter tread pattern but still perform well in dirt, snow, and rain. All-terrain tires typically have small cuts within the tread called sipes that allow the tire to grab smaller surfaces and increase traction dramatically on wet and smooth slippery surfaces.

All-terrain tires offer a semi-aggressive appearance with their tread pattern, which can be very attractive on a Jeep instead of the

All-Terrain Tire Ratings

The following condition ratings are provided as a reference to the intended terrain for which a tire was designed. This information is a compilation of many brands, manufacturer claims, and Jeep community observations.

Condition	Rating
Rain	better
Snow	better
Ice	good
Mud	marginal
Rock	good
Sand	good

In the Middle

Perhaps the most interesting tires in recent years are the Goodyear DuraTrac tire and Toyo Open County R/T. These tires resemble mud tires but maintain a slightly tighter tread to reduce road noise. In addition, they add siping for better snow and rain performance over true mud tires. Mud and general off-road performance is not quite as strong as a true mud tire but these particular tires are very capable. Their aggressive looks and excellent overall performance make these tires a great daily driver tire as well as all-around trail tire in one package. ■

Condition	Rating
Rain	good
Snow	good
Ice	good
Mud	better
Rock	better
Sand	better

The Duratrac is an interesting tire that falls somewhere between mud and all-terrain tires. A comparison between the BFGoodrich Mud Terrain on the left and the Duratrac on the right shows the difference in tread style. The tighter gaps and sipes allow for a quieter ride and better wet-weather performance. Size and width difference is obvious, too, with the BFG at 32 inches and the Duratrac at 35 inches.

Mud tires give the optimum performance for an off-road Jeep, along with a great aggressive visual appearance. Many brands and sizes of this style tire provide a plethora of choices for a Jeep owner. All are typically constructed with a common design: large tread blocks with large voids. It's unusual to see other types of tires than these on the trail.

...actory-style tires often found on a CJ. Many varieties of all-terrain tires are available from numerous manufacturers. These all-terrain tires vary from traditional tread designs to styles that skew the line between street and mud tires. Notable all-terrain tires include the BFGoodrich All Terrain, Toyo Open Country A/T, and Mickey Thompson Baja ATZ.

Mud-Terrain

The mud tire is likely the most common tire found on a Jeep, especially one that is used regularly on the trail. Interestingly, the mud tire is generally the favored variety off-road, regardless of the type of terrain the Jeep experiences. From thick mud to snow, sand, or rocks, these tires excel in many varieties of poor-traction conditions. Notable mud terrain tires are the BFGoodrich Mud Terrain, Mickey Thompson Baja ATZ, and Interco Swamper.

The thick tread blocks and large voids allow the tire to throw away mud to allow the tread to stay clean, thereby allowing the tire to maintain traction. The large tread blocks dig into dirt and mud, searching for traction. In addition, the blocks grip many types of hard surfaces such as rocks, helping the Jeep to crawl up using the side blocks in a gear-type action.

Mud tires are notoriously loud on the street due to the large tread blocks and wide voids between them. Better brand and street-conscious mud tires minimize road noise by altering the size and shape of the blocks around the diameter of the tire. These alterations reduce the continuous hum experienced in many mud tires. Most mud tires become louder as they wear, especially if they are not rotated and/or have off-road tread damage. Many Jeep owners believe that the sound of the tires is a natural and expected attribute of a Jeep.

Because many mud tires do not have sipes and are constructed from

Mud-Terrain Tire Ratings

The following condition ratings are provided as a reference to the intended terrain a tire was designed for. This information is a compilation of many brands, manufacturer claims, and Jeep community observation.

Condition	Rating
Rain	poor
Snow	good
Ice	poor
Mud	best
Rock	best
Sand	better

Rarely are tires as tall as they are labeled. Tire pressure, rim size, and vehicle weight can all play into the actual measurement of the tire. This tire is labeled as a 33-incher but mea sures not quite 32 inches.

stiffer compounds, their performance in rain and slippery road conditions is poor. The large, solid blocks can act like a slick on slippery surfaces that the blocks can't dig into. An exception is their performance in fresh, soft, deep snow, which can be excellent because the tires can dig through the snow and throw it out of the way.

Tire Size

Tire size is quite important. Even a 1-inch-larger size can be the difference between stuck and not stuck. That is, of course, bearing in mind that a 2-inch-taller tire, such as a 35-inch tire instead of a 33-inch tire, results in only 1 inch of extra ground clearance. In addition to the added clearance, a larger tire passes over an obstacle with less effort than a smaller one. Picture a small wheel on a cart getting stuck on a small pebble, while a larger wheel passes right over the pebble.

How Big?

In general, a 33- to 35-inch tire is the optimum size for a CJ used both on- and off-road. The CJ wheel openings can tolerate these sizes, and lift kits with proper bump stops prevent fender and tire damage. As discussed

SAE tires are very easy to understand by just knowing what each number or letter stands for on the side of the tire. The sequence 33x12.50R15LT trans lates to 33 inches tall, 12½-inch-wide section, and mounts on a 15-inch wheel. The final letters mean Light Truck, which is typical for most off-road tires.

earlier, the 33-inch is optimum for the CJ-5; 33- to 35-inch for the CJ-7 and Scrambler.

Tires larger than 35 inches often require fender trimming and/or larger lifts that impact street driving at normal speeds and off-road handling due to the increased center of gravity. In addition, tires larger than 35 inches create increased stress on the driveline, negatively impact effective gear ratio, and require more braking pressure. Popular sizes of CJ tires are 33x12.50R15 and 35x12.50R15.

Advertised versus Actual

Nearly all tires are smaller than their advertised size. Looking through a specification sheet on a particu lar tire can boggle the mind with al the numbers. Researching the actua tire size can sometimes help in th decision-making process when yo are seeking a tire for your Jeep. Fo example, a 33-inch BFGoodrich Mu Terrain KM2 tire for a CJ is adver tised as 33x12.50R15. Decodin those numbers indicates the tire is 3 inches tall, 12½ inches wide, and fits 15-inch wheel. Seems simple enough but in reality the specifications o the tire show the tire as actually 32. inches tall when mounted. Althoug that particular tire is pretty close t advertised size, research shows tha sizes are all over the place.

Mounting the same tire to differ ent width wheels impacts the heigh of the tire. Generally, wider wheel reduce overall height due to th wider spread of the sidewall. In prac tice, using a narrower wheel benefit tire height and protects the whee because the wheel bead is farthe inward from the sidewall. Runnin

In contrast to the obvious markings on an SAE-measured tire, a tire measured in a metric size is relatively confusing and often is best decoded using a size calculator or reading the tire specifications. This Duratrac found on a modern Wrangler JK has markings LT315/70R17, which roughly means 35 inches tall, 12½ inches wide, and mounts to a 17-inch wheel.

low tire pressures off-road with wide wheels can increase the likelihood of popping the tire off the bead.

Metric Confusion

The 15-inch wheel was the standard size offered on all AMC-era CJs and is often the most popular wheel size still used on them. Fortunately, the 15-inch wheel is often still sized using the easier-to-understand height and width measurements instead of metric. Selecting a tire can be made more complex by having to decode metric measurements.

Actual size is typically simple enough: 33 is about 33 inches tall, but a 318/72/R15 is an almost impossible number to figure out without a calculator. Metric tires are sized by a measurement of width and an aspect ratio. The first number is the width and the second number is the aspect ratio. Converting the metric size to an actual size isn't difficult; the formula can be found online and to make it easier there are calculators online that do it for you. Online tire

resellers such as Quadratec or Tire Rack carry most varieties of off-road tires and can provide quick tire size references and availability.

Tire Weight and Weight Rating

The terms sprung weight and unsprung weight are often a topic of conversation when talking tires and wheels. The springs on a Jeep hold the weight of the vehicle while absorbing bumps and allowing the suspension to conform to the terrain.

When discussing unsprung weight, often it's easiest to understand when viewing the axle on the springs. Everything on the axle side of the U-bolts is unsprung weight, and everything on the spring side, including the springs, is weight supported by the springs. Adding larger tires and axles adds additional unsprung weight.

The BFGoodrich Mud Terrain has been the dominant tire in the Jeep community for many years and is showing no sign of slowing. In both its forms, the original KM version and the KM2 version, the tire is a top performer off-road in almost all terrains. On a CJ, the tire looks very much at home, almost as if Jeep should have put them there from the start.

Without springs, the ride would be horrible and likely damaging to the vehicle and its occupants.

Nearly all of the weight of a Jeep is carried by the springs, with the exception of the axles, tires, and wheels; these components are considered part of the unsprung weight. Why does this matter? Increased unsprung weight means that more force is necessary to move the suspension, which can potentially cause poor road handling. Typically, though, road handling at higher speeds is less of an issue because the Jeep isn't known for excellent street handling and that makes higher unsprung weights less significant.

In fact, higher unsprung weight in a CJ can be helpful on the trail because it lowers the center of gravity, resulting in more stability in off-camber situations. The bottom line is, it's about balance and compromise; heavier tires and axles result in a clumsier feel on the street but may be an advantage off-road.

I'll continue to use the above tire as an example: the BFGoodrich Mud Terrain LT33x12.50R15/C. In addition to size indication, there is labeling on the tire that indicates the tire type, construction, and weight. Typically, the first letter or two indicate the tire style: P for passenger, LT for light truck. The middle numbers are the tire size, followed by a letter and number indicating the tire's construction type: B for bias ply and R for radial, followed by the size of the wheel the tire was designed for. (Never mount tires on incorrectly matched rims.) Finally, on most tires the end letter indicates the weight rating, which in this case is C

Weight ratings are important to consider on a Jeep. Although it's unlikely that the Jeep requires any rating higher than C, many tires are only available in D and E ratings. Higher-weight ratings on a light vehicle such as a CJ result in a stiffer ride due to heavier tire compounds and construction, causing stiffer sidewalls and increased unsprung weight from the heavier weight tire. D- and E-rated tires can weigh approximately 10 percent more than a C-rated tire. Most 15-inch tires come in C rating; more modern tires in 16- and 17-inch wheel sizes come in D and E ratings.

In recent years the 15-inch tire size has been fading away because most new Jeeps, among many other vehicles, use the 17-inch wheel, causing the majority of newer tires to have the most options in the 17-inch size. Only the most popular sizes from well-known manufacturers are still offered in the 15-inch wheel. Running 16- and 17-inch wheels on a CJ is certainly possible as long as the wheel mount matches the 5- on 5½-inch hub.

Tire Air Pressure

When driving on the street, tires should be inflated to specified pressures to maintain proper wear and handling. If the pressure is too low, it causes the tires to roll under the rim, causing poor street handling, and pressures too high cause uneven wear and a harsh ride.

When larger tires are installed, it is normal to run lower pressures than factory specified to allow for some extra sidewall cushion, which helps with the unavoidably harsh street ride of a CJ. Pressure can run from 25 to 35 psi and is often at your pref-

The process of airing down the tires in preparation for a day on the trail is a common sight at the trailhead. With the help of tire deflators and a pressure gauge, the job can be done in a few minutes. Choosing the pressure is up to the individual and is often based upon the terrain and obstacles expected on the trail.

erence. Examining the tire contact patch (the area where the tire meets to road) generally helps you find the best pressure to ensure proper wear. Reading the contact patch and determine the ideal pressure is a simple procedure.

Reading the Tire Contact Patch

There are many ways of doing this, but basically marking the tire with something that leaves an impression on the surface shows the contact patch. Using a piece of white paper and a little latex paint gives the best impressions.

On a flat, smooth surface make a mark on the tire and on the surface to match the tire. Roll the Jeep backward or forward to locate the mark at three or nine o'clock. Place a piece of paper centered on the mark on a flat, smooth surface just in front or behind the tire. Taping the paper to the floor prevents it from wrapping

1 *Use a little paint to coat the tread on the Jeep's tire. This can be done with other items such as chalk; paint makes a good mark on a piece of paper and looks good afterward hanging on the fridge as artwork.*

2 *Line up the tire with the paper and roll the Jeep over the paper. A little tape helps prevent the paper from lifting and a smooth surface, such as a concrete floor, helps to get a good impression.*

round the tire. The placement of he paper allows the tire to roll properly over the correct spot.

Use some water-based art or latex paint and roll it across the tire to cover the tread blocks completely, about 6 inches wide. While the paint still wet, roll the Jeep over the paper completely.

Examine the patch created by the paint. The pattern indicates the size of the contact patch and whether the pressure is too high or too low. In addition to pressure, this test can indicate poor camber. Note that the factory CJ Dana 30 typically has no camber and no factory provision for adjustment. Indication of positive or

negative camber can indicate a bent axle tube or worn ball joints. Further investigation would be warranted if excess camber were detected.

Make any pressure adjustments and run the test again using new paper. Compare results to find the contact patch's happy spot for your Jeep.

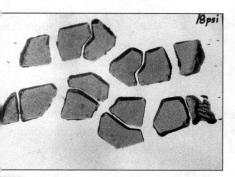

3 At 18 psi, nearly all the tread blocks from the tire can be een. This pressure, 15 to 18, is pically a good off-road pressure iving maximum tread coverage. riving on the street with these ressures makes the ride spongy and ss responsive.

4 At 24 psi, the tire shows good tread coverage at good street-driving pressure for a CJ. Different tires show different results due to vehicle weight and tire construction. About 24 to 26 psi on this CJ with these tires appears to be the best pressure. Running this pressure allows the tires to wear evenly and the Jeep to perform well on the road.

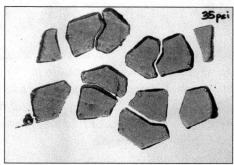

5 At 35 psi, the outer tread blocks are practically not visible. This pressure causes the center of the tire to wear quicker than the outer edge and causes a rougher ride due to the stiffer tire sidewall from the increased pressure.

ff-Road Air Pressure

Driving a Jeep off-road differs uite a bit from street driving, and ften, one of the first tasks performed efore setting out on a trail is airing own the tires. There is no set standard to air-down pressures; it really a matter of preference. Moreover, he style and type of off-road driving hanges the amount of airing down. My Jeep is built for on- and off-road riving, typically slow and controlled ff-road driving, not racing.

Airing down a tire serves a few urposes but most importantly o improve traction and ride. An ired-down tire can conform to the urface it is in contact with, allowing to grip the surface better, there-

fore, increasing traction. Aired-down mud tires can cause the tread blocks to compress, actually gripping and holding the obstacle like fingers.

Perhaps the second most important fact of airing down is the improvement in off-road handling. Lower pressures allow the tire tread and sidewall to flex while driving, acting like an addition to the suspension system. The softer tire absorbs bumps and obstacles, making for a more comfortable ride and better control.

Having an idea of the terrain can indicate the extent of airing down. Rock and sand are the types of terrain that are easier to navigate with tires running lower pressures. Tires mounted to regular wheels

can't be aired down nearly as far as ones mounted to bead-lock wheels, which can go much lower (more on this later).

A typical Jeeper on a rocky trail might use a tire pressure of about 15 to 20 psi. Lower pressure improves traction but can cause a loss of ground clearance. Perhaps more important, lower pressures can cause the tire to separate from the bead on the wheel, causing a flat and possibly tire/wheel damage. Sticking to 15 to 20 psi typically keeps the tire on the wheel. Care is needed while driving; remembering the low pressure will help keep you out of trouble.

Another consideration is the ability to air-up after the trail. Driving a

Large off-road tires are expensive and can wear unevenly if left in the same position through their the lifetime. Rotation keeps the positions

An aired-down tire can conform to the surface for maximum grip. Determining the proper air-down pressure on a Jeep is a matter of testing. An aired-down tire has that noticeable bulge and/or fold that is seen as the tire moves over changing surfaces.

moving to allow the tires to wear evenly and extend tread life. Excess wear of the tires from trail abuse is the only form of early wear a Jeep owner should have to accept.

At 35 psi, the high pressure keeps the sidewall of the tire firm, along with preventing the tread from conforming to the obstacle. Off-road driving with this kind of pressure impacts traction and causes a rough ride because the tire cannot help but absorb the bumps.

CJ on the street with 15 psi makes for an extra-sloppy ride. Cornering and handling is worse than normal with underinflated tires, and is potentially dangerous. Before lowering the pressure to an extreme, make sure there is an available way to air-up before the drive home.

Tire Rotation

Tire rotation at regular intervals keeps tire wear even and increases tire life. The solid axles in the CJ and near-zero camber keep the tire running at nearly 90 degrees to the road but steering and toe-in cause the front to wear more than the rear. Jeepers spend a lot of money on tires to have them chewed away from neglect seems foolish. Generally speaking, rotating tires every 5,000 miles is sufficient on a CJ. Directional tires are rare on a Jeep but would require a different rotation procedure and consulting the tire manufacturer for the particular tire's requirements.

Rotating four tires is slightly different than five. Some Jeepers only

At 24 psi, the medium pressure (or correct pressure for this CJ), the tire still maintains a firm sidewall but allows some give to help absorb the bumps and slightly conform to obstacles. This pressure does not provide optimum performance off-road.

At 18 psi, the tire still maintains its form and is likely safe from being pushed off the wheel; however, the pressure is low enough to allow the tread to conform to the obstacle and grip it with the blocks. In addition, lower pressure allows the sidewall to flex, absorbing bumps and helping maintain vehicle control.

If the Jeep only runs four tires or the spare is of a different size/type of tire, implementing a four-tire rotation scheme helps maintain even wear but allows the tires to serve in a location for a set amount of time. Follow the arrows.

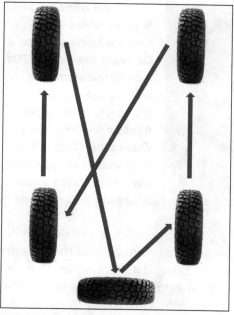

When all five tires are matching, rotating the spare with the others keeps all the tires wearing evenly. Like the four-tire rotation, each tire spends a set amount of time at each location, including the spare, in which the tire accrues no miles.

rotate the four, thinking that the fifth does not wear and it saves the need to purchase five in the future. This thinking often leads to a dry-rotted spare that is likely to not match. Unless you are using a lift, having an impact wrench, floor jack, and several jack stands make rotation easy.

Four Tires

Rotating four tires is a simple enough process. The rear tires move forward on the same side and the front tires move rearward to the opposite side. This method eventually places each tire in every position, returning to the original position on the fourth rotation.

Five Tires

Rotating five tires is a little more complex and it's best to keep a reference. Similar to the four-rotation

sequence, the rear tires are moved forward on the same side. The spare becomes the rear passenger's side and the passenger-side front becomes the rear driver's side. The driver-side front becomes the new spare. In this method, every tire is eventually used at each position and the tire that is the spare gets no wear during its time there. This can allow a set of tires to

wear for longer miles because one sits out for 5,000 miles at a time.

Spare Tire

Many Jeepers go cheap with a spare tire, a practice that leaves them vulnerable. When you're out in the middle of the trail, a punctured tire is high risk and a bad spare tire makes things worse. Having and maintaining a properly sized spare is part of the process of building a Jeep that shouldn't be overlooked. By including the spare in the tire rotation, you keep the spare in good condition and ready for action if needed.

Running a smaller spare, especially if it's a stock size, can be problematic when used on a Jeep with an automatic locker. The difference of size can cause the locker to unlock and lock continuously, possibly causing damage to the locker. If the need to use a small spare arises and the Jeep is equipped with an automatic locker, it's best to run it on the front. If the front has an automatic locker, disengage the lockout hub on the side where the spare is mounted.

Wheels

Wheels or rims, the words mean the same thing and some use them interchangeably. Wheels serve many

A matching spare in both size and type is really the only way to go with an off-road Jeep. If the spare is needed, running a smaller size causes loss of ground clearance and may interfere with locker operation. Less important, a small spare just looks silly on the back of a well-built Jeep.

Aluminum wheels come in many styles and nearly all look good on a CJ. From the retro 1970s look of the aluminum slot reproduced by US Mags, to the more modern-looking Mickey Thompson Classic II, the light weight of the aluminum wheel helps keep unsprung weight lower.

Measuring backspace is best done by placing a straightedge across the span of the wheel rim and measuring to the hub side of the wheel mount. Typical and optimum Jeep CJ wheel backspacing is 3½ to 4¼ inches.

more purposes than just a mounting point for the tires. Wheels are an important component for setting the location of the tire, referred to as backspacing and, probably most important, while not having an effect on function, wheels play a big role in the Jeep's appearance.

Construction

In the early days of Jeep, steel was the only material used for wheels until aluminum wheels were offered on certain AMC-era Jeeps such as the Renegade. Aluminum offers unsprung weight savings and just looks good. Sadly, the aluminum slot was discontinued as a factory offering after 1977, when both painted and chrome steel wagon wheels became common on CJs. The plain white painted steel wheel continued as the standard wheel on base-model CJs.

Most aftermarket wheels used on Jeeps are aluminum, and there seems to be no end to the styles that are offered by many manufacturers. The lightweight and strong construction makes them a good choice. The cost of aluminum is often a drawback when compared to a standard steel wheel.

Steel wheel options are much more limited, but a steel wheel on an AMC-era CJ still maintains a classic look. It's common for Jeepers to use chrome steel wheels or black steel as an inexpensive but strong choice for their Jeep. Steel wheels can take much more abuse from the trail and do not shatter or crack as aluminum does.

Backspacing and Offset

Backspacing is a measurement that indicates the distance between the mounting point and the inner edge of the wheel. This measurement

indicates how far in or out the wheel is located. Knowing what works best on your Jeep can help with proper wheel selection. Narrow-track axles can tolerate a shallow backspacing better than Wide Trak axles due to the added 2½ inches of width. The factory CJ 15 x 7 wheel typically used 3¾ inches of backspace and the 15 x 8 wheel used a 4-inch backspace.

Wheels using 3⅕ to 4 inches of backspace work well on a CJ running a 12½-inch-wide tire; this includes a Jeep running the Wide Trak axle width. Using less backspacing on a Wide Trak width causes the tires to stick out past the flare more than may be legal. Wider aftermarket flares are always an option in this case if the tires exceed the flares too much.

Offset is an additional measurement found on many newer wheels. This measurement indicates the distance from the hub-mounting surface to the centerline of the wheel. Positive offset, when the wheel center is located toward the outside of the wheel, is often found in modern vehicles. Negative offset, when the wheel center is located toward the inside of the wheel, is commonly found in older

Steel wheels are often less expensive than aluminum and tend to take off-road abuse much better by not cracking or breaking. Steel wheels bend under enough stress but almost always continue to function and can be trail repaired, if needed. Notice the low tire pressure on the Swamper tires on this CJ-7.

vehicles. Negative-offset wheels are the most popular type found on Jeep CJs. Larger negative offsets can impact wheel-bearing wear because the wheel is located farther from the centerline.

Spacers

Wheel spacers are common on CJs equipped with narrow-track axles; they give some extra track width and provide extra clearance for wider tires. Wheel spacers are technically defined as adapters because they differ from real wheel spacers in that adapters bolt to the existing lugs and provide new lugs for the wheel to bolt to. Actual spacers sit between the wheel and hub using the same lugs as the wheel. Actual spacers can be dangerous and should be avoided; adapter-type spacers, when installed and maintained properly, are considered safe. Common sizes used are 1½ to 2 inches.

Brake System

Even at the end of the AMC era, the CJ never had great braking power. A Jeep equipped with factory power brakes were better off than others, but the additional braking power provided by the booster wasn't particularly impressive.

During the AMC-era, braking systems did improve a few times through the years by adding a proportioning valve, an optional power booster, and more importantly, front disc brakes in 1977 (standard equipment in 1978). Stopping an early AMC-era CJ with drum brakes can be a nail-biting experience on a dry road with stock-size tires; add larger tires and conditions get worse. To further add difficulty, introduce water and/or mud into the drums and stopping is worse yet.

Drum brakes and water/mud don't mix particularly well; disc brakes are

Optional power disc brakes were a CJ first in 1976, helping further improve stopping power. Although brake pressure was better than ever before, many Jeep owners claim there wasn't much difference between manual brakes and power assisted.

much better at cleaning off from exposure to water and/or mud. Drums can trap contaminants within the drum, causing wear or, worse, brake failure.

Factory Brake Swapping

Owners of non–disc brake Jeeps can improve the braking capacity by swapping outer disc brake knuckles from a later-model Dana 30. This is a relatively straightforward bolt-in swap and works best if the master cylinder and proportioning valve from a disc brake–equipped CJ is used instead of the drum version.

Front Drum to Disc Conversion Kit

SSBC makes a complete conversion kit to change the Jeep's front drum brakes to disc. This kit takes the guesswork and parts matching out of the process. The expense of the kit can be prohibitive but results speak for themselves.

Rear Disc Conversion

Usually the rear drum brakes are sufficient in a CJ equipped with 33- to 35-inch-tires. However, converting the rear to disc brakes only

further enhances and improves the Jeep's stopping power, especially in wet conditions. Although no CJ came from the factory with rear disc brakes, it is not uncommon for owners to convert their Jeep's rear axle to disc brakes.

SSBC also offers a rear brake conversion kit for the AMC 20, as well as other axle types that are bolt-on. Many Jeepers convert to disc brakes using parts from other Jeeps and other vehicles such as Cadillac, Corvette, Geo, and Toyota. These homemade conversions require a significant amount of fabrication and parts gathering with mixed results. It's definitely a project for the adventurous type.

Factory Power Brakes

In 1977, Jeep began offering optional power brakes on Jeeps until the AMC era ended in 1986. The Jeep used the vacuum-style booster, which was often criticized by owners of Jeeps used off-road because of the (almost) lack of brakes if the engine stalled. In the opinion of many, manual brakes and a strong leg were the best thing in a trail-used Jeep.

Due to the less-than-stellar factory power brake system, many Jeep owners developed stronger, more powerful systems using parts from other vehicles. The aftermarket responded by offering bolt-in systems that drastically improve stopping power.

A hydroboost brake system uses the Jeep's power steering pump to increase brake pressure without relying on engine vacuum. A drawback to this system in a trail Jeep is the loss of pressure if the engine stalls.

In truth, power brakes become difficult if the engine is not running, but many Jeep owners learn that they get one or two good presses of the pedal before braking fades. To ensure brake pressure if the engine stalls, you should hold the brakes and start the engine before proceeding.

Brake Boosters

The factory power brake booster was never known for adding much more braking capability over manual brakes. When adding power brakes to a CJ or replacing the factory booster, Jeep owners usually install an aftermarket system or adapt a system from another vehicle that increases braking power significantly.

Adapted Systems

Jeep owners often create their own adapted systems using parts from other vehicles, such as the Corvette, GM K series trucks, full-size S series Jeep Cherokee, and others. As with any adapted system, researching, planning, and testing are essential for success. Brake failure is not a problem to take lightly.

Aftermarket Systems

Several aftermarket systems are available to outfit (or refit) a CJ with power brakes. Off Again 4x4 sells a complete bolt-in power brake system properly tuned for a Jeep called the Navajo Brake system. Reviews of the power and effectiveness of this system are quite favorable from the Jeep community. Several other versions are available from a few manufacturers such as Crown Automotive and Summit Racing.

For years Vanco has been making a hydroboost brake system for the CJ. Unlike traditional power brakes, the hydroboost system uses the power steering pump to increase brake pressure sufficient to stop tires of up to 53 inches. The Vanco system incorporates a nitrogen cylinder to provide backup braking in the event of pump failure or stalling.

Putting It All Together

Tires and wheels might be one of the most noticeable changes a Jeep owner may make from both an appearance as well as performance perspective.

- Radial mud tires provide the best off-road performance and acceptable on-road manners compared to bias-ply mud tires and brands such as Swampers. Other brands, including BFGoodrich, Mickey Thompson, Toyo, and Goodyear, pay close attention to finding a good compromise of on- and off-road performance.
- Aluminum wheels provide good looks, light weight, and many styles. An 8-inch-wide wheel with a 3½- to 4-inch backspace is excellent on both narrow and Wide Trak Jeeps. A 10-inch wheel on a narrow-track-axle Jeep or 1½-inch spacer can help with track width, if desired.
- Disc brakes on the front are essential; rear discs are a plus.
- A quality aftermarket power brake system provides extra stopping power for a Jeep equipped with larger tires.

This 1980 CJ-7 runs a set of 35-inch mud tires, aluminum bead lock wheels, and added rear disc brakes. This setup provides good looks, excellent ground clearance, traction, and stopping power.

ELECTRICAL AND LIGHTING

The electrical system of a vehicle is an often ignored and misunderstood system that can be the cause of a great deal of frustration and mystifying problems. Fortunately, the electrical system of an AMC-era CJ is relatively simple compared to modern Jeeps but it can still leave an owner stumped. When abused, it can be a source of failures and worse, fire.

The fact that the newest AMC-era CJ is more than 30 years old means that most of them have aging wiring, which can be corroded and brittle. Some owners find that just touching

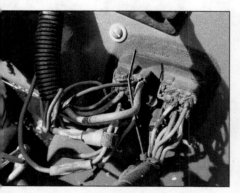

Old wiring is a fact of life in a CJ due to the age of even the newest ones. Living with this wiring takes some care and attention unless it's completely replaced. Over time, wires become brittle; added accessories usually result in taps and splices.

connections can break them because of excess corrosion. In addition to age, owners often hack into the wiring and use electrical tape, incorrect connectors, and poor wire-gauge choices. When you build or modify a Jeep, use matching-gauge wire and automotive-type connectors to prevent failures and the chance of fire.

Electrical System Upgrades and Modifications

Upgrades and modifications to the Jeep's electrical system are often somewhat unglamorous but the improvements increase performance and reliability. These upgrades and modifications can include a better battery, higher-output alternator, external circuit blocks for added accessories and lighting, and headlight relays that brighten the headlights.

Battery

Through the years, battery technology has improved and a CJ can benefit from a newer battery (or batteries) that provides longer life and improved performance. Perhaps the Optima Red and Yellow top batteries are the perfect battery for a trail-used CJ. The sealed, spiral-wound design

allows them to be mounted almost anywhere and in any position.

Vibration, bouncing, and heat that are so commonly experienced on the trail don't affect the Optima battery. For normal trail operation on a CJ, the Red Top performs well in most cases while the deep-cycle Yellow Top performs better when heavy winching is expected. In addition, Optima batteries feature dual terminal posts that are very useful when connecting a winch and extra accessories.

The Optima is one of a few batteries available that serve the demands and environment a Jeep can put on a battery. The sealed design allows mounting in non-standard locations and orientations, plus the dual posts allow several options of powering extra equipment.

Dual Batteries

It's common to find a CJ equipped with dual batteries to help keep up with high-draw (high-drain) accessories such as a winch or on-board welder. Aftermarket dual-battery trays allow installation of two batteries in the same location as the factory tray. You can wire in dual batteries in a few ways. The most common is a simple parallel configuration that wires together like poles. Although this simple design works, in a proper setup parallel alone is not a good method.

This setup requires similar batteries, as well as similarly aged batteries. Installation of an isolation system protects the batteries as well as the charging system. The simplest of isolation systems install a solenoid between the positive poles of the batteries to allow use of one or both. The solenoid should be a continuous-duty version rated at the minimum of the alternator capacity. The Stinger SGP32 is a 200-amp dual battery solenoid is well suited for dual batteries.

For a more advanced setup, Jeep owners install a sophisticated isolation system from companies such as Genesis Offroad or Painless Wiring that controls charging and discharging automatically. Using these kits, both batteries charge and discharge until the starting battery drops below a voltage threshold; it is automatically isolated to save the battery for starting. When this happens, the second battery can continue to power the accessories without risking starting power. The isolation circuit also prevents excess load on the charging system when both batteries are low because of cycling charging.

The Genesis isolation system is simple to install with little need for guesswork and low potential of

incorrect wiring creating a short/fire/overload hazard, which is common with home-built systems.

Alternator

The AMC-era CJ came with a Delco SI alternator typically rated around 60 amps. These alternators are nearly indestructible and will operate for years, even with abuse. AMC-era CJs didn't require much electrical power; even the latest models used simple electronics only to manage the engine and basic vehicle power needs such as starting and lighting. When adding electric powered accessories such as a winch, extra lighting, and

The factory Delco alternator is typically rated around 60 amps, which can be easily exceeded with the addition of extra accessories such as lighting, compressor, and winch. Overloading the alternator causes the battery to lose voltage and the continuous high load can cause the alternator to fail prematurely.

When running dual batteries using an isolator system, it saves the starting battery from being drained and prevents the charging system from excess load during recharging. These systems are often fully automatic and ready for installation. (Photo Courtesy Genesis Offroad)

air compressors that demand power, the charging capacity of the factory alternator may be quickly surpassed.

A common upgrade is to install a higher-output alternator that is rated at 100 to 150 amps. Because Jeep used the standard Delco alternator found on so many other vehicles, a large variety of aftermarket alternators are available, some in shiny finishes and one-wire conversions. Converting the charging system to a one-wire alternator simplifies installation and uses newer charging technology.

The one-wire conversion simply requires a single battery-to-alternator wire. Using the factory wire with the original terminal plug removed is possible, but manufacturers

A higher-output alternator is an easy find, due to the number of vehicles the Delco version was used on. Converting to the one-wire style cleans up and simplifies the installation. The solid plate on the pulley helps keep water and debris entering the engine compartment from getting into the alternator.

Mean Green and Powermaster make high-output high-durability alternators for the Jeep. These bolt-in alternators push 140 amps, and Powermaster claims increased output at idle speeds compared to stock.

recommend replacing the original alternator-to-battery cable with a 4- or 6-gauge wire when using 100- to 150-amp alternators.

For the ultimate charging performance, alternators from Mean Green and Powermaster provide increased charging capacity at slower engine RPM and boast longer hardware life through better construction.

Extra charging capacity can put a strain on factory wiring if original circuits exceed capacity. Leaving original circuits with their proper amp fuses protects wiring and prevents overloads and the possibility of a fire. (Later in this chapter I discuss extra circuit systems that can distribute circuit load properly.)

Starter

Another component that is often ignored and only thought about when it doesn't work is the starter. It is used regularly, and on the trail it's likely to be used more in one day than in a year of normal driving. Although a stock-style starter is often sufficient for many Jeeps, if it is old, you would

be wise to consider a replacement before failure. Dirt, mud, and water often find their way into a starter and eventually cause failure.

Many Jeep owners choose to replace stock-style starters after a season or two of off-road use to avoid failures. In contrast, many upgrade the starter to a higher-performance, higher-life starter made by Mean Green or Powermaster. These starters provide higher torque and longer life through sealed bearings and better components. The aluminum design saves weight and the rotating nose allows for clearance adjustments, if needed.

Wiring Harness

When building a CJ, the wiring is often an old rat's nest of brittle, dangerous wires that may be difficult to trace and identify, because color-coding fades to strange colors or, more likely, just brown. Tracing circuits can be challenging; having a manual with a wiring diagram of the Jeep is handy to own and is a valuable reference tool.

Painless Wiring makes a few versions of the Jeep wiring harness to completely replace the old and tired factory one. Their products are complete with proper gauge, labeled wire, and use modern blade-style fuses. These kits save time and aggravation compared to a home-fabricated refit.

Centech Wiring replacement CJ harnesses feature terminated, well labeled wire, and can be purchased in a ready-to-install version that completely replaces the stock wiring. Some upgrades and instrument options are available to enhance the kits.

When building a CJ, it is common to gut the original wiring and replace it with a brand-new harness from Painless Wiring. Painless has put together a complete harness custom built for many different years of the CJ. The kit features proper-gauge wire that is fully labeled and cut to length. The factory circuit block and relays are replaced with new modern blade fuses that still mount to the factory firewall location. A few custom varieties are available to allow extra circuits and features, if desired.

Grounds

The CJ, even when new, wasn't well known for quality wiring. Jeep vehicle assembly in the 1970s and 1980s seemed to be driven by the need for speed and high production numbers rather than quality. Over time, the degradation of the Jeep's wiring encourages poor grounds that can cause failing components and confusion during troubleshooting. Replacing main ground wires is a good start, but adding some additional good grounds such as an

Wiring Basics

I could write an entire book to discuss proper vehicle wiring, but practicing good habits keeps components on the Jeep working and avoids electrical fires.

The following is a brief list of the essentials for proper wiring.

- Neat and organized wiring is easier to trace and trouble-shoot.
- Use automotive stranded core wire, not solid core as found in home wiring.
- Maintaining matching-gauge wire to circuit capacity prevents overheating, failures, and fire.
- Using proper automotive connectors and avoiding home-style connectors keeps connections from working themselves apart due to vibration.
- Soldering and covering connections with shrink tube when possible provides the best conduction and most durable electrical connection.

- Using dielectric grease when connecting components helps to seal the connection and prevent corrosion after moisture exposure.
- Secure wire and use loom to prevent rubbing, avoid heat sources, use grommets when passing through metal.
- Good grounds. ■

Keeping wiring neat, as seen on this CJ-7, is key to preventing failures and worse, a fire. Using wire loom and ties keeps wiring from wearing against components and makes for a clean appearance and makes tracing wire simpler.

A good stock of automotive crimp connectors is always handy in both the garage and especially the Jeep's toolbox. Using appropriate connectors to wire gauge, along with a proper crimping tool, makes for good connections. Soldering connections and covering with shrink tube is preferred to crimp-style connections.

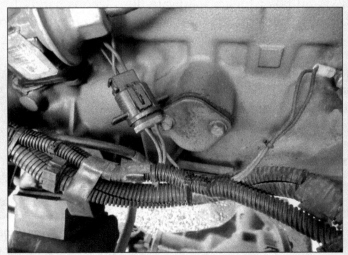

Plastic-wire looms keep wiring clean and protected from rubbing. This stuff can be difficult to use at times and can make tracing a problem harder but the protection trade-off is worth it. Keeping wire within the loom until the split point provides better protection.

auxiliary ground bus keeps things working. The starter, lighting, and electric gauges seem to suffer the most from poor grounds.

Replacing the Jeep's steel body with a fiberglass body changes much of the ground needs from any components that relied on the steel body for a ground. When replacing a Jeep body with fiberglass, it is necessary to add a ground bus with a heavy connection direct to the battery, along with individual grounds-to-body attached components such as lights.

Extra Circuits

As extra components are added to the Jeep, continual splicing into the factory wiring causes failures and makes for messy work. A better option is to install an extra circuit system that extends electrical needs in a safe and organized way.

A few companies make secondary circuit systems, but Painless Wiring is likely the leader in wiring systems used in off-road vehicles. A few varieties of circuit systems are available from Painless that offer multiple circuits in weatherproof enclosures that are perfect for adding extra capacity to a CJ. The attached wiring uses proper-gauge wires for each circuit and blade-style fuses. Several of the circuits use relays along with a master fuse or circuit breaker to protect the entire harness.

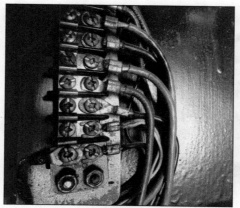

A good ground is the foundation of a vehicle's electrical system, and without one, components can be unreliable. The CJ used the chassis, body, and engine as the primary ground from the factory. Installing a ground bus for important and high-draw components provides better and more reliable power.

Attaching extra accessories that require power is simple if you find a suitable location for the enclosure in the engine compartment. Follow battery attachment procedures as specified by the manufacturer.

Headlight Relays

The factory wiring supplies power to the Jeep's headlights through a rather long path; it causes power loss and results in dim lights. The path directs all of the power through the headlight switch, which degrades over time to cause even dimmer lights

Adding a protected circuit block to added power accessories is the best way to protect from overloaded circuits and the need for excess wiring. Painless makes wiring blocks from seven circuits and up. All feature overload protection and use blade-style fuses. The seven-circuit block provides a main fuse, a combination ignition switch, and always-on circuits.

and increased switch heat. Replacing the switch helps, but installing a set of relays to redirect the power dramatically increases the light output.

Relays are essentially remote switches that use a minimal amount of power to complete a secondary circuit within the relay. By using the Jeep's factory headlight switch to power the relay instead of the headlights directly, only a minimum of power moves through the switch. Heavier-gauge and shorter-length wire is used to provide power to the headlights through the relay.

Installing Headlight Relays

This procedure reroutes headlight power through the newly installed relays and relieves power load on the headlight switch. Clean and organized wiring using the proper gauge ensures a safe and reliable system. The time to allow for this project is several hours.

Parts and Supplies

The procedure requires two automotive weatherproof relays. Choose quality relays from Bosch or Hella because a relay failure means driving in the dark. One relay is used for low beam and the other one for high beam. In addition, a 15-amp fusible

link is close to the battery for the direct battery power side of the relay circuit.

Use 12- to 14-gauge wire for both the positive and ground wire. Stay consistent with gauge: Choose one and stick with it for the complete circuit. Replacing the headlight

Installing headlight relays requires several inexpensive parts: two headlight plugs, two relays, two relay plugs, and 12-gauge wire. Typical relay-mounting location is on the rear of the grille in an accessible location.

A completed installation should be neat and securely mounted. Understanding the installation aids in troubleshooting in the event of a failure. This setup is mounted just below the rear air intake hole on the driver's side of the Jeep.

connectors is a good idea because they are likely old and brittle.

Routing

On a CJ, the headlight wiring runs on the driver's side of the Jeep from the firewall connection. Mounting the relays on the driver's side of the grille is a good location; that allows using the factory headlight switch feeds to switch the relays. Running a fused positive and ground to the new relays in an organized way is often best accomplished by running them down the passenger-side grille supports and across the inside of the grille. Place both wires within an automotive-style wire loom for protection.

Relay Wiring

Here is a simple step-by-step procedure:

- Attach the high-beam circuit feed from the headlight switch to the 86 terminal on the high-beam relay.
- Attach the low-beam circuit feed from the headlight switch to the 86 terminal on the low-beam relay.

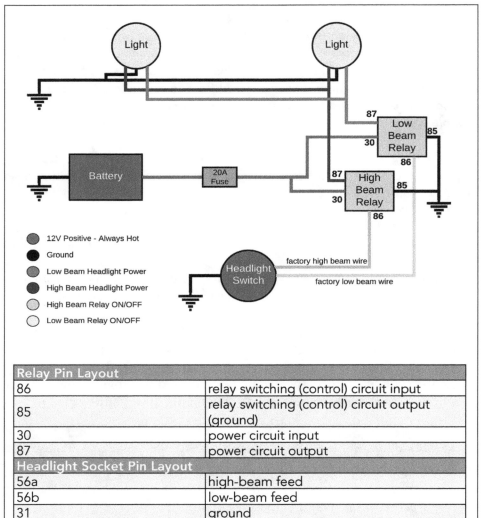

- 12V Positive - Always Hot
- Ground
- Low Beam Headlight Power
- High Beam Headlight Power
- High Beam Relay ON/OFF
- Low Beam Relay ON/OFF

Relay Pin Layout	
86	relay switching (control) circuit input
85	relay switching (control) circuit output (ground)
30	power circuit input
87	power circuit output
Headlight Socket Pin Layout	
56a	high-beam feed
56b	low-beam feed
31	ground

Headlight relay circuit layout consists of using the factory light circuits to switch the relay, while providing power to the lights through higher-capacity wiring switched by the relay.

- Attach the new high-power feed wire to the 30 terminal on both relays.
- Attach the 85 terminals to the new ground source.
- It may be easier to remove the headlights and their bezels to work on the inside grille wires.
- Attach the 56a wires to the high-beam relay.
- Attach the 56b wires to the low-beam relay.
- Attach the 31 wires to the new ground source.
- Final installation steps include making sure the wiring is protected and secured.
- Test light operation on both the low- and high-beam settings.

Headlight Upgrades

Upgrading the headlights in a CJ is common and results in higher light output, which increases night visibility. Many easily installed options are available, including modern LED lighting.

Factory Lights

The AMC-era CJ came equipped with standard 7-inch sealed incandescent bulbs that were around 55 to 60 watts. This is low-light output compared to the more modern lighting available today. A few upgrade options are available that provide improved night visibility.

H4 Halogen Lights

H4 halogen lights are a more modern, brighter replacement to the standard sealed incandescent bulb. Hella and Delta Tech make direct-fit H4 conversion lights that install with only a screwdriver. These bulbs are modular and need to be mounted within a reflector housing. This con-

Converting to H4 bulbs increases light output and only requires installation of new lenses and bulbs. It is recommended to install relays to get the full output potential of this conversion. This Jeep is equipped with IPF H4 conversion bulbs and lenses; the blue color of the bulbs is a hint.

version, along with installation of headlight relays, is often the best result without significant expense.

LED Lights

LED lighting is a relative newcomer to automotive headlights; it consumes far less power and provides brilliant light output. LED lights typically use the same connector as H4 lights. If using LED lights on a vehicle that is exposed to colder temperatures, the lights should have heating elements to prevent snow and/or ice buildup because LED lights often do

LED lighting is rather new to vehicle headlights and it's taken several years for the technology to get to the point of being worth installation from both a light color perspective and semi-reasonable cost. LED headlights such as this one from J.W. Speaker are substantially brighter than stock and use minimal power but still carry a high price tag.

not generate enough heat to melt snow and ice on their own. LED light systems can be expensive when compared to traditional systems.

Quadratec makes direct-fit 50-state-legal LED headlights for the CJ that can be installed in 20 to 30 minutes. These lights use a fraction of the power used by traditional sealed beam lights: 15 watts on low beam versus 55 watts for sealed beams.

Extra Lighting

Most Jeep owners add extra lighting. Adding a variety of lights to the Jeep can improve visibility in many conditions. It's common to add lighting to other parts of the Jeep, including underneath to aid in nighttime off-road adventures. Although traditional halogen lights are still used, LED lights have begun to dominate secondary lighting on off-road vehicles in recent years. LED lights provide brighter light with a fraction of the energy usage. In addition, they are extremely resistant to vibration and have a very long life.

Forward

Mounting extra lights on the front of a CJ is common and useful in poor visibility conditions. Fog lights cover a wide range of area; driving lights provide improved lighting in more focused areas farther ahead in front of the Jeep. Fog lights are generally considered more practical on a CJ that is used off-road.

Light bars have had a return in popularity since the introduction of LED bulbs. Old-school chrome bars with four to six bars are a thing of the past; these bars tended to drag through tight spaces and draw a lot of power. LED light bars come in a variety of sizes, from a few inches to 50 inches wide with very little added height when mounted to the windshield. These LED bars put out a considerable amount of light

Fog lights or driving lights on the front of a CJ look as natural as the winch they sit next to on a CJ. These feature a protective plastic grille to prevent breakage by objects. The 4- to 6-inch round lights are most common, but small, extremely bright, square, and round LED lights are becoming more popular.

This is an example of the light output of the Jeep's relay-powered headlights against a backdrop of trees approximately 40 feet away. Even though the lights put out a brighter beam, this isn't always sufficient on a nighttime trail run.

Adding small low-draw LED lights under the Jeep can help both the driver and a spotter in the dark. These small lights fit nearly anywhere and can even aid in trail repair in the dark, if needed.

Add the brilliant light from a 50-inch windshield-mounted light bar and it becomes obvious how much light these bars flood out in front of the Jeep. Although the picture doesn't show it, a drawback of windshield-mounted bars is the way they completely illuminate the Jeep's hood.

power, considering their low power usage.

One consideration when mounting a light bar to the top of the windshield is the need to get wiring to the top and outside, which is often a challenge when dealing with the top and doors. The intense light generated by the LED bar often completely illuminates the Jeep's hood, which may prove to be a distraction and cause reduction in visibility, especially with a bright paint color.

Rear, Under and Side

Similar to the front, adding lights to the rear, under, and side increases visibility; this can be especially useful on a hazardous off-road trail. The lighting helps both the driver and spotter (if used) see obstacles, helping navigation and preventing possible damage. Mounting lights underneath requires careful planning to prevent damage to the lights and the wiring from trail objects.

Placing these lights under the hood can help illuminate the engine compartment if on-trail repairs are needed; locations are nearly limitless.

It is common to use small 2- to 3-inch LED lights in these locations; most models are in durable housings and are waterproof. KC HiLites, Quadratec, and Rigid make a variety of small LED lights in several configurations. Extra-small LED rock light kits from Rigid are available that can be mounted nearly anywhere.

Wiring Lights

Extra lighting should be wired using manufacturer wire gauge and circuit protection recommendations to avoid overloads and failure. As discussed earlier, a separate extra circuit module can provide a perfect connection point for external lights. Switch panels from Painless Wiring and Daystar that are perfect for a CJ

come in many varieties and make clean work of wiring extra accessories and lights.

Putting It All Together

A lot was covered here on an important topic that is relatively unexciting and often ignored. Some things to take away from this are the following.

- A good charging system and a good battery remove a weak point from the Jeep.
- Headlight relays are a great modification with excellent results.
- Extra lighting is extremely useful when trail running at night.
- Lights facing other directions help both the driver and spotter.
- LED lights are very bright but draw much less power.
- Good grounds are good.

Adding switch panels in convenient locations to control power to accessories conserves space and keeps things organized. Custom switch panels allow an individual Jeep owner's style to show through. Using old-school switches and indicator lights make the panel look era accurate.

Off-road driving at night adds a level of adventure to a possibly uninteresting trail. The lack of visual clues and distance sight can make even a familiar trail seem new. Extra lighting to light up the darkness, especially underneath, makes the going more enjoyable and less risky.

RECOVERY, ONBOARD AIR AND TRAIL GEAR

Building and modifying a CJ is more than the big stuff such as engine, axle, and suspension modifications. The accessories with which a Jeep is equipped increases its trail performance and the ability to get in and out. Showing up with a trail-built Jeep will likely get you through the day, but when trouble arises, having the extras keeps the day going.

The nature of driving a Jeep off-road is to put the Jeep's capability to the test, and Jeepers eventually find themselves or others stuck in or on some trail obstacle. Getting "unstuck" can be a challenge to the unprepared, which wastes time and potentially damages parts.

Getting stuck is inevitable, regardless of how well built a Jeep is. In fact, it's a fact that improved capability creates the desire to do more challenging trails. This circular loop is what makes Jeep owners eventually run 40-inch tires and $10,000 axles, if they don't know their limits. Having the proper recovery gear makes a stuck situation temporary.

Winch

A winch on the front of a Jeep is an iconic look that seems to fit the Jeep in any setting. Not many other vehicles look so normal with a winch sitting front and center. Having a winch is a kind of insurance that makes the word *stuck* only a temporary situation. With a quick attach of the winch line and a flip of the switch, a Jeeper can be underway.

Choosing a winch is not a difficult task but it's best to avoid using "cheap" models to reduce the likelihood of a failure. Major winch brands such as Warn, Superwinch, and Ramsey are among the top manufacturers and can make this investment reliable.

Line Pull Rating

Winches vary in the amount of weight they can pull; higher-rate ratings put less load on the winch and allow for longer pull times. Ratings are based on the first layer of the cable on the winch drum; additional layers reduce capacity due to an effective higher ratio. In general, a weight rating of 8,000 to 9,500 pounds is good for a CJ.

The iconic Jeep grille is not hidden by the presence of a winch on the front. Adding a winch to a Jeep is as common as lift kits and larger tires. Selecting the best one for your Jeep depends on your needs and intentions. Heavier Jeeps with frequent trail use may require premium equipment.

Line Length and Construction

Picking the length of the line, commonly called rope, is really a matter of preference. Longer line length allows farther pull distances but can reduce the winch capacity due to line layers when used in a short pull. The most common line length used on a trail Jeep is 125 feet.

Line construction offers a choice of wire or synthetic rope, each with its advantages and disadvantages. Wire rope, the traditional and more common choice, is made up of strands of carbon steel wire, typically 7 bundles containing 19 strands each. Wire rope weighs considerably more than synthetic but is more resilient to abrasion. Small breaks in the strands cause burrs that will tear your hands; using gloves with wire rope is imperative. Wire rope can crush or kink if not spooled in properly and can be dangerous in a failure without proper precautions.

Synthetic rope is a newer arrival to winches and its higher cost can be justified by its advantages. A length of synthetic rope can weigh approximately five times less than the same length of wire rope. One of the advantages is the absence of flesh-ripping burrs and dangerous recoil during a failure. Synthetic rope drops dead very quickly and offers little, if any, recoil in the event of a failure. Another advantage: Synthetic rope floats. A few disadvantages are that the rope doesn't hold up well to chafing and excess heat from the winch drum during excess winching.

Gearing

The three most common gearsets found in winches are spur, worm, and planetary gears. The long-running Warn 8274 may be the only spur gear winch still widely available, leaving most winches to use worm gears and, most prevalent, planetary gears. Planetary gears allow for smaller sizes, lighter weight, and reasonably low-amp draw. A downside to this style is the increased heat from internal braking to control the load during winching.

Electric versus Hydraulic

Although electric winches are the most popular, the hydraulic winch has many diehard fans. Electric winches are the simplest to install because they only require connection to the Jeep's battery. Depending on the battery, electric winches can be used for a brief time if the Jeep's engine is not running. A division of style exists in electric winches: Internal and external solenoids. Internal-solenoid winches are typically more visually appealing because the internal

Traditional wire cable has been a mainstay on automotive winches until recently. The extremely strong and inexpensive cable in 100- to 150-foot lengths is still standard equipment on most winches. Wire cable is prone to wear, kinking, and crushing, especially when misused. Small breaks can cause burrs that rip flesh easily, making glove use important.

Synthetic rope is considerably lighter and generally safer for use in both protecting hands and spring back, in the event of a break. Most winches are capable of being refitted with synthetic rope. When refitting a winch with synthetic cable, it's often common to change to a hawse fairlead.

solenoid is mounted on a bridge above the spool. External-solenoid models mount the solenoid to the winch itself or to something external.

Hydraulic winches typically attach to the power steering pump and require the engine to be running to work. A big advantage of hydraulic is the ability to perform extended pulls because less heat is generated. Some hydraulic systems recommend or require a replacement power steering pump to operate properly.

Electrical Needs

Electric winches put a high demand on the Jeep's battery and can cause damage to the battery if it is underrated. Using a quality battery or a dual-battery setup for high-winch-use Jeeps keeps things reliable. A dual-purpose battery with both good starting and deep-cycle capability such as the Optima Yellow Top or ProComp HDX off-road gives the best performance and longest life.

It is always best to attach the winch directly to the main battery

Dual posts on Optima batteries make attaching a winch even easier. The top posts are preferred for winch attachment because the forward posts are extensions. Disconnecting the winch when not in use isn't required but most Jeepers do it anyway. The Optima Red Top battery is a conventional automotive battery; the Yellow Top battery is a deep-cycle battery.

posts. A dual-post battery such as the Optima gives two posts on each pole, allowing easy connection. Use the direct-connect post instead of the cable-connected post on an Optima. Many Jeep owners install a disconnect to cut power to the winch when not in use.

A good charging system in the Jeep helps the battery recover more quickly from winch use. Most AMC-era CJs came with low-amp alternators because electrical requirements were low in pre-computerized and pre-fuel-injected engines. When replacing an alternator, consider adding one that provides increased output in the 100- to 150-amp range. As discussed earlier, converting a Jeep to a one-wire alternator simplifies the installation.

Mounting

The extended front section of the CJ frame is a natural location for mounting a winch. Unfortunately, the crossmember at the front of the frame makes mounting the winch higher necessary. The higher mounting helps keep the winch out of the mud but cuts down on radiator airflow. Many versions of stand-alone mounts are available, as well as bumpers with integrated mounts. Most winches use a standard mounting pattern that makes installation easier.

A fairlead is used to help guide the line in and out of the winch. In

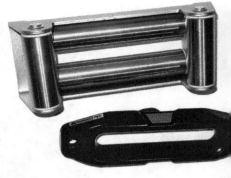

The fairlead is used to provide a guide for the winch cable as it is pulled inward. It allows the cable to freely move without binding or wearing against the surface when the cable is moving at an angle. Traditional wire cable usually uses a roller fairlead (top); a hawse fairlead (bottom) is typically used with synthetic cable.

the past, a roller lead was used and worked best with a wire rope. In the early days, a hawse fairlead was needed to prevent damage to synthetic line that became caught in the edges of the rollers. Redesigned roller fairleads are now available to safely use with synthetic line. In reality it's up to the Jeep owner.

Accessories and Extras

Some winches integrate other accessories such as an air compressor and wireless controls. A Jeep equipped with a winch should also carry other items used in conjunction with the winch.

Winch mounts come in many varieties, some built into bumpers and some stand-alone. In addition, they often provide a fairlead mounting area and bolt on using existing

frame holes. The Warn 13910 is a standard mount that can accommodate most winches; its simple design, strength, and reasonable price make it a favorite.

A pair of good gloves is especially important with wire rope.

A tree-saver strap is used when attaching the line to a tree. The strap prevents the line from damaging the tree or becoming stuck in the tree's bark. D rings are a safer method to connect a line or strap than a hook; having two or three is typically sufficient.

Finally, a snatch block is useful when a directional change is necessary in the line or additional pulling power is needed. Using the snatch block to reconnect the line to the Jeep doubles the pulling power of the winch while it cuts the line speed in half.

Having a kit at the ready for use when winching should be standard equipment in a trail Jeep. Gloves, tree strap, clevis, and controller should be part of the kit. In addition, have something to hang on the cable to prevent snap back, such as a floor mat or blanket.

Installing a Winch

A CJ could possibly be one of the easiest Jeeps to mount a winch to. A simple Warn bolt-on mount, A Warn VR10-S winch, and some easy wire routing is about all it takes to add this valuable tool.

2 *The mount may need some adjustment to fit the CJ frame because they can vary in exact width. Elongating the holes slightly with a Dremel allows a proper fit.*

3 *Attach the fairlead to the mount prior to mounting the winch.*

1 *Loosely attach the plate frame mounts on the forward section of the frame. Test fit the winch plate before mounting the winch, making adjustments if needed.*

4 *Position the winch on the plate, passing the line through the fairlead, and insert the square bolts within the winch body. Attach the plate to the bottom of the winch using the supplied bolts.*

5 *Place the winch mounted to the plate on the frame mounts and tighten all fasteners.*

6 *Determine a good route to get the winch wiring into the engine compartment for attachment to the battery. Removing the passenger-side headlight eased wire routing within the grille.*

7 *You can route into the grille and exit using the oval hole at the top.*

8 *Cables can be attached to the grille support bars to make a clean installation.*

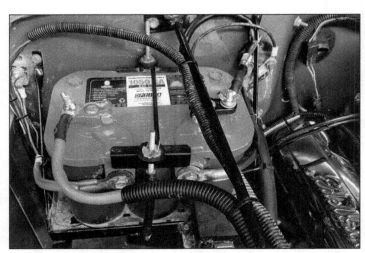

9 *Attaching to the battery should be done properly to avoid overloading the connection. A direct connection to the battery terminals is best. A disconnect to detach the positive side of the battery or a high-amp plug set cuts power to the winch when not in use.*

10 *Securing the battery leads to the grille opening prevents rubbing and wear.*

11 *Attach the line hook and clean up any remaining wiring; test the winch operation.*

For manual recovery or situations where a front-mounted winch will not do, using a "come-along" puller does the trick. Perhaps the ultimate in come-along pullers is the More Power Puller from Wyeth Scott, which is pull rated at 12,000 pounds. (Photo Courtesy Ralph Hassel)

Manual Recovery

On occasion, recovery is needed when a winch isn't available or usable. A few tools can make this job much easier and safer. A cable puller, or "come-along," is a ratcheting manual winch available in many sizes and capacities. These require some human muscle and really can't fully take the place of a winch. They are most useful to hold a vehicle in place, especially from the side.

Many styles and capacities of come-alongs are available, but perhaps the best-known manual puller is the More Power Puller, which is capable of handling 3 tons. When needed, a high-lift jack can serve as

a limited distance puller. The short length of the jack allows movement of only about 3 to 4 feet without resetting the jack.

Onboard Air

As was discussed in Chapter 9, having the ability to air-up after a day on the trail is handy and saves having to drive on the street with squishy tires. In addition, having the ability to air-up a flat tire or run air tools adds convenience.

Onboard air systems can come in nearly any combination of equipment. Typical setups use either an electric-driven or an engine-driven air compressor. Many engine-driven systems consist of homemade designs using converted belt-driven compressors that were originally used for air-conditioning systems. Engine-driven systems are capable of supplying a considerable amount of air, allowing the continuous use of air tools.

Air Tanks

An onboard air system needs an air storage tank to be effective because most compressors can't deliver a consistent or sufficient amount of air to be usable. Even a small tank that can

Having an air tank to hold a supply of compressed air allows for quicker air-ups and the use of tools. Two- to five-gallon tanks are common, as well as special bumpers that can serve double duty as air tanks and provide plenty of options to a Jeep owner. This CJ has front and rear bumpers that serve as air tanks for the onboard air system.

store 100 to 150 psi of air is able to run tools or air-up tires very quickly. At a minimum, use an air tank that is 2 gallons or more and is rated for pressures of 100 to 150 psi.

Because space is nearly always an issue with a CJ, finding a good mounting location for an air tank can be a challenge and requires a little creativity. Tanks tucked away between the frame rails and above the rear axle area fit well and conserve interior room. When mounting a tank under the Jeep, make sure the lines are capable of withstanding heat and possible trail objects. Some Jeepers purchase or fabricate their own bumpers that are capable of serving as air tanks, another example of a space-saving measure.

Electric Air Compressors

Electric air compressors are easy to install and can be mounted nearly anywhere. ARB, Viair, and Smittybilt manufacture electric compressors of varying sizes and capacities. In general, electric compressors are compact, which lessens their capability of running tools on their own. When combined with a storage tank, stored air is used for most of the work and the compressor is used to refill the tank, which often can take several

minutes. This refill time can cause the tank to run out quickly, allowing for short tool usage time or slow increase of tire air-up time.

When selecting a compressor, compare CFM and pressure ratings. Higher CFM allows quicker tank recovery and faster air-up times.

Electric compressors offer simple installation and can mount nearly anywhere. Air locker–equipped Jeeps can use the compressor for both the lockers and air-ups. Electric compressors are typically noisy and slow due to their compact size.

Engine-Driven Compressors

An engine-driven compressor can supply air in much larger capacity because it's a pump driven by the Jeep's engine. On a CJ, the most commonly used compressor is a York style that probably served as an air-conditioning compressor. Due to their common use, locating used compressors from junkyards or new/rebuilt compressors from auto parts stores isn't difficult.

AirBoss sells a complete onboard air kit for CJs running stock engines but most systems are homegrown. I the Jeep is still equipped with the factory engine, mounting a York compressor is not too difficult and can be done by using the proper factory mounting brackets and pulleys from an engine equipped with factory air conditioning.

Of course, re-purposing the compressor on a CJ equipped with factory air eliminates the air conditioning. Non-AMC engines may require some additional brackets and/or fabrication. Additional components, including an oil catch and air filter, are needed to properly run an engine-driven system.

Designing an Onboard Air System

Home building an onboard air system should start with the compressor. It dictates the components needed for a basic system. Both electric- and engine-driven systems are illustrated here. There are many ways of customizing, but the essentials remain the same.

Engine-Driven System

Assuming the compressor is mounted and functional, the following components are needed.

- Air filter: filters the air entering the compressor
- One-way valve: prevents compressed air from leaking back through the compressor
- Oil trap: filters oil from the compressor and prevents it from entering the air system
- Safety valve: prevents exceeding rated psi.
- Auto shut-off switch: allows the compressor to automatically

cycle on and off when pressure reaches max or min
- Connectors: quick-release air hose connection points
- Air tank
- Hoses and fittings, as needed
- Hand throttle to run the engine

An onboard air system supplied by an engine-driven compressor such as a York compressor can supply enough air to power tools and air tires in a short time. Because the York compressor was used on factory Jeep engines, they mount easily. Visible here is the compressor and air filter.

at higher RPM to increase compressor speed

The components of an engine-driven system vary from an electric compressor. Seen here are the components that make up the engine-driven system. From left to right: coalescing filter, one-way valve, and manifold (blue). Attached to the manifold from left to right: pressure gauge, air supply hose, pressure relief valve, hose attachment, pressure sensor. On the end is a pressure switch to cycle the compressor. Below are the tank supply lines.

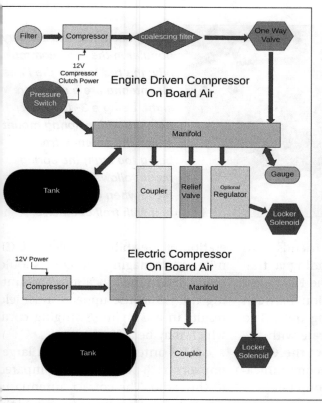

These diagrams are of a typical engine-driven system and an electric-driven system. Options and configurations can be endless, but these components are common on most systems. Constructing a system can mean hours of searching for fittings and components. Off-road shops and online resources can discuss exact parts needed.

Electric System

Assuming the compressor is mounted and functional, the following components are needed. Most electric compressors have self-pressure regulation that does not require additional components.

- Connectors: quick-release air hose connection points
- Air tank
- Hoses and fittings, as needed

Options

Because no two systems are the same, many customizations and additions are possible. If the Jeep is equipped with air lockers, they may be tied into the system to use the stored air. It may be necessary to add a pressure regulator to the air locker system to avoid overloading the locker seals. Adding quick couplers in the front and rear as well as under-hood adds convenience.

Compressed Carbon Dioxide Tanks

These systems use a high-pressure bottle to hold carbon dioxide gas and are ultra portable, to the point of being easily removed from the Jeep to help others. The Power Tank brand of portable tanks is the carbon dioxide tank leader in the Jeep community.

A variety of systems and mounts to satisfy nearly any need or installation location are available. The 10-pound tank is the most common size, which is small enough to store in a Jeep and provides plenty of air for airing-up and running tools. According to specs, a single 10-pound tank can add 10 psi to a 33-inch tire 20 times; that's several trail runs on a single tank. An empty tank can be refilled at many types of locations including fire extinguisher service shops, welding gas supply stores, beverage carbonics companies, and paint ball supply stores.

Air Tools

When the Jeep is equipped with an air system capable of running tools, carrying the right tools makes

the best use of the installation. A length of air hose, tire inflation chuck, blowgun, impact wrench, and small air wrench are some of the basic tools to carry on the trail.

Communication

Today, nearly everyone has a cell phone with them at all times. However, in the Jeep community, slightly older technology is still common for staying connected when traveling in a group; Citizens Band (CB) and Family Radio Service (FRS) radio systems are used often. These systems allow quick, convenient communication to everyone on the same channel. Many Jeepers use both systems at the same time for different purposes.

Running air tools can make the work easier and quicker. Most engine-driven systems and systems with tanks can power impact wrenches and inflation attachments on the trail.

FRS radios are excellent for quick private communication on the trail instead of a CB. Reserving the CB for trail group use keeps the channels open and reduces annoying chatter.

Fiberglass antennas are very popular in the Jeep community; the red tops of the Firestik antenna are a common sight. Using a 3- to 4-foot antenna with a spring mount keeps the antenna from being too high; the spring mount allows the antenna to move when coming in contact with trail obstacles.

Many off-road parks monitor certain CB and FRS channels to provide aid, if needed.

CB Radio System

The CB on the trail is used for group communication and can easily keep everyone informed about upcoming obstacles or alert the leader to trouble somewhere within the group. FRS radios are handy to allow more specific communication between smaller groups within a larger one.

Space is limited in a CJ and the Cobra 75WXST uses a hidden base that leaves just the handset and cord to conserve space. Small CB radios such as the Cobra 19DX and Uniden PRO 510XL fit well under the dash in a CJ.

For example, three friends with their vehicles are attending a trail run in a larger group. The FRS radios can allow communication between the three while reserving the CB to monitor and communicate with the whole group. This allows the CB to stay clear of personal communication and available for group talk.

A simple, quality CB often serves a Jeeper well. Expensive, gimmicky radios just waste money perhaps better spent elsewhere. The FCC limits a CB to 4 watts of output power and most radios use this power, which is more than sufficient for the purpose of on-trail or small-group communication. It's rare for a Jeeper to need long-distance communication, which is likely better performed using a cell phone.

The common theme with a CJ is the lack of space that makes installation of nearly any accessory a challenge, so choosing a smaller-footprint CB helps save space. Common CB locations in a CJ are below the dash, in or on a center console between the front seats, or on a mount at the top of the windshield. Finding the best location is owner preference. Consid-

eration of the ability to reach the CB mic and managing the cord should help determine location. Mounting the CB at the upper windshield results in a dangling/swinging cord which may be a distraction.

A CB antenna often has a large impact on CB performance compared to the radio. The correct antenna in a proper location provides the highest performance and results in clear communication and good range. There is a bit of science involved in choosing and tuning an antenna but thankfully CB experts who are off-roaders have perfected the combinations for a Jeep. Fine-tuning a CB using an inexpensive SWR meter maximizes the CB's performance.

Using a quality 3- to 4-foot fiberglass antenna mounted at the top of the bodyline or higher provides the best performance while being durable during off-road use. Many fiberglass antennas have a bit of flex so they don't break when coming in contact with branches and other trail obstacles. Adding a spring to the mount adds some extra flex to the antenna.

Adjusting CB SWR

After taking the time to install a CB into a Jeep, it's not just time to pick up the mic and start talking. Tuning the CB's antenna for proper operation maximizes the CB performance. Using an inexpensive standing wave ratio (SWR) meter, tuning takes only a few minutes.

If the SWR on channel 40 is higher

than that on channel 1, the antenna is too long. Conversely, if the SWR on channel 1 is higher than that on channel 40, the antenna is too short. The goal is to reach a 1:1 to 1.5:1 ratio

between the two channels. On most fiberglass antennas, the tip is adjustable to allow altering the antenna length.

High SWR readings are often a result of ground problems or poor

coaxial cables. On a CJ, a no-ground plane antenna is sometimes the best solution. Using proper length and quality coaxial cables reduces the likelihood of high SWR readings.

1 A standing wave ratio (SWR) meter is an inexpensive tool for tuning a CB antenna to obtain optimum output. With the Jeep in an open area, attach the SWR meter to the radio side of the CB antenna wire.

2 Put the CB on channel 1 and the meter on FWD. Key the microphone and hold the button; adjust the SWR meter knob to make the meter reach the set area. This step prepares the meter to take an actual measurement.

3 Flip the switch from FWR to SET, record the reading, and release the key. Adjust the antenna by its tip or base, as required. Repeat the test as needed to obtain optimum measurements. Repeat on channel 40.

For CJs that are equipped with a fiberglass body, CB performance can be poor due to the lack of a ground plane. Without getting into the science, the ground plane is essentially the surface that the transmitted

signal uses to reflect into the atmosphere. A Jeep has a poor ground plane from the start, and a fiberglass body makes things worse. Installing a no-ground-plane antenna system dramatically increases CB performance.

FRS Radio Stystem

Introduced in 1996 as an improvement in walkie-talkie–type radio systems, these small, inexpensive, battery-operated radios allow for personal communication. Having

a set of these in the Jeep for the trail allows you to keep in contact with nearby Jeepers. Be skeptical with range claims on FRS radios because most normal situations prevent a range of more than 1 mile.

Fuel and Water Storage

Some Jeepers may choose to spend an extended time on the trail, which necessitates bringing extra fuel and water. Using externally mounted portable storage tanks, generally

The CJ is notorious for having a poor ground plane, which affects CB performance. Fiberglass bodies make matters worse. If needed, a few companies make no-ground-plane antennas that can improve performance. Firestik is a popular choice among Jeep owners.

Jerry cans date back to World War II and have been modified and refined since then. They are handy for carrying extra supplies of fuel and water. Companies have created many clever designs of these through the years. Rotopax offers ingenious container shape and mounting designs that make the most of space.

called jerry cans, is the preferred method. It's rare to see metal cans being used; high-strength plastic is lighter and less prone to damage. It is important to use purpose-built cans for different liquids. Fuel and water should be stored in cans that are designed for each type. In addition, look for cans that are specifically designed to carry potable water.

The most common location for mounting external tanks is at the rear of the Jeep, likely integrated into the spare tire/rear bumper setup. Several clever systems make the best use of space, mounting, and ease of access. Bear in mind that carrying extra fuel and water adds extra weight quickly.

Tools and Parts

It's inevitable that something will break or need attention while on the trail. Keeping a smartly chosen set of tools gives you the best chance of a successful repair without carrying an entire shop toolbox full of tools.

Carrying some special tools and parts for the Jeep can often save the day. Some components are prone to failure on the trail; carrying them can get you back underway instead of being towed out. A universal joint is often a point of failure that can be changed on the trail with some special tools and having a spare joint on hand.

Hand Tools

Because most AMC-era CJs use mostly SAE nuts and bolts, reducing to an SAE-only set of hand tools can save space and weight. Carrying a set of wrenches, ratchets, deep sockets, and shallow sockets gives you all you may need on the trail. In addition, a variety of screwdrivers, pliers, and cutters should be in the toolbox. Carry adjustable tools such

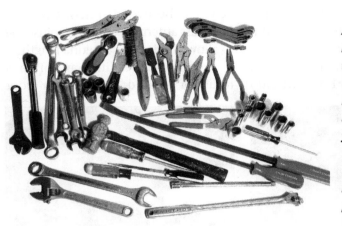

as clamps, wrenches, and locking pliers. A soft-side tool bag can save space and weight compared to a rigid plastic or metal box.

Jeepers often attempt to keep the number of tools to a minimum to conserve weight and space. A trick is to use your trail tool set when performing maintenance on the Jeep. If a necessary tool is missing, it may be something to be added to the trail set.

An assortment of hand tools for the trail should be among the items you pack. Knowing your Jeep and its needs will help you decide what to take. Packing enough to cover potential trail repairs without over packing is a matter of trial and error.

Jack

Carrying a jack that is capable of lifting the Jeep is an indispensable tool that often can serve more purposes than just jacking. The Hi-Lift jack set is the standard that many others are based on. The Hi-Lift which is available in 36- to 60-inch lengths, is capable of raising the Jeep from nearly any sturdy lifting point. Replacing a flat tire on the trail on a lifted Jeep without a proper jack can be a challenge. Although the Hi-Lift jack is an essential tool, retaining the factory jack is a good idea. The factory jack can serve a multitude of purposes besides jacking.

Electrical Tools

An electrical failure because of a bad crimp or ripped wire can be repaired easily with a set of electrical tools that includes cutters, crimpers, tape, lengths of wire, and connectors. Spare fuses are essential.

The Hi-Lift jack is similar to an automotive bumper jack that uses climbing pins to raise or lower a vehicle in a safe and secure manner. The Hi-Lift can serve as a manual puller, if needed. Mounting a jack to the Jeep can be achieved in a variety of ways; keeping the jack from rattling is a challenge.

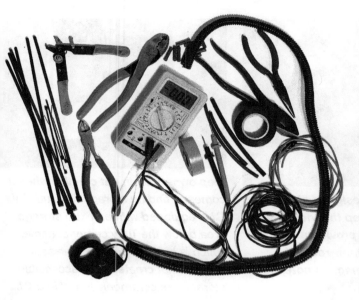

Electrical problems can spring up out of nowhere and can be troublesome to repair without some basic tools and supplies. Wire, wire ties, tape, and a meter are essential tools.

Carrying hand tools and knowing your Jeep helps in deciding what specialty tools may be needed on the trail. Clamps, pullers, lights, and safety equipment should be on the list.

Tool List

This list can serve as a starting point for putting together a set of tools to accompany you and your Jeep on the trail.

- Hi-Lift Jack
- U-Joint Tool
- Standard Jack
- Breaker Bar
- Pry Bar
- Clamps
- Engine Belts
- Ratchet Straps
- Fold-Up Shovel
- Cutters and Pliers
- Sandpaper
- Bungees
- Socket Sets
- Screwdrivers

- Penetrating Oil
- Adjustable Wrench
- Ratchets
- Locking Pliers
- RTV Silicone
- Allen, Torx Wrenches
- Socket Extensions
- Zip-Ties
- Electrical Repair
- Metal Saw
- Hammers
- Tire Repair Kit
- Fix-Flat
- Wood Saw

- Jumper Cables
- Multi-Meter
- Work Gloves
- Vinyl Gloves
- Snap-Ring Pliers
- Multi-Tool or Knives
- Work Light, Flashlight
- Fire Starters
- Epoxy or Adhesives
- Tire Air Gauge
- Fire Extinguisher
- Lighter or Matches

Parts and Supply List

You should carry some extra parts and supplies. Depending on your Jeep, you may require other or extra things.

- Driveshaft U-Joint
- Wire
- Grease
- Engine Oil
- Cotter Pins
- Paper Maps
- Food and Water
- Tape
- Gear Oil

- Lengths of Hose
- Radiator Repair
- Duct Tape
- Water
- Tie-Rod Ends
- Nut and Bolt Assortment
- Electrical Components

- Wood Blocks
- Chargers, Batteries
- Trash Bags
- Small Metal Pieces
- Hose Clamps
- Toilet Paper
- Hand Cleaner
- Parts Cleaner
- Safety Glasses

Safety

Carrying a fire extinguisher or two can save a vehicle fire or other type of fire. The risk of fire when using a Jeep off-road is higher than normal driving due to the conditions, slow speeds, and lack of pavement. Checking pressures and maintenance should be part of a normal routine.

The trail's location dictates what clothing you need to take. Over packing, especially in a cold environment, with gloves, hats, and extra layers, is never a bad thing. Wet-weather gear is always an essential item needed on the trail, as is quality footwear. Thinking ahead and being prepared keeps you dry and warm.

In addition to proper clothing, carrying camping blankets in cold weather can be a lifesaver if the need to spend extra time in the cold arises.

Carrying a basic first-aid kit covers most simple injuries on the trail. If you have allergies, including potential or known reactions to insects such as beestings, make sure you have proper medication. In addition to a first-aid kit, include soap to clean hands and other body parts as needed.

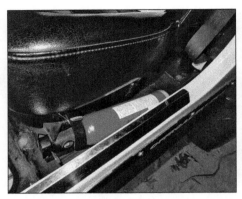

Having a fire extinguisher can prevent a bad situation from getting worse. Many Jeepers mount an extinguisher next to the driver's seat. It's important to check the charge in the extinguisher periodically.

Tuffy makes well-designed storage products for the Jeep that not only look good but also provide a secure storage location. Open-roof vehicles expose belongings to potential thieves.

Jeep owners often get creative when it comes to finding storage for stuff. This CJ is equipped with an extra storage area below the Tuffy center console, which is hinged. Custom rear-seat mounts that create easily accessible storage are commonly found in a CJ.

This should seem like common sense but often people set out on the trail without extra food. Finding a restaurant on the trail isn't a normal thing, and going all day without provisions can be dangerous. Pack extra food to provide good energy that doesn't need refrigeration. Water is essential and having more than you need is always best. Avoid drinks that are high in salt or caffeine because these can actually make you thirstier.

Storage

Finding places to keep all the gear, food, and drink in a CJ is a challenge, but smart thinking always prevails. Many companies make storage components that provide organized and secure storage for many models of the CJ. Tuffy has a reputation of making tough, secure storage components that make the best of available space in a CJ. The center console and rear storage console are among the most popular additions to a Jeep.

Carrying tools and storing items in soft-side bags allows storage for more items because the bags can con-

form to the spaces, as well as what's in the bags around them. Securing items within the Jeep is necessary to prevent items from bouncing around or falling out of the Jeep. In addition to keeping items in, securing items keeps them from hitting the Jeep's occupants in the event of a rollover.

Putting It All Together

When choosing a winch, here are a few tips.

• Invest in a quality, well-known name brand with a proper

A good winch on the front of a Jeep adds peace of mind for the owner and completes the look. Testing the winch before a trip avoids any surprises, and re-spooling after use keeps the line in good working order.

weight rating for your Jeep; 9,000- to 12,000-pound winches are perfect.
• Synthetic line is much lighter and typically safer.
• A Hi-Lift jack is almost standard equipment.
• A small CB with a quality antenna gets much use.
• Carry a set of FRS radios for private trail conversation.
• Plan ahead with tools, food, and clothing to avoid taking too little and forgetting too much.

Fitting everything into a tool bag is a good way of knowing whether too much or too little is being packed. Packing smart reduces weight and increases space; soft-side bags keep the noise down and stack better.

OTHER USEFUL STUFF

Now that your mind has been filled with ideas and your wallet is empty, there are more items worth throwing into the mix. The stuff that isn't necessarily bolted on or part of the Jeep when building, modifying, and using the Jeep is the extra percentage that adds up to 100 percent.

Choosing a Vehicle

Buying a CJ is getting a bit more difficult as the years pass, and buying a good one that hasn't rusted away or been hacked up too much is even harder. When buying a CJ, you need to understand the desired result and

the work that may be involved. Realistically, the majority of AMC-era CJs need work, and the ones that don't are expensive. When you find a CJ for sale, try to place it within the categories below, and consider your particular situation.

Some years of AMC-era CJs are preferable, but it really comes down to 1972–1975 and 1976–1986 and the particular body style of the CJ that you are looking for. The 1976–1986 CJ has more aftermarket support, which makes finding parts easier with more choices. Actually, only minor differences separate the 1976–1986 CJs and these include engine, transmission/transfer case, and axle options.

Because of the advanced age of the CJ, some general items may not apply and may be irrelevant. Rust, leaks, and wear are to be expected and their extent may have an impact only on the price. In general, mileage may not matter either because it's likely many components are either replaced or rebuilt.

Probably the most important thing is a clean title. Getting a title that matches the type of Jeep and matches the VIN plate on the Jeep is extremely important. Purchasing

Finding a used AMC-era CJ is not particularly difficult but finding one in usable shape is getting tougher as the years pass. Because the last CJ rolled off the line in 1986, many CJs have faded away into piles of rust or been hacked to bits by previous owners.

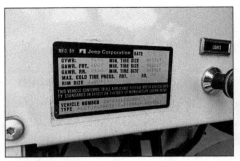

The VIN can be located in a few places on a CJ; most obvious is on the dash or on the firewall inside. Obtaining a good title is important to properly register the Jeep in most states. A missing VIN plate could create difficulties and could mean trouble.

Many states offer replacement VIN plates in the event the original is lost, decayed, or damaged. Often, obtaining replacement plates requires vehicle inspection by an authority to verify ownership. Typically a notice appears on the vehicle's title when a replacement VIN plate is issued.

a Jeep with a bad title or no title is essentially buying an assembled pile of parts, which may be okay if your intent is to use the Jeep for parts. Getting a good title with no VIN plate requires additional work to have the Jeep properly registered. Many states offer replacement VIN plates for old vehicles; most require some sort of proof that the Jeep is the one on the title. AMC-era CJs often had VINs stamped on the top of the frame above the passenger-side rear wheel.

Project Types

This book is about building and modifying a CJ for maximum performance on- and off-road, and almost any AMC-era CJ has potential to serve in this way. If the price is right for the base, changing or modifying the Jeep makes the most of your funds.

The Basket Case

A basket case is the Jeep that has a badly rusted body and/or frame, missing parts, no engine, non-running engine, etc. This kind of Jeep seems like a hopeless mess; however, it could be a good start for

a project or serve as parts in a combination build. A good title here is often the best part of the deal. Expect to scrap much of this Jeep and retain what is useful. Little parts, brackets, mounts, etc., that are hard to find are worth saving from a basket case.

The Survivor

Finding a stock Jeep that hasn't been modified can be as rare as finding a four-leaf clover. They exist but often come at a high price. As the years pass, it becomes a matter of

questioning if preserving the Jeep in its stock form is better than modifying it and dragging it over the rocks. AMC-era history is getting more difficult to retain. A relatively untouched vehicle to serve as a history reference is probably worth more than a built-up Jeep. Unrestored vehicles left as original are growing in value and appreciation.

The Trail Rig

Buying someone else's Jeep that was modified and used off-road may seem like a good idea, and it can be. It takes a thorough examination of the Jeep to determine the quality of the modifications and the capacity to deal with the unknown ability of the Jeep. If done right, a trail rig is often a good bargain because a lot of the work may already be done. Moreover, it's a well-known fact that the money put into a vehicle is never recouped, so you can potentially pay a fraction of the original investment put into it.

Inspect the trail rig for poorly made modifications, especially if components are cut and/or welded. Bad welds can cause metal damage and compromise structural integrity.

The basket case Jeep purchase is often wise for the sake of gaining a specific part or adding to a parts supply. Many times these Jeeps end up for scrap after anything valuable has been stripped away.

A trail rig is risky unless you know what you are looking for. These can be a bargain if put together correctly and not totally abused. It's well known that the money put in never comes back out. Look for welds and weld quality as a judge of work skill; poor welds, especially on the Jeep's frame, can mean further trouble ahead.

Correcting these problems can be troublesome and possibly expensive.

If the Jeep is equipped with a non-factory engine, transmission, and/or transfer case, make sure you get the details from the previous owner about the components and specifics of the swap. Trying to figure out what was done later is time-consuming and can be expensive.

When considering a trail rig, do a test drive on the street and take note of the driving characteristics. Pay attention to cornering, wandering, vibration, and especially braking. Strange driving behaviors can indicate problems that you'll have to deal with later.

The Lost Project

Occasionally, an owner starts a project that either moves beyond the budget or life gets in the way of the Jeep getting back on the road. Buying a lost project requires a keen eye to spot items of value and make sure that all of the needed parts are included or they can nickel and dime the project later. A benefit of obtaining a lost project is that it can often be acquired at an excellent price because the owner may be looking to move it quickly.

The Base

A CJ that is in usable condition but not perfect or pristine gives a good starting point for a build and modification project. It may need some bodywork or even a fiberglass replacement but has a solid frame and good working running gear. Simply, a V-8 or I-6 AMC-era CJ that is drivable and has a solid frame makes a perfect base from which to start.

It comes down to the moment of the sale and knowing the desired end result. It's often best to take a trusted friend along for an extra set of eyes and to prevent an impulsive decision. Buying an old Jeep is much harder than buying a new one. Experience, knowledge, and attention to detail are key.

Registration and Insurance

Some states have special vehicle registration classes that allow a vehicle older than a certain age to be registered within these classes. Usually these classes are designed for special vehicles and are often referred to as classic, antique, or collectible. Rules are often different for these classes and can be a benefit to an old vehicle. The rules often limit mileage and driving frequency but as a plus, they exempt the vehicle from exhaust emissions rules and allow for specialty insurance policies.

Because AMC-era CJs aren't known for carrying a high "blue book" value, the owner is often short changed in the event of an accident or loss. Specialty insurance companies can offer higher insurance values, often at a less expensive premium, that may cover a loss entirely. These specialty companies typically have restrictions such as mileage, storage, and type of use that usually don't get in the way of how CJs are

The base is the best starting point for a Jeep build. This Jeep has some rust and is showing its age but is in fair working order to warrant a second life. These Jeeps are too degraded for keeping as is and being called a survivor for history purposes but not too far gone to be usable. (Photo Courtesy Craig Brown)

VIN Guide

Knowing the particular Jeep being looked at is part of the knowledge needed before purchasing a used Jeep. Knowing some particulars of your own Jeep will come in handy as well. Most CJ VIN plates are located on the driver-side firewall near the master cylinder.

Here are some things to note from a Jeep VIN. It does not carry vehicle-specific information such as trim level, color, or special options. Later-model Jeeps had a sticker attached to the underside of the driver-side door that contained trim codes. Some earlier years had codes stamped on the VIN plate. The codes listed often had only certain trim information that has proven to be difficult to decode due to lack of information resources available.

As people have located information, they post it online; the Internet is the best resource to decode this information. ■

1972–1974 CJ

Character	Code			Description
1st	J = Jeep			Make
2nd	2 = 1972	3 = 1973	4 = 1974	Year
3rd	A = Toledo auto/LHDPlant/Transmission F = Toledo 3-speed/left-hand drive M = Toledo 4-speed/left-hand drive			Transmission
4th and 5th	83 = CJ-5	84 = CJ-6		Model
6th	5 = Open			Body Type
7th	R = 4,750 pounds	S = 4,500 pounds	T = 3,750 pounds	GVW (Gross Vehicle Weight)
8th	A = 258 standard B = 258 low compression	E = 232 standard F = 232 low compression	H = 304 standard	Engine
9th to 13th	#####			SSN (Sequential Serial Number)

1975–1980 CJ

Character	Code			Description
1st	J = Jeep			Make
2nd	5 = 1975 6 = 1976	7 = 1977 8 = 1978	9 = 1979 0 = 1980	Year
3rd	A = Auto	F = 3-speed	M = 4-speed	Transmission
4th and 5th	83 = CJ-5	84 = CJ-6	93 = CJ-7	Model
6th	A = 3,750 pounds	E = 4,150 pounds		GVW (Gross Vehicle Weight)
7th	A = 258 ci, 1-barrel C = 258 ci, 2-barrel	E = 232 ci, 1-barrel H = 304 ci, 2-barrel		Engine
8th to 13th	######			SSN (Sequential Serial Number)

1981–1986 CJ

Character	Code				Description
1st	1 = USA				Country
2nd	J = Jeep				Make
3rd	C = MPV	E = Export left-hand drive	F = Export right-hand drive		Type
4th	B = 151-ci L = 232-ci	C = 258-ci H = 304-ci	F = Diesel		Engine
5th	A = Auto, Column	M = 4-speed	N = 5-speed		Transmission
6th and 7th	85 = CJ-5	86 = CJ-6	87 = CJ-7	88 = CJ-8	Model
8th	A = 3,750 pounds	E = 4,150 pounds			GVW (Gross Vehicle Weight)
9th	Check #				Check #
10th	B = 1981 C = 1982	D = 1983 E = 1984	F = 1985 G = 1986		Year
11th	T = Toledo				Plant
12th to 17th	######				SSN (Sequential Serial Number)

often used. Daily-driver AMC-era CJs are less common as the years tick by. Consider protecting your investment in your Jeep by looking into specialty insurance.

Garage Tools

Owning an AMC-era Jeep almost requires you to have the proper tools in your garage to work on it. Although some extra specialty tools are a luxury and are for the extra skilled builder, most tools are essential. Below is a list of the heavily used tools in a Jeeper's garage.

Jack Stands

Safety while working should be the top priority, and having tools to ensure that safety is simple. High but strong and stable jack stands can support the weight of the Jeep securely when you are working underneath. A proper weight-rated quality floor jack allows the Jeep to be raised and lowered without sudden drops or sinking. Never rely on a jack to

support the vehicle while working underneath.

Hand Tools

Complete sets of hand wrenches in both open-end and box-end styles, along with full 3/8- and 1/2-inch socket sets in both shallow and deep types are necessary. Ratchets of varying lengths and a breaker bar help get the extra-tight fasteners loose. Toolboxes keep everything organized.

- Set of screwdrivers, pliers, chisels, and drifts
- Hammers and mallets
- Pry bars
- Clamps
- Measuring tools

Specialty Tools

These tools have more specific purposes and either help get the job done correctly or with less of a battle.

- Torque wrench
- Drum brake tools
- Hub sockets
- Ball joint socket

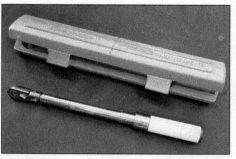

Specialty hand tools such as a torque wrench help get a job done properly. These tools can last a lifetime, and used ones can often cost a fraction of the original.

- Timing light
- Vacuum gauge
- Ball joint and tie-rod tools
- Hydraulic press
- Pullers

Welder

Small, cheap flux-core welders are okay for minor home repairs but they do not do well when fabricating

Multiple sets of jack stands are good for safety when working under a supported Jeep. Stands should be properly weight rated and not supported on blocks or angles. Tall stands are good for supporting the Jeep by its frame when working on suspension.

In contrast to carrying tools on the trail, there is no such thing as having too many tools in your garage. Large toolboxes keep tools organized and accessible.

A quality welder capable of welding up to 1/4-inch steel should be sufficient in a Jeep garage. Often the 220-volt MIG-type welders perform the best and provide years of service. Keeping a fire extinguisher handy when welding is wise.

An oxygen/acetylene torch set is an invaluable tool for the advanced Jeep builder. A torch makes quick work of loosening a stubborn bolt or cutting off an old rusted part.

For steel fabrication, a metal chop saw can cut steel pieces cleanl[y] and quickly. Inexpensive abrasive discs are readily available and easily changed. Minding the area behind the saw prevents fires from sparks.

A good assortment of electric power tools helps with the job. A metal-bladed reciprocating saw, drills, and angle grinder are tool[s] that see the most use in a Jeeper's garage. Keeping a supply of spare blades and discs keeps the work moving.

or repairing components on a Jeep. A 220-volt MIG welder has enough power and is perfect for most DIY Jeepers in both capacity and cost. Sticking with a reputable, well-known brand of welder such as Miller or Lincoln is worth the investment.

Acetylene Torch

The torch isn't for the timid and can be very dangerous. However, it serves a purpose that makes it difficult to do without, especially with an old Jeep. Although it's destructive, heat is the ultimate way to remove old steel parts and loosen stubborn bolts. Fabrication with a torch makes cutting steel pieces a quick job.

Power Tools

When fabricating and customizing, certain power tools are needed in a Jeep owner's garage. These are some of the most useful tools.

- Grinder/angle grinder
- Metal chop saw
- Reciprocating saw
- Drill, 3/8- and 1/2-inch
- Drill press, 1/2-inch
- Soldering iron
- Heat gun

Air Compressor

Choose an air compressor that is capable of maintaining the set pressure when air tools such as a grinder, chisel, or sander are in continuous use. An upright compressor with a CFM rating that is for extended-use

tools saves space and gives the bes[t] performance. Piston-style compressors are the quietest and are generall[y] best at keeping up with tools under continuous use.

Air Tools

Air tools are a valuable time save[r] when working on your Jeep, especially wrench type air tools. Keepin[g] a reasonable assortment will mak[e] garage life easier on both you an[d] your Jeep.

- Impact wrench
- Air ratchet
- Grinder

A compressor in the 30- to 60-gallon range provides plenty of air for running common air tools. Upright compressors save space and can be squeezed into corners out of the way.

Towing

Towing a CJ is often a way to get the Jeep to and from the trail without the need to drive it the full distance or require a trailer. Flat towing requires a few things to securely attach the Jeep to the tow vehicle and an understanding of transfer case towing differences. Homemade tow bars are risky; using a properly

built and rated tow bar protects the Jeep from a towing disaster.

The Jeep can be secured to the tow vehicle by one of several methods. Bumper-mounted plates supplied by a tow bar manufacturer are secured to the bumper and allow easy attachment/removal of the tow bar. Currie makes shackles that have tow bar mounts integrated into them. These allow the bar to be attached without the need to attach tow bar tabs. In addition to the bar, you should use safety chains or cables.

Attaching the Jeep to the tow vehicle also requires either wiring the Jeep's taillights to the tow vehicle or using a set of removable lights attached to the rear of the Jeep.

If the Jeep is equipped with a Dana 20 transfer case, it is necessary to remove the rear driveshaft to avoid damage. The Dana 20 rear output bearing receives lubrication from the intermediate shaft, which does not turn when the engine is not running. It is possible to flat tow a Dana 20 CJ with the driveshaft attached

for short distances; longer distances starve the rear bearing of lubrication and cause damage.

A Dana 300 transfer case can be flat towed for slightly longer distances than a Dana 20; some Jeep manuals indicate 150 miles. It is recommended to disconnect the driveshaft similarly to the Dana 20 to preserve transfer case life.

When flat towing for a short distance, place the transfer case into neutral and the transmission in a gear. If the Jeep is subject to frequent flat towing, installing a set of rear full-floating axles with lockout hubs alleviates the need to disconnect the driveshaft.

On the Trail: Before and After

Most Jeep owners have a ritual before a trail run, which often includes checking the Jeep for its readiness. It is a good practice to check over many parts of the Jeep to make sure they are ready for action. Inspect the driveshafts and suspension components. Check the fluid levels in the drivetrain, and lubricate tie-rod ends or other joints with grease fittings. Keeping a list of items to take helps reduce over-packing (or under-packing) and the likelihood of forgetting things.

Attaching a tow bar to the front of the Jeep can be done in a few ways, from bumper-mounted tow tabs to clever shackles that provide tow bar–mounting provisions. Using safety chains and lighting is a must when flat towing.

Disconnecting or removing the rear driveshaft is the best way to flat tow because the possibility of transfer case damage is eliminated. If not fully removing the shaft, the differential end should be disconnected and tied up out of the way. Taping the bearing caps prevents them from falling off and spilling the bearings.

Putting It All Together

A pre-trail ritual involves spending some time under the Jeep checking for loose nuts and/or bolts. Lying underneath with a pile of wrenches makes the job quicker. In addition, check the lubrication in the differentials and other parts of the drivetrain before a trail run.

Here are a few tips from this chapter.

- Knowledge and patience is key when buying a used Jeep.
- Consider special registration classes, if available.
- Protect your investment with specialty insurance.
- Building and modifying a Jeep requires good tools and a nice place to work; the correct tools save time and get better results.
- Towing is a handy way of getting a CJ to and from the trail but knowing the towing requirements will save broken parts.
- Proper before and after trail care keeps the Jeep and driver happy.

It's a shame that a few minutes of playing in the mud can create a few hours of cleaning. Many Jeep owners don't clean their Jeeps after the trail, but over time this can cause problems with rust, corrosion, and contamination of components. Water and mud have a way of getting into areas they don't belong. Cleaning exposes areas that may have been damaged on the trail and are hidden beneath the dirt.

Cleaning after the trail can be done in a few stages by cleaning the globs and chunks first, followed by more detailed cleaning underneath; it's a messy job. Avoid using a pressure washer because it can force water into areas that may not be well protected. Use an automotive soap and a wash mitt to clean underneath; starting from the middle and moving outward help keep you cleaner. Another idea is to clean the Jeep on gravel or grass to prevent making a mess of a driveway.

After a trail run that is especially wet, muddy, or dusty, it is good practice to check the oil in the differentials, transmission, and transfer case for water that may have entered. Drain and replace the oil to prevent damage. Front wheel hubs can trap water, too, causing wear to the bearings. Cleaning wheel hubs is a time-consuming job but it's worth the effort. In addition, if the Jeep is equipped with drum brakes, they can trap small gravel and dirt inside that can cause excess and uneven wear to brake shoes. Removing the drums and cleaning preserves the brakes.

Having a garage to work on a Jeep is a privilege, and even a small one can allow a big job. Many Jeep owners do their work without the benefit of a lift or large shop supply of fancy tools. This garage measures only 14 x 30 feet but is very usable and features air conditioning, radiant floor heat, and plenty of LED lighting.

SOURCE GUIDE

Advance Adapters
4320 Aerotech Center Way
Paso Robles, CA 93446
805-238-7000
advanceadapters.com

ARB/Old Man Emu
4810 D St. N.W., Ste. #103
Auburn, WA 98001
425-264-1391
arbusa.com

Barnes 4WD
34 McKinney Rd.
Etowah, NC 28729
828-551-7616
barnes4wd.com

BFGoodrich
P.O. Box 19001
Greenville, SC 29602
877-788-8899
bfgoodrichtires.com

Carter
101 E. Industrial Blvd.
Logansport, IN 46947
574-722-6141
carterfuelsystems.com

Cobra Electronics
6500 W. Cortland St.
Chicago, IL 60707
773-889-3087
cobra.com

Crabtree Tool & Die
28886 Hwy. B
Perry, MO 63462
573-565-0004
crabtreetool.com

Crown Automotive
83 Enterprise Dr.
Marshfield, MA 02050
crownautomotive.net
781-826-6200

Dynatrac Products
7392 Count Cir.
Huntington Beach, CA
    92647
714-421-4314
dynatrac.com

Edelbrock
2700 California St.
Torrance, CA 90503
310-781-2222
edelbrock.com

Energy Suspension
1131 Via Callejon
San Clemente, CA 92673
888-913-6374
energysuspension.com

Firestik Antenna Company
2614 E. Adams St.
Phoenix, AZ 85034
602-273-7151
firestik.com

Flaming River Industries
800 Poertner Dr.
Berea, OH 44017
440-826-4488
flamingriver.com

Four X Doctor
1033 N. Victory Pl.
Burbank, CA 91502
818-845-2194
fourxdoctor.com

Genesis Offroad
P.O. Box 1038
Byhalia, MS 38611
901-214-5337
genesisoffroad.com

Goodyear
200 Innovation Way
Akron, OH 44316
330-796-2121
goodyear.com

Hi-Lift Jack Company
46 W. Spring St.
Bloomfield, IN 47424
812-384-4441
hi-lift.com

Holley
1801 Russellville Rd.
Bowling Green, KY 42101
270-782-2900
holley.com

Howell Engine
    Developments
6201 Industrial Way
Marine City, MI 48039
810-765-5100
howellefi.com

Interco Tire
2412 Abbeville Hwy.
Rayne, LA 70578
800-299-8000
intercotire.com

JB Conversions
P.O. Box 2683
Sulphur, LA 70664
337-625-2379
jbconversions.com

Jeff Daniel's Jeep
    Customizations
495 Indian Creek Rd.
Harleysville, PA 19438
215-256-8090
jeffdanielsjeeps.com

K&N Engineering
1455 Citrus St.
Riverside, CA 92507
951-826-4000
knfilters.com

KC HiLites
2843 W. Avenida De Lucas
Williams, AZ 86046
928-635-2607
kchilites.com

Kentrol
550 W. Pine Lake Rd.
North Lima, OH 44452
330-549-2235
kentrolinc.com

Lokar Performance Products
2545 Quality Ln.
Knoxville, TN 37931
865-824-9767
lokar.com

Lucas Oil Products
302 North Sheridan St.
Corona, CA 92880
800-342-2512
lucasoil.com

Mean Green
3 Imaging Way
Derry, PA 15627
724-694-8290
mean-green.com

Mickey Thompson
4600 Prosper Dr.
Stow, OH 44224
330-928-9092
mickeythompsontires.com

Midway Industries
2266 Crosswind Dr.
Prescott, AZ 86301
928-771-8422
centerforce.com

Mile Marker Industries
2121 Blount Rd.
Pompano Beach, FL 33069
800-886-8647
milemarker.com

Mountain Off-Road
   Enterprises
685 Hwy. 92
Delta, CO 81416
877-533-7229
mountainoffroad.com

Novak Conversions
648 W. 200 N., Ste. 1
Logan, UT 84321
877-602-1500
novak-adapt.com

Off Again 4x4
508 E Murray Dr.
Farmington, NM 87401
505-325-5761
offagain4x4.com

OK Auto
2621 NJ-57
Stewartsville, NJ 8886
908-454-6973
ok4wd.com

Optima
5757 N. Green Bay Ave.
Milwaukee, WI 53209
888-867-8462
optimabatteries.com

Ox Off Road
11405 Challenger Av.
Odessa, FL 33556
727-230-7803
ox-usa.com

Painless Performance
2501 Ludelle St.
Fort Worth, TX 76105
817-244-6212
painlessperformance.com

Performance Distributors
2699 Barris Dr.
Memphis, TN 38132
901-396-5782
performance
   distributors.com

Power Tank
43 Commerce St.,
   Unit 103
Lodi, CA 95240
209-366-2163
powertank.com

Powertrax
1001 W. Exchange Ave.
Chicago, IL 60609
800-934-2727
powertrax.com

Quadratec
1028 Saunders Ln.
West Chester, PA 19380
800-743-4927
quadratec.com

Rock Hard 4x4
P.O. Box 186
St Paul, NE 68873
844-762-5427
rockhard4x4.com

Rocky Road
1920 S. Wendell Ln.
Heber City, UT 84032
435-654-1149
rocky-road.com

Rugged Ridge/Omix-Ada
460 Horizon Dr., #400
Suwanee, GA 30024
770-614-6101
ruggedridge.com

Spidertrax
174 12th St. S.E.
Loveland, CO 80537
800-286-0898
spidertrax.com

SSBC Performance Brake
   Systems
11470 Main Rd.
Clarence, NY 14031
800-448-7722
ssbrakes.com

Steerco
4920 Rondo Dr.
Fort Worth, TX 76106
817-626-9006
steerco.com

Summit Racing
P.O. Box 909
Akron, OH 44309
800-230-3030
summitracing.com

TeraFlex
5680 W. Dannon Way
West Jordan, UT 84081
801-713-3314
teraflex.com

Toyo Tires
5665 Plaza Dr., #300
Cypress, CA 90630
714-236-2080
toyotires.com

Uniden
3001 Gateway Dr., Ste. 130
Irving, TX 75063
817-858-3300
uniden.com

US Mags
19200 S. Reyes Ave.
Rancho Dominguez,
   CA 90221
us-mags.com

Vanco Power Brake Supply
6342 Jonathan St.
Lancaster, CA 93536
800-256-6295
vancopbs.com

Warn Industries
12900 S.E. Capps Rd.
Clackamas, OR 97015
800-543-9276
warn.com

Warrior Products
16850 S.W. Upper Boones
   Ferry Rd.
Durham, OR 97224
503-691-8915
warriorproducts.com

Xenon/GTS
2891 E. Via Martens
Anaheim, CA 92806
800-999-8753
teamxenon.com

CPSIA information can be obtained
at www.ICGtesting.com
Printed in the USA
LVHW050539201122
733280LV00012B/903